Violence and Solace

Reconsiderations in Southern African History
Richard Elphick and Benedict Carton, Editors

Violence and Solace

The Natal Civil War in Late-Apartheid South Africa

Mxolisi R. Mchunu

University of Virginia Press
Charlottesville and London

University of Virginia Press

First published 2020 by UKZN Press
Published in the United States by the University of Virginia Press under license of UKZN Press
Printed in the United States of America on acid-free paper

First University of Virginia Press edition published 2021

ISBN 978-0-8139-4636-8 (hardcover)
ISBN 978-0-8139-4637-5 (ebook)

9 8 7 6 5 4 3 2 1

Library of Congress Cataloging-in-Publication Data is available for this title.

Jacket photo: Vulindlela youths marching at KwaVulisaka, Natal, South Africa, 1987. (Courtesy of KwaZulu-Natal Museum)

Contents

Foreword to the US Edition

Always illuminating, *Violence and Solace* is at times deeply unsettling. Mxolisi Mchunu's study focuses on memories of trauma as South Africa transitioned to democracy. These painful recollections in turn evoke legacies of a Zulu warrior past—both real and imagined—which require critical investigation. Of particular importance are political histories, namely the alliances, divisions and realignments of Zulu groups and their interactions with Boer and British agents of white supremacy.

The antagonists of *Violence and Solace* favoured either the Zulu nationalist Inkatha Freedom Party or isiZulu-speaking members of the African National Congress (ANC) and its affiliated United Democratic Front (UDF). By the mid-1980s, these opposing blocs were fighting a civil war in the Midlands, a region on the outskirts of Pietermaritzburg, capital of the Natal province.[1] Advocating democratic socialism, the ANC/ UDF repudiated the 'reactionary' president of Inkatha, Mangosutho Buthelezi, who also served as chief minister of Pretoria's KwaZulu homeland.[2] Many older Inkatha members rallied behind Buthelezi's invocation of Shaka, the 'warrior' of legendary Zulu might.[3] Meanwhile, Natal became a proving ground for the apartheid government's strategy of using paramilitaries to stoke ethnic feuds. The lethal rivalry ravaged the Midlands, killing 12,000 people over ten years.

While journalists called this civil war a 'tribal' vendetta, academics investigated Zulu origins and the stereotypes that seemingly animated the violence.[4] Historians critically examined the reputation of King Shaka kaSenzangakhona, who had been lauded for forging a Zulu empire but also blamed for the Mfecane, a period of decimating warfare in southern Africa during the early nineteenth century. One historian traced tales of Shaka's carnage to white writers who published lies and half-truths about this 'Black Napoleon' in an effort to conceal the rogue activities of Europeans and their African henchmen trafficking in firearms and, possibly, in slaves.[5]

Another historian depicted Shaka as a state-builder who incorporated defeated enemies into single-sex (male and female) regiments, *amabutho,* and, while executing elite foes, allowed recalcitrant chiefdoms to migrate away.[6] Along similar lines, a third historian emphasised that Shaka, though authoritarian, was no genocidal leader. The Zulu founder secured fealty from privileged loyalists, *amantungwa,* by giving them tribute obtained in raids. He also absorbed commoners disparaged as *amalala,* menials in the margins of a royal heartland that included the Natal Midlands.[7] Thus, historical research revealed that even in the era of its ambitious founder, the Zulu kingdom was neither stable nor cohesive.

Shaka was murdered in 1828 by assassins sent by his brother Dingane. Thereafter the Zulu kingdom was reduced in scope, particularly when fratricidal conflicts coincided with colonial encroachments.[8] In the 1830s, the Voortrekkers, Dutch-speaking Boers, streamed into Natal. Dingane ordered their massacre. After several bands of their compatriots were slaughtered, Boer commandos exacted decisive revenge at the Battle of Blood River, cutting down waves of Zulu troops.[9] Sensing Dingane's declining power, Prince Mpande, another of the monarch's brothers, lured his subjects to the Boers, thus 'breaking . . . the rope that held the nation together', as one Zulu sage recalled.[10] In January 1840 a combined Voortrekker and Zulu army roundly defeated the king's military, forcing Dingane to flee to his Swazi enemies, who killed him. While the rout guaranteed Mpande the throne, he lost half of his domain. Thousands who had settled in Shaka's heartland after their chiefs were subjugated by him pulled up stakes and returned to their ancestral regions, including the Midlands.[11]

In 1843, the British annexed Natal, prompting many Boers to depart for the hinterland over the Drakensberg mountains. Governing a vast isiZulu-speaking population and a small number of mostly

English-speaking settlers, the new colonial power recalibrated African rights. In the mid- to late 1840s, Theophilus Shepstone, the future secretary for Native Affairs, laid out 'native reserves' to be ruled by chiefs. Blending indigenous patriarchal prerogatives with British legal procedures, he then created a hybrid system of 'customary law', which became the load-bearing beam of 'Native Administration'. A thin colonial bureaucracy depended on a thick layer of indigenous functionaries. Each white magistrate adjudicating customary law was assisted by local chiefs who acted as 'deputies . . . [of] the Crown'.[12] Traditional leaders resolved civil cases, punished crimes and pocketed fines. Shepstone learned from his deputies how to manipulate chieftaincy to serve colonial ends and to transform African social order by enhancing the subordination of women and youths to male elders. Classified in the 1878 Code of Native Law, his policies carried over into the twentieth century. In the era of apartheid, customary law would inform the design of black 'Bantustans,' among them Buthelezi's KwaZulu 'homeland' in Natal.[13]

The mineral revolution that catapulted South Africa into global prominence disrupted Zulu family obligations. By the 1870s, boys and men were being lured to dig in the diamond fields near Kimberley, and, in the 1880s, to work in the gold mines of Johannesburg. The outflow of labour gutted chiefdoms of able-bodied males. As a consequence, women had to shoulder greater domestic burdens.

Confronting the dual shocks of mining capitalism and British imperialism, Zulu society repeatedly split along generational lines. Young soldiers in the kingdom's *amabutho* were inspired by tales of Shakan-era glories when regiments were enriched with captured livestock. The fourth Zulu monarch, Cetshwayo, played on these sentiments by promising to confront the whites and give his bravehearts (*amaqhawe*) the spoils of battle. Against him were prominent Zulu chiefs with their own *amabutho* who sought commercial partnerships with Europeans. Fatal clashes ensued.[14] Perceiving an opportunity to subdue Cetshwayo's apparent militancy, the Colonial Office in London ordered a military invasion of his realm.[15]

The Anglo-Zulu War began in January 1879 with *amabutho* annihilating redcoats at the Battle of Isandlwana. For Zulus, it was an epic, if Pyrrhic, victory. Seven months later, they were overwhelmed by

British forces. Yet even with this grave loss, the image of the kingdom's martial culture had captured 'the world's attention' with such ferocity that its renown obscured a startling fact: Zulu independence had been a 'short-lived if spectacular phenomenon' lasting 'no longer than a single lifespan'.[16] Civil strife between feuding royals subsequently wrecked Cetshwayo's nation and drove him to the grave.[17]

In 1887, Zululand was made a colony of the Crown, and in 1893, Natal was granted responsible, or self-governing, status. Settler dominance was irrevocably ascendant. Increasingly, the Midlands became an attractive area for colonists buying farms. African poverty worsened after ecological disasters during the 1890s, from locusts to rinderpest, destroyed crops and cows. When in 1906 an onerous poll (head) tax was imposed on unmarried men over eighteen, popular anger exploded and again Zulu society was riven by tensions between elders and youths.

A chief named Bhambatha channeled the disaffection into an insurrection dubbed *impi yamakhanda,* the 'war of the heads'. African patriarchs who acquiesced in colonial authority were being challenged by young men protesting the incursions of white rule. The rebels looked to shield themselves from enemy bullets and shells by being doctored with protective medicines (*muthi* and *intelezi)* derived from the bodies of slain settlers. With its superior firepower, the government militia crushed *impi yamakhanda.* In the ensuing courts martial, fathers were summoned to testify against sons charged with treason.[18]

Zulu resistance to colonial domination took another form following the Union of South Africa in 1910, which merged four colonial territories—British Natal and the Cape as well as the Boer Transvaal and Orange Free State—into a white-ruled nation determined to exclude black people from citizenship. A decade later Zulu intellectuals and representatives of Cetshwayo's monarchy established Inkatha, with the aim of achieving modest political and economic reforms. Their cultural nationalist organisation derived its name from a sacred coil woven from many fibers, symbolizing the strands, or lineages, bound in loyalty to Shaka's royal house. Inkatha relied on the patronage of Zulu king Solomon kaDinuzulu, the brother of Mangosuthu Buthelezi's mother. Solomon's benefactors were wealthy white advocates of Shepstone's ideal: upholding the stability of provincial Natal through the customary authority of cooperative homestead fathers and husbands. In the 1920s, Zulu patriarchs needed money from wage-earning kin to buy the food that sustained subsistence in barren and congested chiefdoms. Over the ensuing decades cash-strapped elders expected their children to enter the capitalist economy and send their income home. That younger Zulus, or any Zulus, might challenge law and order rather than work for the family was considered an existential threat by Inkatha ideologues. As the regime of racial segregation asserted intrusive control over African institutions, Inkatha went into decline and had unraveled by King Solomon's death in 1933.[19]

The electoral triumph of the Afrikaner-led National Party in 1948 introduced apartheid, a social-engineering project that categorised four groups—European, Coloured, Asian and African—and subjected them to differentiated legislation as unassimilable populations. Zulu appeals to ethnic chauvinism were soon drowned out by ANC calls for diverse protest groups to coalesce into a democratic front willing to oppose draconian divide-and-rule.[20] In response, Afrikaner nationalist leaders, some of whom descended from the Voortrekkers, outlawed the ANC in 1960, thus prompting its radical strategists to flee the country and inaugurate guerrilla operations.

As state repression intensified, Buthelezi in 1975 launched a new Inkatha to contest apartheid. His activism initially energised the underground ANC. However, a schism developed two years later when Pretoria created the KwaZulu Bantustan and asked an agreeable Buthelezi to become its chief minister. The rupture between Inkatha and the ANC reenacted, very loosely, rifts that had surfaced before, pitting fathers against sons, Shaka-oriented traditionalists against nation-state modernisers, monarchists against democrats and collaborators against militants. Under pressure, Buthelezi henceforth struggled to explain his participation in an institution of white supremacy.[21]

In the 1980s, the UDF—a coalition comprised of unions, churches and civic organisations—linked arms with the ANC to coordinate mass civil disobedience and rolling strikes. Denounced as a stooge by his detractors, Buthelezi faced accusations that he was colluding with Pretoria's security forces. Running skirmishes between Inkatha and UDF/ANC supporters in Natal flared into prolonged campaigns. By decade's end, human rights monitors had reported thousands of casualties. With the release of Nelson Mandela from prison in early 1990 and the promise of negotiations between the ANC and the National Party, Inkatha transformed itself into a political party. Internecine conflict raged on the edges of Pietermaritzburg in areas where Bantustan officials defended Buthelezi's directives and township youths targeted Inkatha strongholds.[22]

Countering the stereotype of warrior manhood, armed mothers and wives fortified their Midlands community in keeping with a longer tradition of female *amabutho* mobilisations.[23] To help their families cope with devastating fear and loss, African women expressed their 'gendered construction of [martial] Zuluness' through reverential gestures of solace in worship and mourning.[24] Meanwhile, journalists glibly described the belligerents as senseless marauders answering the tribal cry 'Go and fight'.[25]

Violence and Solace recounts a tragic drama at the center of South Africa's tumultuous interregnum. With unsparing candour, Mxolisi Mchunu illustrates how people in the throes of civil bloodshed did not simply embrace primordial urges unleashed by Shaka. On the contrary, their experiences revealed the influence of changing political alliances, divisions and realignments which had shaped Natal and Zululand since the early 1800s. In the war-torn Midlands, men, women and children had to be aware of this complex centuries-old history. Their lives depended on it.

Benedict Carton

Notes

1. J. Aitchison, 'Numbering the Dead: Patterns and Meaning in the Midlands Violence', in *Collected Seminar Papers* (London: Institute of Commonwealth Studies, University of London, 1988), pp. 117–90; M. Kentridge, *An Unofficial War: Inside the Conflict in Pietermaritzburg* (Cape Town: David Philip, 1990); D. Bonnin, G. Hamilton, R. Morrell and A. Sitas, 'The Struggle for Natal and KwaZulu: Workers, Township Dwellers and Inkatha, 1972–1985', in *Political Economy and Identities in KwaZulu-Natal: Historical and Social Perspectives,* edited by R. Morrell (Durban: Indicator Press, 1996), pp. 151–2.
2. J. Sithole, 'Preface: Zuluness in South Africa: From "Struggle" Debate to

Democratic Transformation', in in *Zulu Identities: Being Zulu, Past and Present,* edited by B. Carton, J, Laband and J. Sithole (New York: Columbia University Press, 2009), pp. xii–xx; G. Hamilton and G. Maré, *An Appetite for Power: Buthelezi's Inkatha and South Africa* (Bloomington and Indianapolis: Indiana University Press, 1987).

3. P. Harries, 'Imagery, Symbolism and Tradition in a South African Bantustan: Mangosuthu Buthelezi, Inkatha and Zulu History', *History and Theory* 31(4), 1993: 115–8; M Buthelezi, 'The Empire Writes Back: Re-examining the Legacies of Shaka and Zulu Power in Post-apartheid South Africa,' in *Zulu Identities: Being Zulu Past and Present,* edited by B. Carton, J. Laband and J. Sithole (New York: Columbia University Press, 2009), pp. 23–34.
4. J. Kelly, *To Swim with Crocodiles: Land, Violence and Belonging in South Africa, 1800–1996* (East Lansing: Michigan State University Press, 2018), p. xxviii.
5. J. Cobbing, 'The Mfecane as Alibi: Thoughts on Dithakong and Mbolombo', *Journal of African History* 29, 1988: 487–519. A critique of Cobbing's argument: C. Hamilton, *The Mfecane Aftermath: Reconstructive Debates in Southern African History* (Johannesburg: Wits University Press and Pietermaritzburg: University of Natal Press, 1995); E. Eldredge, 'Sources of Conflict in Southern Africa, c. 1800–1830: The "Mfecane" Reconsidered', *Journal of African History* 33, 1992: 1–36. New scholarship re-establishing slaving as a source of 'Mfecane' violence: L. Chewins and P. Delius, 'The Northeastern Factor in South African History: Reevaluating the Volume of the Slave Trade out of Delagoa Bay and Its Impact on Its Hinterland in the Early Nineteenth Century', *Journal of African History* 61(1), 2020: 89–110.
6. J. Wright, 'Revisiting the Stereotypes of Shaka's "Devastations"', in *Zulu Identities: Being Zulu, Past and Present,* edited by B. Carton, J. Laband and J. Sithole (New York: Columbia University Press, 2009), pp. 69–81; J. Wright, 'The Dynamics of Power and Conflict in the Thukela-Mzimkhulu Region in the late 18th and early 19th centuries: A Critical Reconstruction', unpublished PhD thesis, University of the Witwatersrand, 1989.
7. C. Hamilton, 'Ideology, Oral Tradition and the Struggle for Power in the Early Zulu Kingdom', unpublished MA thesis, University of the Witwatersrand, 1985), pp. 465–9; C. Hamilton and J. Wright, 'The Making of the *AmaLala:* Ethnicity, Ideology and Relations of Subordination in a Precolonial Context', *South African Historical Journal* 22(1), 1990: 3–23.
8. P. Colenbrander, 'The Zulu Kingdom, 1828–79', in *Natal and Zululand from the Earliest Times to 1910: A New History,* edited by A. Duminy and B. Guest (Pietermaritzburg: University of Natal Press, 1989), pp. 96–109.
9. C. Ballard, 'Traders, Trekkers and Colonists', in *Natal and Zululand from the Earliest Times to 1910: A New History,* edited by A. Duminy and B. Guest (Pietermaritzburg: University of Natal Press, 1989), pp. 121–3; J. Sithole, 'Changing Meanings of the Battle of Ncome and Images of King Dingane in Twentieth-Century South Africa', in *Zulu Identities: Being Zulu Past and Present,* edited by B. Carton, J. Laband and J. Sithole (New York: Columbia University Press, 2009), p. 322.
10. Testimony of Mbovu, 7 February 1904, in *The James Stuart Archive of Recorded Oral Evidence Relating to the History of the Zulu and Neighbouring*

Peoples, Vol. 3, edited by C. de B. Webb and J.B. Wright (Durban: Killie Campbell Africana Library and Pietermaritzburg: University of Natal Press, 1982), p. 49.

11. Colenbrander, 'The Zulu Kingdom, 1828–79', in *Natal and Zululand from the Earliest Times to 1910: A New History*, edited by A. Duminy and B. Guest (Pietermaritzburg: University of Natal Press, 1989), pp. 96–109.
12. D. Welsh, *The Roots of Segregation: Native Policy in Colonial Natal, 1845–1910* (Cape Town: Oxford University Press, 1971), p. 15; T. McClendon, *White Chief, Black Lords: Shepstone and the Colonial State in Natal, 1845–1878* (Rochester, NY: University of Rochester Press, 2010); J. Guy, *Theophilus Shepstone and the Forging of Natal* (Pietermaritzburg: University of KwaZulu-Natal Press, 2013).
13. Kelly, *To Swim with Crocodiles: Land, Violence and Belonging in South Africa, 1800–1996* (East Lansing: Michigan State University Press, 2018).
14. Testimony of Baleni, 14 May 1914, *in The James Stuart Archive of Recorded Oral Evidence Relating to the History of the Zulu and Neighbouring Peoples*, Vol. 1, edited by C. de B. Webb and J.B. Wright (Durban: Killie Campbell Africana Library and Pietermaritzburg: University of Natal Press, 1976), p.32; J. Laband, *Zulu Warriors: The Battle for the South African Frontier* (New Haven: Yale University Press, 2014), pp. 207–21.
15. R. Cope, *Ploughshares of War: The Origins of the Anglo-Zulu War of 1879* (Pietermartizburg: University of Natal Press, 1999).
16. J. Laband, 'The Rise and Fall of the Zulu Kingdom', in *Zulu Identities: Being Zulu Past and Present*, edited by B. Carton, J. Laband and J. Sithole (New York: Columbia University Press, 2009), p. 87; E. Eldredge, *The Creation of the Zulu Kingdom, 1815–1828* (Cambridge: Cambridge University Press, 2014), pp. 270–82.
17. J. Guy, *The Destruction of the Zulu Kingdom: The Civil War in Zululand, 1879–1884* (Pietermaritzburg: University of Natal Press, 1994), pp. 80–209.
18. B. Carton, *Blood from Your Children: The Colonial Origins of Generational Conflict in South Africa* (Charlottesville: University of Virginia Press, 2000), pp. 105–6, 121–39; J. Guy, *The Maphumulo Uprising: War, Law and Ritual in the Zulu Rebellion* (Pietermaritzburg: University of KwaZulu-Natal Press, 2005), pp. 111–254.
19. N. Cope, *To Bind the Nation: Solomon kaDinuzulu and Zulu Nationalism 1913–1933* (Pietermaritzburg: University of Natal Press, 1993); P. la Hausse de Lalouvière, *Restless Identities: Signatures of Nationalism, Zulu Ethnicity and History in the Lives of Petros Lamula (c. 1881–1948) and Lymon Maling (1889–c. 1936)* (Pietermaritzburg: University of Natal Press, 2000) pp. 77, 86–8, 205–8.
20. G. Mare and G. Hamilton, *An Appetite for Power: Buthelezi's Inkatha and South Africa* (Bloomington: Indiana University Press, 1988), p. 141. T. Waetjen and G. Mare, 'Shaka's Aeroplane: The Take-off and Landing of Inkatha, Modern Zulu Nationalism and Royal Politics', in *Zulu Identities: Being Zulu Past and Present*, edited by B. Carton, J. Laband and J. Sithole (New York: Columbia University Press, 2009), pp. 352–62.
21. Mzala, *Gatsha Buthelezi: Chief with a Double Agenda* (London: Zed Books, 1988).

22. See note 1 above.
23. S. Ndlovu, 'A Reassessment of Women's Power in the Zulu Kingdom', in *Zulu Identities: Being Zulu, Past and Present,* edited by B. Carton, J. Laband and J. Sithole, (New York, Columbia University Press, 2009), pp. 111–21; E. Timbs, 'The Regiments: Cultural Histories of Zulu Masculinities and Gender Formation in South Africa, 1816–2018', unpublished PhD thesis, Michigan State University, 2019; S. Hassim, 'Family, Motherhood and Zulu Nationalism: The Politics of the Inkatha Women's Brigade', *Feminist Review* 43, 1993: 1–25; L. Jarvis, 'Gender, Violence, and Home in the Nazareth Baptist Church, 1906–1939', in *Ekhaya: The Politics of Home in KwaZulu-Natal,* edited by M. Healy and J. Hickel (Pietermaritzburg: University of KwaZulu-Natal Press, 2014), pp. 107–30.
24. J. Kelly, '"Women Were Not Supposed to Fight": The Gendered Uses of Martial and Moral Zuluness During *uDlame* (1990–1994)', in *Gendering Ethnicity in African Women's Lives,* edited by J. Shetler (Madison: University of Wisconsin Press, 2015), pp. 180–1.
25. *Weekly Mail,* 30 August–5 September 1991; this newspaper article referred to political violence that moved from Natal to the Rand; S. Taylor, *Shaka's Children: A History of the Zulu People* (London: HarperCollins, 1994), pp. 356–70.

Foreword

There are innumerable ways that human beings travel the long journey to healing. Mxolisi Mchunu tells us in *Violence and Solace: The Natal Civil War in Late-Apartheid South Africa* that writing his PhD and now this published book has helped him to heal. As he says, 'It is about sacrifices, emotional agony and its psychological impact on unrecorded victims, who were invariably women and children.'

No two people read a book or watch a movie in the same way. We read in the light of our own journey.

Before I finished reading this book, I contacted the author to ask him which department his PhD had been submitted to and he replied that it was history. I asked because it could equally have been offered to political science, social anthropology, social psychology, psychiatry or theology, or as part of a series of case studies on trauma healing.

There are many striking aspects in the text and I want to mention just a few. As Mchunu notes, the major players in the killing fields were black men fighting black men. However, the most affected were women and children but we seldom hear their voices and almost never in the first person. This is one of the remarkable aspects of this book, especially as Mchunu recalls his childhood memories. Through his willingness to self-disclose and give himself permission to be vulnerable, he gives us, as the readers, priceless insights into the immediate impact of trauma.

As I read, I felt that the whole book was a kind of private soliloquy written to himself, which we are privileged to witness.

The book illustrates the value of many different lenses to examine the same reality. Each lens can bring us to a certain set of conclusions.

This happens through the ongoing literature review and the way Mchunu comments on much other contemporary writing.

So many books written by academics about Africa, especially by non-Africans, lack the telling insights of a participant observer who is from that culture and speaks the local language. In addition, many scholars often omit reference to the full range of human, and even conflicting and apparently contradictory, emotions that people experience in war. I particularly appreciated the way Mchunu spoke about his anger towards his mother and how he had reflected on its genesis later in life.

Many articles see the conflict in the Natal Midlands as primarily arising from the struggle for power, influence and control between the Inkatha Freedom Party (IFP) and the United Democratic Front/ African National Congress.

Mchunu makes reference to the significance of what I would call the psychopathology of some leaders, who were described as megalomaniacs. Some have also commented on a leader in Natal who was a religious man of peace when speaking English but not so when speaking Zulu. This made his religiosity a form of mystification if not obscenity. It is also possible to argue that some leaders in the Natal Midlands were warlords. Chris Hani told me that listening to some leaders in the Natal Midlands made him feel that he was conservative in comparison. I do not think enough has been written about the implications for societies when leaders are seriously damaged human beings.

Moving the lens wider, Mchunu says, 'A crucial factor was state backing, both overt and covert, for the IFP before 1994.'

There are factors that Mchunu references that throw more light on what happened.

To what degree was it also a battle for dominance between the generations? What did it mean to be a man in patriarchal Zulu culture, and what happened when one side felt threatened or emasculated, even, or especially, if it was your own relatives?

We can also see a battle between democracy and traditional society, with the Zulu king at the apex. The recent rumblings around the Ingonyama Trust suggest that compromises that were made shortly before 1994 may cause long-term contestation. These will need to be managed very wisely to avoid major multidimensional strife in the future.

Mchunu reminds us that there was a long history of faction fights going back decades that had become part of the DNA of Zulu warriors. One could also reflect on just how colonial, followed by apartheid, experiences of domination, humiliation and exploitation shaped consciousness, including the competition for scarce resources.

The role of *muthi* in the conflict is a dimension that has been largely ignored by commentators. Some writers have referenced the importance of *muthi* in relation to the bravery of Zulu *impis* in the Battle of Isandlwana, despite the superior firepower of the British forces.

I was struck by the horrendous story of a relative who was abandoned because, as she had Alzheimer's disease, she would give away their hiding place and endanger everyone else. Such understandable choices are what haunts survivors and leads to moral and spiritual injury. The obvious temptation is to seek to bury the memory but unhealed memories have a way of coming back to haunt us, even into old age.

According to Mchunu, there are those who claim that there is now complete peace in the community but many of the interviewees tell another story. Several interviewees, who were survivors of the violence, indicate that some of their relatives had gone mad. I sometimes feel in such a context that those who run crazy are the only sane ones. The ones we should really worry about are those who participated in the violence and appeared to be unaffected.

This book makes it clear that many of the people in the community have had lifelong mental health issues, including the inability to have healthy, long-term relationships. These findings speak to the importance of healing memory processes, whether or not people need clinical intervention as most people do not.

As the Institute for Healing of Memories, we made a conscious decision many years ago to open an office in KwaZulu-Natal precisely because of the post-1994 ongoing political violence. We soon came to see that many people in different communities suffered from multiple woundedness. It is not accidental that KwaZulu-Natal also has the highest level of HIV infection rates.

There is reference in the book to one person who framed the conflict in terms of the battle between good and evil.

It is striking that, for Mchunu, a watershed moment in his journey to wholeness was his conversion to Christ and the experience of himself as deeply loved. Fortunately, he did not then make the mistake of thinking that he had arrived with no more healing to be done. The comments of his colleagues about unhelpful ways he responded under pressure assisted him to introspect on the long-term effects of old wounds.

Mchunu's conclusion that the greatest need of the community is not so much for reconciliation but rather for healing is something with which I concur wholeheartedly. It is still true for countless individuals and communities across South Africa, not to mention the whole human family.

Reading this book will be a rich and illuminating experience on many levels. For those who are willing, it will also be a mirror for self-reflection and help others on their journey to healing and wholeness.

Thank you, Dr Mxolisi Mchunu, for your life and witness.

Father Michael Lapsley
Founder and Director of the Institute for Healing of Memories

Acknowledgements

There are people without whom this book *could* not have been written and those without whom, I suspect, it *would* not have been written. My interest in the subject stems from my experiences as a child observer of political violence in KwaShange in the Natal Midlands. Many people of my age, born in this region, have similar memories. Undoubtedly, my desire to understand the impact and trauma caused by this violence, and how people recovered from it, is, at heart, a personal one. This book would not have been written without the survivors of the violence, perpetrators and/or victims – to whose memory it is dedicated. I am grateful to them for what they taught me about our dreadful recent past. I have tried to represent their experiences with as much accuracy as possible. I hope this book fulfils their wish to record this history.

Many people provided substantive contributions to the text; others commented on early drafts and engaged in thoughtful discussions of the ideas presented here. I would like to record my gratitude to Philippe Denis for, first and foremost, our camaraderie, which developed over the years as he supervised the PhD thesis that has culminated in this book. He guided me from the early stages of this research and throughout the work. His critiques shaped my scholarship.

I acknowledge Mbongiseni Buthelezi for our companionship and his immense contribution to my research and the writing of this book. He intellectually and elegantly engaged with my ideas. I am grateful in every way and hope to keep up our collaboration in the future. Special thanks go to Jill Kelly and Ben Carton, who read the manuscript, critically engaged with me and offered guidance that sharpened my arguments. They were always available to assist and replied promptly to my emails.

I benefited a great deal from the following outstanding scholars, who sadly passed on before this book was published: Margaret Lenta, who edited and commented on each and every chapter of my thesis; Yvonne Winters, to whom I am indebted for her unstinting gift of reading my manuscript and giving me her insights; Jeff Guy and Philip Bonner for reading and commenting on chapters.

Thanks to my lecturers and colleagues at the History Department of the University of KwaZulu-Natal: Keith Breckenridge, Julie Parle, Vukile Khumalo, Thembisa Waetjen, Jeff Guy, Catherine Burns, Marijke du Toit, Stephen Sparks, Ian Macqueen, Nafisa Essop Shaik, Mandisa Mbali, Prinisha Badassy, Barbara Wahlberg, Steve Kotze, Bernard Dubbeld and Julian Brown. This department shaped me like a potter moulding clay. It was not easy, but it was worth it.

I also benefited from Sonya Keyser and Richard Bell's expertise. They devoted their time to edit the manuscript and make it read better. Other specialists in the field who helped me were Jabulani Sithole, Debby Bonnin, Marinus de Haan, Lou Levine, Wendy Leeb and Bongani Ndhlovu. John Aitchison presented me with a book on the KwaZulu-Natal violence, to which I often referred. Their confirmation of my understanding was most reassuring. Thanks to Carolyn Hamilton and all my fellows at the Archive and Public Culture Research Initiative at the University of Cape Town for reading and commenting on some of my chapters.

Thanks go to Pearl Sithole, Sipho Malembe, Thenjiwe Meyiwa, Robert Morrell and Michael Hudson for reading some of the chapters and for recommending literature. Special thanks to my companions Zibonele Nxele, Zaynab Essack, Nondumiso Mkhize, Zipho Phakathi, Siphamandla Chili, Sthandiwe Mthuli, Nkosinathi Mzelemu, Mbongeni Hlengwa and Sibusiso Ntsele. Their support and critiques enriched my growth as a researcher and an academic. Thanks to my cousin, Philani Zuma, who recorded some of my interviews and videotaped most of them, under unfavourable conditions.

My colleagues at the Alan Paton Centre and the University of KwaZulu-Natal Archives in Pietermaritzburg helped me with information when I needed it. I must also thank staff at the Pietermaritzburg Archives and PACSA. My colleagues at the Campbell Collections were an essential source of research insight. Their companionable lunch conversation and support were invaluable.

The research work that is done at this library is rare: special thanks go to Senzo Mkhize, Mwelele Cele, Mthunzi Zungu, Stacie Gibson, Yvonne Winters, Bobby Eldridge, Vusi Buthelezi, Emily Krige and Nellie Somers.

I thank everyone at UKZN Press, especially Debra Primo, Kholeka Mabeta, Sally Hines and Adele Branch. Special thanks to Jacob Dlamini for writing an emotionally powerful endorsement for the book and Father Michael Lapsley for graciously acceding to my request to write the foreword. I thank many of our struggle heroes and heroines who sacrificed their lives for us to be liberated. Thanks to my spiritual leaders and life coaches, Merrick and Tshidi Habile; their support was unswerving.

To my mother, Jabulile Mchunu: there is no substitute for the unshakeable faith and love she has always given us as her children. My father and siblings have also been supportive throughout my career; I will forever be indebted to them.

I could not have written this book without my wife, Bongiwe, and children, Kuhle, Kuphelele and Kwandile, whose presence encouraged me to work hard. I cannot imagine how anyone could make me happier and prouder than they do. My wife helped me stay focused. She gave freely of her wisdom, patience and love. I am grateful to her for her help in this project and spending most of her time with our boys while I was busy researching and writing.

I acknowledge financial support I received from the Johannesburg Institute for Advanced Study (JIAS) at the University of Johannesburg, under the leadership of Bongani Ngqulunga. I thank him and all my fellows at JIAS for their expertise and guidance.

Finally, I thank the National Research Foundation (NRF) for the funding I received through my supervisor Philippe Denis and the University of KwaZulu-Natal Black Academia Scholarship. The NRF bears no responsibility for the opinions expressed within this book.

Abbreviations

ANC	African National Congress
CODESA	Convention for a Democratic South Africa
COSATU	Congress of South African Trade Unions
FOSATU	Federation of South African Trade Unions
IFP	Inkatha Freedom Party
MK	uMkhonto weSizwe
PAC	Pan-Africanist Congress
PFP	Progressive Federal Party
PTSD	post-traumatic stress disorder
SACP	South African Communist Party
SAP	South African Police
TRC	Truth and Reconciliation Commission
UDF	United Democratic Front
UWUSA	United Workers' Union of South Africa

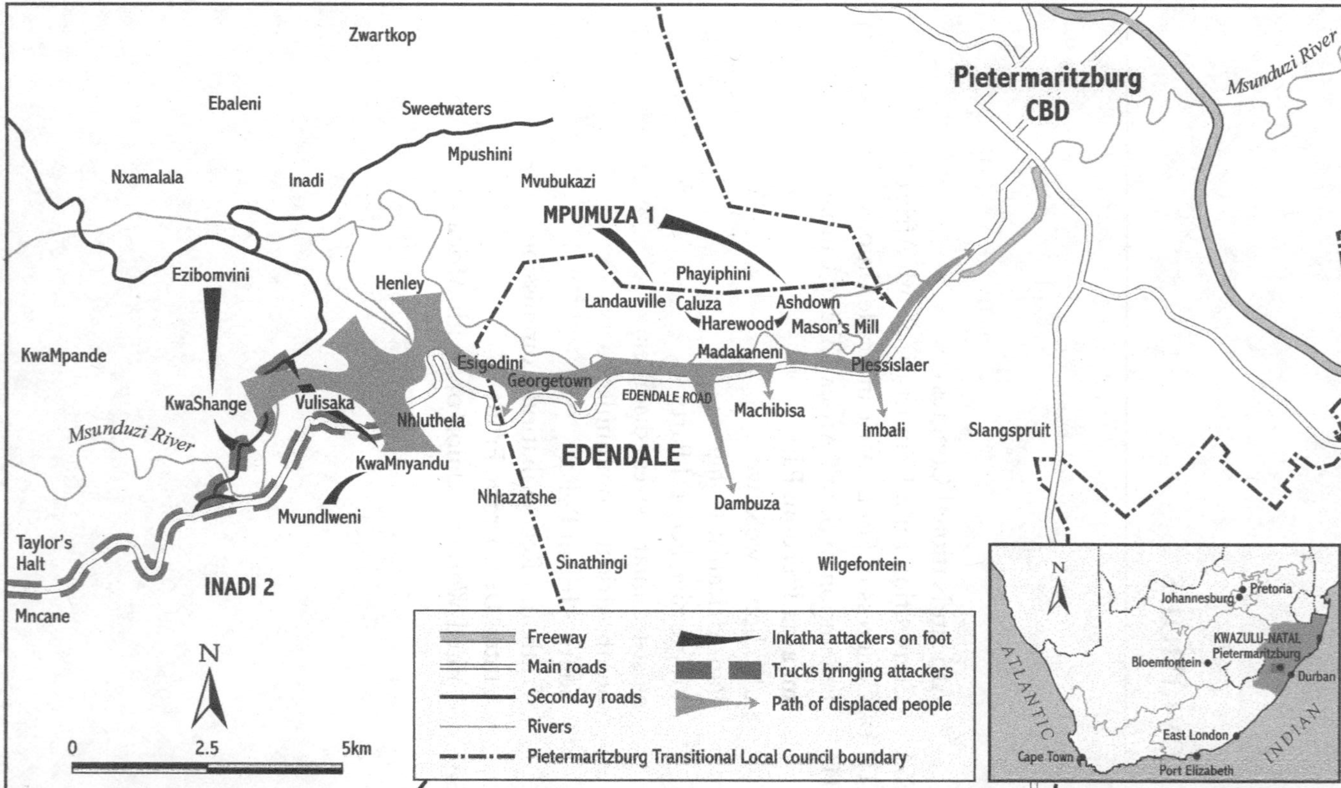

Map showing Seven Days' War, Vulindlela, 25–31 March 1990 (adapted from Cartographic Unit, University of Natal, 1999).

Introduction

THE POLITICAL VIOLENCE and vigilante activities that occurred in Natal and Zululand from 1985 to 1996 had numerous causes. The formation of the United Democratic Front (UDF) in 1983 contributed to the rise of vigilantism and political violence. The establishment of the Congress of South African Trade Unions (COSATU) in 1985 compounded this situation. Both these movements were known to be sympathetic to the African National Congress (ANC), which was still banned; hence they had similar objectives to the ANC. During this time, Inkatha was the only strong black political movement in the country, and particularly in Natal and Zululand. The Inkatha movement and its leader, Mangosuthu Buthelezi, regarded the formation of the UDF and COSATU as a challenge to the hegemony of Inkatha in the region, following Buthelezi's fallout with the ANC leadership in exile. Local leadership of political movements, the UDF and COSATU, on the one hand, and Inkatha, on the other hand, mobilised their support bases and took up arms against each other. The imposition of the state of emergency in 1986 intensified political violence and vigilante activities in the region. The Natal Midlands violence saw a high number of deaths and casualities. Local communities, such as Vulindlela, suffered a great deal.

Clan faction fights were characteristic of KwaShange, a rural community in Vulindlela in the Natal Midlands, from the 1940s to the 1970s,[1] but from the late 1980s onwards (especially 1987) political unrest and struggle against the National Party apartheid regime changed into conflict between Inkatha and the UDF, which gradually worsened into civil war. The violence impacted upon families and inter-generational relationships. According to some senior residents of KwaShange, a number of youths were ill-disciplined. Issues of disciplining youths had been obscured during the political struggle and violence, making it hard to disentangle them. The violent nature of different incidents within this struggle period affected people, both psychologically and physically.

The South African government was accused of secretly provoking acts of violence in Natal and Zululand, and it was furthermore accused of having sent Inkatha troops to the Caprivi Strip in Namibia for training in guerrilla combat. The government later acknowledged this, explaining that the KwaZulu Legislative Assembly needed specially trained forces for its officials. The unbanning of political parties and the release of Nelson Mandela in 1990 saw Natal and Zululand entering a new phase of random vigilante activities and violence. The security forces (the South African Police and the South African Defence Force) were accused of supporting Inkatha vigilantes. All this led to the 'Seven Days' War' in 1990 in the Natal Midlands, particularly in Vulindlela.

As a result of the violence between Inkatha and the UDF, some 12 000 people died from 1985 to 1996 in KwaZulu-Natal (formerly made up of the province of Natal and the KwaZulu homeland). This is a conservative figure. The number of deaths from political violence is notoriously difficult to establish and the real numbers are probably higher. Extensive damage was inflicted on private and public property.[2] According to John Aitchison, in the Natal Midlands alone, arson and petrol bomb attacks destroyed or damaged 1 103 houses between 1987 and 1989.[3] During the same period, 291 vehicles – 126 of them buses – were damaged through arson or stoning. It is estimated that between 200 000 and 500 000 refugees fled the conflict in the province between 1984 and 1994.[4]

In KwaShange, this violence created divisions in families and the community. All efforts to put an end to the violence and vigilantism failed. And the announcement that the first democratic election in South Africa was to be held in 1994 triggered even more violence.

Exhaustion in the area and a national climate that promoted peace were elements that eventually brought the conflict to an end. Socially and economically, the region is still experiencing problems. Survivors and generations born during and after the turmoil talk about endless psychological and emotional suffering. Trauma experienced as a result of this violence and its consequences influenced the lives of all persons affected by it, and this was transmitted across generations, through families and communities. The social structure of the community was affected by it, and, by implication, that of successive generations will also be affected.

This book presents a historical overview of the violence in Vulindlela, KwaShange Location. It describes what happened during the years of political violence and records testimonies of the survivors in the area. It is an account of how they coped (or failed to cope) with their experiences, both then and fifteen years after the end of violence. It is a social inquiry that focuses on the way KwaShange survivors of violence make sense of their experiences and the world in which they live.

KwaShange is part of Vulindlela. It is a rural area about 30 kilometres from Pietermaritzburg and the population is largely traditional.The settlement was established in the nineteenth century as the Natal Zwartkop Location under the colonial administrator Sir Theophilus Shepstone's location policy. Under the National Party government's homeland policy, it was renamed Vulindlela in 1975 and made part of greater KwaZulu.[5] After the first democratic elections in 1994, the area was absorbed into the province of KwaZulu-Natal.

Vulindlela is located within the greater Msunduzi Municipality and is one of the seven sub-districts in the uMgungundlovu District Municipality. It is situated to the west of both the Pietermaritzburg and the greater Edendale areas. It is peri-urban in character with tracts of agricultural land interspersed with settlement. Most of the land is owned by the Ingonyama Trust Board, and land allocation is undertaken by five traditional councils. Vulindlela is made up of nine wards, of which five are under traditional leadership and four are under the ward councillors of the local government municipal system. Its population of just over 150 000 is predominantly Zulu-speaking.[6]

I am aware that earlier academic historical writings purport to be scientific and objective as opposed to writing autobiographical life stories, which are regarded as subjective and influenced by the vagaries of memory and the intentions of their authors. An opposite concern is raised by contemporary, progressive scholars such as Robert Morrell, who argues: 'For some time, history has been searching for lost voices

– those of workers, the peasants, the children, and most recently the subaltern. But there is another voice which historians have been less anxious to access – that of the writer him- or herself.'[7]

Arguments concerning self-study (autobiography) and 'insider-outsider' research have been addressed in several studies and disciplines in the Social Sciences and Humanities faculties, particularly in disciplines such as Literature (in which field autobiographies are generally considered) and Anthropology (insider-outsider research). History tends to undervalue autobiographies because of their subjective nature, but not biography, which is considered to be in the area of historical study. I believe that personal narratives are an invaluable form of intellectual discourse and an important source of social history. Morrell contends that even an apparently objective document bears the distinctive and unique mark of its author and his or her past, predilections and disposition.[8]

The subject of this book is my personal odyssey: how I experienced the traumatic events of 1987 to 1996, from the age of eight up to my early teens. This period of uncertainty and violence marked my life and affected my identity. Thus, this book could not be written without frequent reference to my historically constructed self. The study was shaped by my own history and past experience. It was only after reflection that I was able to grasp the nature of memory and its relationship to the violence-induced trauma, which characterised the civil war that marred my childhood. Mine was a childhood that in its interactions among parents, children and siblings was echoed in many other families in KwaShange. I have used the opportunity to write this book in order to understand some of the effects of war on family dynamics. The aim is for the reader to catch a glimpse of a complex 'truth' about the nature of the violence in KwaShange and what was happening within the survivors, a truth not limited by the mask that the survivors so often hide behind. The aim is also to shed light on the largely hidden experiences of women and children in this conflict via an examination of and reflections on myself and my parents' experiences. That is why I have permitted my own voice to come through. My aim is to produce conclusions that will add an authentic dimension to existing knowledge of the experiences of violence in the Natal Midlands. At the same time, I hope that this will help to rationalise the methodological use of the self in research.[9]

I do not focus on great incidents or historical moments, but on the multitude of 'small emotional and psychological effects' that stemmed from my mother's and my own experience of the political violence.[10] In other words, the book tries to answer these questions: how did this 'abnormal' situation of war affect everyday life; how did this imprint the mind and soul of the ordinary KwaShange community member? And what happened to those who were children at the time? By reflecting on myself, I explain the effects of the violence on many of the children in the Natal Midlands.

Memories that are painful or do not fit with our present identity may be repressed or reconfigured so that they are easier to live with.[11] Yet, this process of interpretation and reinterpretation is never totally accomplished, as Peter Coleman writes: 'There can be no such thing as a final account of a person's life. Any coherent account is shaped by an underlying and continuing search for meaning, whether on the part of the subjects or their biographer.'[12]

The hardest hit

The political upheaval tore whole communities and families apart – from Vulindlela to Edendale to Howick. Generations grew up in the midst of brutal armed conflicts. Children as young as ten observed. Some were involved in the violence as either victims or perpetrators. Some children were forced by circumstances to get involved and fight to defend their communities. Children have, of course, always been caught up in warfare. They usually have little choice but to experience at least the same horrors as their parents – as casualties or even as combatants. When they have to sleep in forests, hide in streams at night, and when food runs short in refugee camps, it is children who are the hardest hit since their growing bodies need steady supplies of nutrients. The trauma of exposure to violence and brutal death has emotionally affected generations of young people for the rest of their lives.[13] One woman in Pietermaritzburg commented on her experience of political violence:

> I am bitter that all my children died within a short space of time in this [tragic] way. They respected me. And one of them was supporting the family, but I am thankful that they are now free from these times of hatred and distrust. I am also free from

> an endless life of fear, fearing for their safety. Nonetheless, it is still a horrible experience to be a parent of any black family: in these days [speaking of the then civil war] our male children are being slaughtered.[14]

Newspapers at the time reported that children as young as ten years old were killing people in the Pietermaritzburg area, and it was feared that the war was spawning a generation of hardened killers. This observation resulted in community leaders calling for the urgent establishment of rehabilitation programmes for the thousands of children who were 'roaming wild', witnessing brutal mob murders, copying their elders and playing violent games.[15]

At this time, schools were affected by a lack of teachers. Many teachers were reported to be seeking employment elsewhere (especially those from rural Vulindlela), where people belonged to the Inkatha movement, while teachers who taught in these schools came from Edendale and Imbali and belonged to unions that were affiliated to COSATU and the ANC. Large numbers of children were reported to be on the run and others were abandoned by parents who fled in fear of their lives. According to the South African Council of Churches at a meeting in the Midlands, children had been so badly traumatised that they might never recover. 'We are deeply concerned about children who have been drawn into the violence. Some are only eight years old.'[16] Many children were seriously damaged psychologically: some reacted by becoming fearful but others turned highly aggressive. At that time, children less than ten years old were emulating their parents and adopting violence as an exciting new game, such as stabbing, verbally abusive insults, destroying property, using vulgar terminology and petrol-bombing. Reverend Musa Zondi commented that 'their future is being permanently paralysed by what they are learning now'.[17]

The violence disrupted normal family life and destroyed the fabric of society. At the most impressionable and sensitive age, children got used to seeing people being brutally killed. They were being subjected to things they should never have experienced at that age. Reverend Zondi compared the situation in Pietermaritzburg to Beirut and Northern Ireland 'where you see children throwing stones even though they don't understand the conflict'.[18] Peter Kerchhoff, the founder of Pietermaritzburg Agency for Christian Social Awareness (PACSA) and an ardent campaigner for social justice in the 1980s and 1990s,[19] said that children were being psychologically traumatised and undoubtedly needed care. Others were proposing rehabilitation but there was doubt whether the programmes would work while violence and injustice continued. There was a need to end the violence first.[20]

'The children are scared because they can see the adults are scared. People really do not know what is happening,' said one woman in Elandskop.[21] This woman was suffering from the anguish of being a parent in a troubled area. Many people were frightened, especially at night 'when a knock at the door could set your heart racing'.[22] Families had taken to sleeping in the veld for fear that their homes would be set alight in the night. The woman in Elandskop said she had taken three young children, whose parents left them in the care of relatives as they worked in other areas, to her employer's home where they had stayed for a week until things had calmed down. Many children got lost in the ensuing confusion and some were sent to relatives in more peaceful areas. The number of children killed in the turmoil is largely unrecorded. The plight of children amid that turmoil was an area of grave concern to the violence monitors.[23] A thirteen-year-old boy from Edendale said he had left home about three months before when political tensions had prompted him to take to the streets with his friends:

> I had to make a choice between my friends, who are politically active in organisations such as UDF, and the traditions of my family. My father is a chief and an Inkatha member. I have no fight with either organisation but even friendships become political and at home my loyalties were continually questioned. It was easier to leave although this has meant quitting school.[24]

Many academic articles have been written on the effect of political violence on children.[25] All these authors agree that violence has a negative impact on families and children are seriously affected. Some authors have highlighted the role of inter-generational tensions as a result of young people being more inclined to take a militant line and elders upholding traditional tribal authority.[26] There has been very little academic research on the experiences of children during the political violence in the Natal Midlands. It is mostly in newspaper reports that reference is made to the status of children at the time of the civil war. There were predictions that children's futures were being permanently paralysed by what they were learning.

Notes

1. For the history of faction fights in Natal and Zululand, see J. Sithole, 'Land Disputes, Social Identities and the State in the *Izimpi Zemibango* in the Umzinto District, 1930–1935', *Journal of Natal and Zulu History* 27(1), 2009: 60–82.
2. P. Denis, R. Ntsimane and T. Cannell, *Indians versus Russians: An Oral History of Political Violence in Nxamalala (1987–1993)* (Pietermaritzburg: Cluster Publications, 2010).
3. John Aitchison, 'Numbering the Dead', unpublished mimeograph, 1988.
4. Quoted in A. Jeffery, *The Natal Story: Sixteen Years of Conflict* (Johannesburg: South African Institute of Race Relations, 1997), p. 2.
5. E.H. Brookes and N. Hurwitz, *The Native Reserves of Natal.* Natal Regional Survey, Volume 7 (Cape Town: Oxford University Press, 1957), pp. 2–3.
6. Vulindlela local area plan spatial framework accessed from Msunduzi Municipality, www.msunduzi.gov.za.
7. R. Morrell, *From Boys to Gentlemen: Settler Masculinity in Colonial Natal, 1880–1920* (Pretoria: Unisa Press, 2001), p. x.
8. Morrell, *From Boys to Gentlemen*, p. x.
9. Morrell, *From Boys to Gentlemen*, p. x.
10. This type of research into oral sources, as Alessandro Portelli reminds us, 'tell[s] us not only what people did, what they wanted to do, what they believed they were doing, and what they now think they did'. See A. Portelli, 'The Peculiarities of Oral History', *History Workshop Journal* 12(1), 1981: 99–100. In other words, oral histories are sources with multiple layers of meaning that help historians investigate complex questions of memory, myth, experience, identity, narrative, power and the role of the historian in the construction of history.
11. A. Thomson, 'The Anzac Legend: Exploring National Myth and Memory in Australia', in *The Myths We Live By*, edited by R. Samuel and P. Thompson (London: Routledge, 1990).
12. P. Coleman, 'Ageing and Life History: The Meaning of Reminiscence in Later Life', in *Life and Work History Analyses: Qualitative and Quantitative Developments*, edited by S. Dex (London: Routledge, 1991), p. 122.
13. UNICEF, *The State of the World's Children 1996* (Oxford: Oxford University Press, 1996).
14. *Sunday Tribune,* 21 February 1988.
15. *Sunday Tribune,* 21 February 1988.

16. Reverend Ben Nsimbi, a Methodist minister from Georgetown, a township in the Edendale valley, in *Sunday Tribune*, 21 February 1988.
17. *Sunday Tribune,* 21 February 1988.
18. *Sunday Tribune,* 21 February 1988.
19. A. Koopman and J. Deane, 'New Names for Old: Transformation in the Streets of Pietermaritzburg', *Natalia* 35, 2005: 87.
20. *Sunday Tribune*, 21 February 1988.
21. *Sunday Tribune*, 21 February 1988.
22. *Sunday Tribune*, 21 February 1988.
23. Reports from the 24-hour Monitoring Group of the Midlands Crisis Relief Committee, 25 March to 28 July 1990, Alan Paton Collection, Pietermaritzburg.
24. *Sunday Tribune*, 21 February 1988.
25. See J. Aitchison, 'The Origins of the Midlands War', in *The Role of Political Violence in South Africa's Democratisation*, edited by R. Greenstein (Johannesburg: Community Agency for Social Enquiry, 2003); J. Aitchison, 'KwaZulu-Natal: The Pre-election Wars of the 1990s', in *The Role of Political Violence in South Africa's Democratisation*, edited by R. Greenstein (Johannesburg: Community Agency for Social Enquiry, 2003); S. Stavrou, 'Underdevelopment: Natal's Formula for Conflict', *Indicator SA* 7(3), 1990: 52–6; A. Minnaar, *Conflict and Violence in Natal/KwaZulu: Historical Perspectives* (Pretoria: HSRC, 1990); R. Taylor and M. Shaw, 'The Natal Conflict', in *Restructuring South Africa*, edited by J.D. Brewer (London: St Martin's Press, 1994); A. Johnston, 'Politics and Violence in KwaZulu-Natal', in *Violence in Southern Africa*, edited by W. Gutteridge and J. Spence (London: Frank Cass, 1997); Jeffery, *The Natal Story*.
26. See A. Guelke, 'Interpretations of Political Violence during South Africa's Transition', *Politikon* 27(2), 2000: 239–54. For a study of young people involved in political violence in Natal, see A. Sitas, 'The Making of the "Comrades" Movement in Natal, 1985–91', *Journal of Southern African Studies* 18(3), 1992: 629–41. See also M. Mchunu, 'Culture Change, Zulu Masculinity and Intergenerational Conflict in the Context of Civil War in Pietermaritzburg (1987–1991)', in *From Boys to Men: Social Constructions of Masculinity in Contemporary Society*, edited by T. Shefer, K. Ratele, A. Strebel, N. Shabalala and R. Buikema (Cape Town: UCT Press, 2007); C. Campbell, 'Learning to Kill? Masculinity, the Family and Violence in Natal', *Journal of Southern African Studies* 18(3), 1992: 614–28.

1

An Autobiographical Narrative

MOST OF WHAT I describe here did not take place in the public eye. Nor did my experience relate only to the death and suffering of men (talking from a patriarchal society's viewpoint) who fought heroically to fend off attack in KwaShange. It is also not about prominent men who founded local United Democratic Front (UDF) or Inkatha branches and acted as 'warlords' or organised vigilante groups that perpetrated the violence in the area. But it is rather about sacrifices, emotional agony and its psychological impact on unrecorded victims, who were invariably women and children. It is about ordinary people, who were caught up in a circle of political violence for almost a decade. It is easy for the 'outsider' to get the wrong idea about the daily lives of these people, and perhaps pity those who were fighting for survival. This was an unrelenting struggle for life itself, on the part of parents, for their own lives and for their children.

Children of the violence did not understand the genesis of the war. What they knew was gleaned from fearful mothers, from siblings and from actual experiences of hunger, fleeing, hiding and panic. They became orphans or were abandoned. The newspaper reports of the time predicted their identity crisis. My question is: what happened to these children?

The violence started when I was eight and only subsided when I was sixteen. I could be considered 'lucky' in having retained my parents, siblings and my home. I survived my experiences, but at what cost? My teenage years were marked by anger and distrust.

There is a second category of 'children' of violence – youths (*izinsizwa* – aged between fourteen and twenty), who were differently affected: they were instigators, party members, 'soldiers', if you like.

Often in the case of war-torn societies, where the conflict has continued or has broken out sporadically for years, these behaviours may eventually become accepted and may be common to large portions of the population and may be considered cultural phenomena. Research shows that post-conflict societies sometimes experience levels of violence comparable to those in times of civil war.[1] Adam Curle notes, regarding societies torn by civil conflict, that alienation tends to escalate into post-traumatic stress syndrome. Violence generally continues to exist within the social fabric of societies coming out of conflict for decades after the conflict has ended.[2]

Personal experiences of the violence in the civil war arguably affected many people to a greater or lesser degree. This is the inside story of KwaShange, told by two of its survivors, namely, my mother and myself.

Theatre of the mind: Living in a violent era and area

Imagine a domestic worker: my mother, Jabulile Mchunu, who was working for an Afrikaner family in Pietermaritzburg. She came from rural KwaShange, 30 kilometres from the city. She worked six days a week, from Monday to Saturday, travelling backwards and forwards daily. It was 16h00, time for her to go home to KwaShange. Her employer gave her a lift to the bus stop at East Street in Pietermaritzburg because walking in the street alone was dangerous. This was where all those who lived in Vulindlela commuted to and from the city. She noticed that only a few people were waiting for buses to go back home. This had become the norm because people opted to stay at their respective employers' houses to avoid commuting, and on this day there were very few women. Only people who had to go to town urgently did so at that time. My mother waited for the 17h00 bus, which arrived on time. She got onto the bus with a lot of men. These men were forced to return home; there was a war going on and they had to patrol to protect the area at night. They had to relieve those who had been patrolling during the day. While she was still waiting at the bus stop, she heard that many women and children had already left KwaShange and fled for their lives because a message had come that Inkatha would attack the area that same night.

In telling me later, she exclaimed, '*ngaphelelwa asonzwaneni! ngicabanga izingane zami*' (I just lost the little energy I had, thinking about my children). My mother was not sure if the bus would reach KwaShange. There were many reasons why this might not happen. Firstly, this bus could be stoned when passing Edendale. Even though Edendale was a UDF-aligned area, it was dangerous to go through, because *amaqabane* (comrades) stoned any bus that passed through Edendale going to '*ngaphezulu*' (the outskirts of Pietermaritzburg in the north), as almost all villages described as *ngaphezulu* were Inkatha Freedom Party (IFP) strongholds. There IFP supporters attacked those who were not obviously of their party. My home area of KwaShange fell under Chief Shayabantu Zondi, who refused to allow his people to become UDF party supporters; hence it was singled out for attack by Inkatha in an attempt to displace those UDF-supporting families. So UDF people in Edendale, in support of KwaShange, would stone buses passing by, even though the bus could well contain people from the latter area. KwaShange buses would usually be accompanied by an Edendale car to allow them safe passage. In addition, this same bus could be stopped by Inkatha people in Mvundlweni, the area opposite KwaShange, another IFP stronghold. They were known to be merciless killers of UDF supporters. That same morning, my mother had had the experience of being in a minibus that was shot at in Mvundlweni, and the person who had been sitting next to her was injured by a bullet. Many people lost their lives in the Mvundlweni area. And this bus was also in danger because police patrols could think it contained people returning from a rally somewhere – potential troublemakers. The police were known for wasting no time shooting to kill.

Luckily that day my mother arrived home at about 17h45. She was safe, but fearful. It was quiet with no people moving around. You could hear a dog barking from afar, but you could see no fire smoke, no one leading a normal life. People had gone to seek refuge somewhere far from the area. Others were hiding. You could hear a whistle as a warning of possible attack – comrades communicating with each other from different parts of the area. Women and children had been instructed to move out of the area, but those who had nowhere to go were hiding.

My mother often claimed that throughout this time 'the only thing that I was concerned about was my children's whereabouts'. She would come home only to find the younger children waiting for her arrival. Anything could have happened on her way back home.

As the oldest of the three younger children, I would be filled with anxiety for her return. I could not imagine what I would have done without her as some children were left as orphans. 'I did not expect to find your older brothers anyway,' she said. My older brothers had gone. She did not know where they were, but wherever they were, they were patrolling and they had weapons to defend the area from Inkatha attackers as well as from policemen, who often came as part of a 'third force'.[3] On her return, my mother would pace up and down, locking the house and surrounding rondavels and preparing herself and the younger children for another night in the nearby forest. Her eyes would be full of tears, but she was not crying. Later, she explained: 'I had to be brave because if I showed fear, all of you would cry, and I would not know how to control myself.' She would tell her children: 'Let us go, everything will be fine after all, tomorrow we will sleep in our home and nothing will happen to us.' When my mother said this, I did not understand what was really happening, and I did not know who to talk to because my mother was too anxious. Her body was there but her mind was miles away. I did not know where my father was, but subsequently I realised that he had stayed at work because there was no transport from town to KwaShange. I was unsure whether to believe my mother's promises that 'things would get better' because she had been saying this for some time, but it never happened. I thought she was not telling the truth and I felt afraid at the time, and later I felt angry. Perhaps I would have preferred to have been told the truth. I loved my mother and I wanted to believe her, even though what she was claiming sounded contradictory to what was happening. Yet, when I did not believe her, I felt guilty and it was like I was betraying her in some way that I could not fully explain.

My mother was also anxious about her two elder sons, who were patrolling. She knew that they were angry with her because she worked for the 'dogs' (*amabhunu* or Boers as they were called at that time) who oppressed black people. The context was the UDF's policy to make South Africa under the National Party government ungovernable. My mother explained: 'The reason why I was so scared was because it had happened to other neighbours, whose children turned against them [parents]; people had gone mad.' My mother eventually went to sleep in the forest with her three children; her employer had given her three sleeping bags for the cold outdoors.

She got up in the morning of the following day, not too early because Inkatha would attack the village at that time of the morning. She eventually left the forest with us children at 04h30 because she had to catch the bus at 05h30 in order to go to work. Her explanation was: 'One had to respect the employers because I knew that I would need their assistance one day, so I had to pretend that things were normal.' She was not sure if she would reach work because the bus might be attacked in the neighbouring Inkatha area. So the stressful journey of the previous day was repeated. She left us children in fear because we were not sure if everything would go well at school. At this time, there were few children at school as many had left the area. It was not a normal situation; teachers we knew were no longer there and our primary school was in danger because it had Inkatha children and UDF children. Each organisation wanted to come and look after its members' children.

One day my mother came back in the afternoon to hear that her uncle, Zakhele Makhathini, had been stoned to death by UDF boys in the area. They accused him of being a spy and having a relationship with Chief Shayabantu Zondi, the Inkatha leader. My mother could not go to see her uncle's body because she was afraid that she would be killed next. As she locked herself in her room, crying, she heard the news that her uncle's wife had been killed too. Her aunt had threatened to mention the killers' names to the police as she knew the people who came to kill her husband, some of whom were relatives. The aunt's family had a mentally challenged daughter. She had slept with her parents the whole night because she did not realise that they were dead. My mother's later comment was, 'I remember myself losing my mind, the whole night I could not sleep, and I was shouting "blessed are those who are dead".' In her anger and frustration, she decided not to go to the forest that night, but to sleep in her own house. She explained: 'If I am to die, I would like to die with my children in my house.'

This narrative is but one story of my mother with her children in the area of KwaShange; there are many other women in this and surrounding areas who experienced similar ordeals. I have only described what I saw of my mother then and what she tells me now. This is individual and collective memory, added to my knowledge of historical events in the area. Others, who were children at the time, told me what they went through in the civil war. When questioned about what they felt about their parents' states of mind, almost all described their parents as people who had 'lost it'. Two sisters described their mother's condition as 'needing psychological therapy', but other family members described her as being 'possessed by spirits' (they thought she was being called to become an *isangoma* – traditional healer). Others thought their mother was at the initial stage of *ukuhlanya* (madness).[4]

My personal experiences and memories of violence

My memories of childhood are swamped with political violence. I only remember bits of my life up to seven years old: my first day at school, how I missed home. I ask myself what I missed when I went to school. I think it was childhood games, playing with clay and mud, building houses and wire toy cars. We would escape from home to a small stream, known as iNembe, to swim. Along with my siblings, we were always happy because we knew that after working hours my mother would come back from work with slices of bread and jam, and occasionally with fruit and cakes. These are good memories but they were short-lived because the political violence started in 1987. I was then in Standard 2 (Grade 4) in Henley Combined School. I was only ten years old. I was the seventh child in a home of nine. I had five brothers and three sisters.

My father worked for the Department of Agriculture at the University of Natal, and my mother was a domestic worker. My father's second wife lived in KwaShange, some distance from us. She was unemployed. My grandmother, who was a pensioner, my aunt and her three children, and my eldest sister with her two small children lived with us. Not far from home were my paternal uncles. They had their own nuclear families. Our neighbours were my maternal uncles and aunt, while other neighbours were close family friends, who had come to the area of KwaShange at the same time as my grandparents in the 1960s.

In 1986, when I was in Standard 1 (Grade 3) at school, we did a subject called *ubuntu-botho*, which is an African philosophy that places emphasis on 'being human through other people'. It has been succinctly reflected in the phrase 'I am because of who we all are'.[5] It was 'a compulsory non-examinable subject in all KwaZulu schools under the Department of Education and Culture'.[6] It was 'part of Inkatha's ideological strategy to control youth who had rebelled against parental authority'.[7] It was my favourite subject because it meant that we stopped normal classes, and we joined together with groups from other classes and we sang. I remember there was a song that went '*Uphilela ntoni wena, uShenge uyasiphilela isizwe*' (What are you living for? Shenge lives for the nation). We would sing these songs at home too. One of my paternal uncles used to enjoy it and encouraged us and sang these songs along with us. He often came to school to meet with our principal and teachers. We did not know what it was about, but we felt important because our uncle knew the principal. In retrospect, from my interviews with him, I realised that as a leader of the local Inkatha branch, he was campaigning for the teachers to join Inkatha.

In 1987, there was serious tension between my parents and this 'Inkatha' uncle. We were warned to stop going to his home, but no explanation was given. My grandmothers interceded and calmed the situation down, but still my parents were not happy when we played at my uncle's house. In the same year, there was a group of young people who gathered at school every Friday afternoon for meetings. On these occasions, they would come out and sing slogans on the road, persuading people to join Inkatha. I still remember some of the songs: '*yibambeni mabuth'eNkatha, yibambeni mabuth'eNkatha, abanye baya le, beye le, siyaphambili*' and '*joyini, joyina, joyina Inkatha. Inkatha leyo eyesizwe*' (join, join, join Inkatha, Inkatha of the Nation). As children we would follow them and sing.

One day my mother came back from work to find my elder brother and I had attended one of these meetings. She reprimanded us severely and warned us to never again go to such gatherings. Later, I realised that she may have known more than I thought about the political situation. The tension between my parents and my uncle stemmed from his attempts to persuade them to join Inkatha. It was at such meetings that the first violent conflict of 1987 was discussed. This led to the killing of thirteen boys, so my mother had unknowingly saved her sons.

Later that year, I remember it was cold and had been raining the whole night; this was the time of the 1987 floods. In the morning, I was seated near the fire in my maternal uncle's house, opposite our own home. Through the door, I saw a number of yellow police cars struggling along the muddy road. My mother and my aunt were outside, talking in low voices, almost whispering. I could not hear what they were saying. All I remember is my mother called me to go home with her and instructed all of us not to go anywhere. My older brothers were all at home that day. It was indeed a strange day: I had never seen such quiet people in my life. Worry was written in everybody's eyes. Outside, it was silent: everybody was indoors. KwaShange was still and the bad weather probably contributed. It was a strange atmosphere.

When my grandmother, in the silence, broke into loud praying, I realised that something had gone wrong. Secret talks between my mother and my older brothers worried me. That day marked the beginning of the end of my childhood, and that of many of my age group. I heard in my grandmother's prayer that some people had been killed. I remember feeling deeply disturbed but not knowing the whole story. It only became clear when another aunt, who was close to the house where Inkatha youth had gathered to plan an attack on UDF-supporting homes, came and explained. This house had been attacked. She saw flames and heard guns and she was completely panic-stricken, especially because most of the boys who had died were her husband's extended family members.

From 1987 to 1990, KwaShange changed completely. Many people I had known since I was small were no longer there – either they had died or relocated without us knowing. We would wake up in the morning and hear that so-and-so family was no longer in KwaShange, and no one could tell us children where they had gone.

One morning we heard that my paternal uncle (the one who knew the school principal) had fled. No one knew where his family had gone into hiding. His sons, who were our close family members and friends, had gone, and that meant we would never see them again. I remember how I desperately missed them. By that time, I understood that there was a war between the UDF and Inkatha. *We* were obviously UDF and *they* were Inkatha. The UDF was 'cleaning-up' the area and any person who was suspected of being an Inkatha supporter was attacked and killed and his house burnt. Almost every day, we would receive threats from neighbouring Inkatha areas that KwaShange would be attacked. People were 'on the run' all the time. As children, we were trained by our older brothers to make petrol bombs for self-defence. We were told to hold up plastic bottles at arm's length and they would aim and shoot at them. Later I realised that this was to toughen us up to become young combatants in order to defend our homes. During this period, we were often woken up at night or early in the morning, and we had to run into hiding at a moment's notice, so we slept fully clothed, even down to our shoes.

This continued until 1990 when the greatest horror started – the Seven Days' War. I was in Standard 5 (Grade 7). I was entering adolescence and I was aware of what was happening in the area. My understanding of politics started when Nelson Mandela was released from prison in 1990. I remember my brothers and sisters talking about it and we heard the news on the radio. At that time, I had no clue who Mandela was. I had never heard of him except in slogans we chanted and songs we sang. In retrospect, I realise that all those who led us in slogans and songs did not know or had not seen Mandela or even his pictures. In my childish mind I thought, Shoo! This person is obviously a white person and he is so important! I had never seen or heard of a black person receiving such attention. I was so interested that I went to our neighbour to watch television. I remember there were drops of rain and obviously it rained in Johannesburg as well, where the television station was based, because the news reader said, '*kwaXhosa imvula isho ukuthi kunama thamsanqa*' (drops of rain mean luck in Xhosa belief). This happiness preceded a great horror for KwaShange.

On 27 March 1990, Inkatha attacked KwaShange and many other areas. It had been raining for a few days and the Msunduzi River was overflowing. It was still early in the morning and we had just woken up. One of my cousins came to tell us that there was going to be an attack. When the message came, many people left their homes and moved away from near the road to hide in the forest. My mother, two younger siblings and I left late, and it was not possible for us to run far. As we were running, bullets were flying over our heads. We knew that if we heard a gunshot, we had to lie down on our stomachs; it was safer that way. My mother realised that if we continued running, we would be killed by the bullets. She decided that we should hide in the nearby stream. The Inkatha attackers were only two minutes away and we could hear them swearing and threatening to kill us. We hid in the stream from approximately 06h00 until 23h30.

While we were in the stream, many things happened. We were joined by a woman of my mother's age. She was followed by her dog, which was drawing attention to us, causing tension between my mother and the owner. My mother wanted her to get rid of her dog, but the owner did not know how. Later the police helicopter flew over us, trying to force us to leave the stream, so we would be seen by Inkatha members who were close to where we were hiding. We could hear them talking and shooting; we could smell the houses burning. Police sprayed tear gas on us. At the time, I did not know that it was tear gas. I remember praying, a frightened thirteen-year-old, and longing for the bank to open up and bury me, my mother and my siblings. I wanted to die naturally rather than be killed by the Inkatha people. Then we saw grass and trees by the stream moving, where we were hiding – somebody was coming towards us. It was our neighbour, an old woman, but I thought people had figured out that we were in the stream and had come to 'finish' us. To me, the tear-gassing was an answer from God. I thought He heard my prayer and this was the process of dying, as by then I was fearful that everyone was dead – my grandmothers, my elder brothers and my sisters. Somehow the knowledge that there was a person – not a power but a person – named Jesus, who could see, hear and answer my prayers gave me the hope that I needed to get through the night. By night-time, we knew that things had calmed down, but we did not know where to go because we thought that our house had been burnt. The neighbour who had joined us in the stream suggested that we go to the local church. She had heard that there were people who had gathered there. We sat in the church until the early hours of the morning. Nobody was prepared to risk going home. Many of those who had gathered in the church – old people and children – walked the many kilometres to Edendale to seek refuge.

My mother encountered many severe challenges and hardships. In my early years, she was virtually a single parent. She was often distressed and her mental suffering caused great hardship to those around her. As the senior woman, she had the burden of giving hope to the family that was steadily disintegrating. She had to deal with my older brothers who complained about their living conditions, dropped out of school and were jailed during the state of emergency. My early childhood is filled with memories of terror at physical and emotional violence, yet it was also filled with tenacity and a will to live. This was also the dawning of my faith. I remember praying earnestly for the first time when I was eleven years old. When my mother's uncle had been killed, stoned to death by KwaShange UDF youths, who accused him of being an Inkatha informer, my mother came back from work worried. Her heart was broken because she was not sure if my older brothers were among those who had attacked her uncle. It was common for UDF people to ask the relatives of a person who was about to be attacked to kill their relatives if they belonged to a rival political group. I recall that at the time my brothers would come home in drunken rages and were using *muthi* (traditional medicine), which meant they were forbidden to talk to women. I was afraid for my life and for the life of my mother and younger siblings, and in desperation I cried many tears.

My life is different now: as I write this I am sitting in one of the oldest and most prestigious academic institutions in South Africa, the Campbell Collections of the University of KwaZulu-Natal. I am altered in other ways too, compared to when I was eight to thirteen. I now have a wife and children; I have a PhD. I am happier, more grateful and much more privileged. Remembering what I lived through to get to this point helps me to savour these moments and experiences. They cannot be taken for granted. Even though my life is different, I am still the same in essence, but I remember my past and long for a better future. My memory makes me more resilient. God has never forsaken me – God heard my prayer when I was eleven, and when I was thirteen in the stream and He still hears my prayers today.

The unrelenting blame game

Rebuttal of evidence and deflection of blame by the parties involved left some irreparably damaged emotions. Instead of finding a solution to the endemic savagery, leaders weaselled out of their responsibility and dodged accountability. Violence continued unabated, the death toll kept mounting and vandalism escalated. We were hopeless and helpless. We were left defenceless and felt abandoned. The violence to which we were subjected was the most serious atrocity of our time.

From 2–7 July 1991, the ANC held its first national conference inside the country since its banning in the 1960s. The 48th conference was the first of its kind to be held internally for over 30 years. The conference brought together leaders and supporters of the ANC from its branches throughout the country, from underground structures of the ANC, from the camps of uMkhonto weSizwe (MK), the Women's League, the Youth League and from the ANC's missions abroad. Under the theme 'People's Power for a Democratic Future', the conference examined the then political situation and charted the path to a united, non-racial, non-sexist and democratic South Africa. There were plenary sessions and various commissions that discussed different themes, including one on political violence. Without doubt, the discussions were intense.

The Commission on Political Violence

The conference was held when violence in the Natal Midlands was at its peak. As detailed in Chapter 5, on 10 February 1991, eighteen people died in one day in Vulindlela, KwaShange Location. This was the second KwaShange massacre and exposed the failure and falsity of the peace initiatives between the UDF and Inkatha leadership in the region. The commission, therefore, was to discuss the violence and formulate the ANC's response to what was viewed as a counter-revolutionary war by some leaders, such as Harry Gwala, the leader of the ANC and the South African Communist Party (SACP) in Natal.[8]

Blade Nzimande, a leader of the ANC and SACP in the Natal Midlands at the time, was one of the delegates who attended the Commission on Political Violence. He opined that the violence was a war waged by the state against black people:

> It is part of a very clear strategy of low-intensity warfare that has been waged by the enemy, particularly in the mid-1980s to try and destroy the liberation movement. Whilst before February 2, 1990, it was very clear, the enemy was throwing us into prison and there were massive trials. After February 2, the state is continuing that kind of violence through different ways and mechanisms. Secondly, we must dispel the notion of the third force. The explanation of a third force is based on

> the premise that [F.W.] De Klerk is honest and he really wants to bring change – it is only a third, unidentifiable force out there undermining the good intensions that De Klerk wants to do. I think that has caused political problems in terms of our strategy as the ANC in terms of how we deal with the violence.[9]

There were many peace initiatives and peace agreements between the UDF/ANC and Inkatha during this time. Nzimande was part of the delegation that represented the UDF/ANC in these talks that led to the signing of the peace agreements. At the commission, Nzimande lamented Inkatha's two-faced nature. They signed a peace agreement but when they emerged from the agreement, they did the exact opposite of what they had agreed on.

> Because we signed a peace agreement with Inkatha on January 29, 1991, we tend to be very reluctant to expose what Inkatha is doing and we tend to be reluctant to analyse Inkatha for what it is. Let me give an example from the Natal Midlands, to show how Inkatha uses these peace agreements to try and hide these atrocities against the people: They try to attack a particular community [KwaShange] and the comrades are able to repel them and Inkatha goes to the press and says the ANC in KwaShange ambushed them [Inkatha] . . . who were from a peace rally that was reporting back on the January 29 peace agreement meeting. A very nice story. When we start responding to the press, raising that Inkatha actually attacked KwaShange community and the community defended itself . . . there was no ambush. When we met with Inkatha at the level of what was called 'Twelve a Side Structure', which was created between Inkatha and the ANC, Inkatha accused us, saying we should not have gone to the press but brought the issue to be discussed at the 'Twelve a Side Structure'. Inkatha used these structures to hide their atrocities. If you expose what they were doing, they accused you of breaking these local peace agreements.[10]

The national leadership of the ANC was heavily involved with negotiations to end apartheid in the country after the unbanning of the ANC and other political parties. The negotiations were facilitated at the all-important Convention for a Democratic South Africa (CODESA), which was held from 4 May 1990 to 27 April 1994. But the negotiations occurred against a backdrop of political violence in the country, including allegations of a state-sponsored third force destabilising the country.[11] The ongoing violence had a potential to shift the focus of the ANC at the negotiations, paving a way for the country that the ANC was *definitely* going to govern. This violence was a nuisance to the ANC leadership.

The violence was discussed at the commission as one of the thorny issues that was an obstacle to the building of the organisation and a peaceful transition. This caused a strain between the national leadership of the ANC and some leaders in the Natal Midlands, who were viewed as pro-violence. Gwala reported to the commission that violence had been going on since December 1987. He verbally attacked both Inkatha for its two-faced conduct and the state under the National Party government for its double-standard tactics:

> The UDF and COSATU tried to find a solution to the violence by entering into peace agreements with Inkatha. But who reneged? It was not UDF and COSATU. Let us look at the role of the state; those who were leading the negotiations to stop the violence were rounded up and thrown behind bars into detention. People want peace but it is a crime [according to the state] to seek peace. The warlords, however, are left free to continue with their carnage, massacres and murders. What did we do? We entered into more peace initiatives [referring to the ANC and Inkatha at the national level]. This was a good thing because people want peace. The fact that we called upon security forces to stop this attack, it is because we want people to leave peacefully. We said warlords must be arrested. I only wish that those who are affected, who are involved in this violence, would be the people who discuss their own fate.[12]

The Lion of the Midlands, as Gwala was affectionately called, roared at the commission when he referred to the KwaShange massacre. The audience, which included Winnie Mandela and other senior leaders of the ANC, broke into thunderous applause:

> The [KwaShange] people gallantly defended themselves and killed more than eighteen of the attackers, Inkatha warlords in the so-called KwaShange massacre, when Inkatha, loaded in buses, went to KwaShange to attack the people. What did we [the ANC National Executive Committee] say? 'We condemn the massacre.' In other words, KwaShange people were condemned for defending themselves. We are accused [by the ANC national leadership] that in the Natal Midlands, we talk war, we do not want peace. I was asked one day if I have ever gone to David Ntombela [a leader of Inkatha in the Natal Midlands] and shaken hands with him. I said I will be the last person to do that.[13]

Gwala argued strongly against describing what was happening between the UDF and Inkatha as violence. He viewed the violence epithet as reducing the 'war of liberation' into a mere feud:

> We call it violence. Once you give it this description, what are you expected to do? You are expected to get all the priests with their Bibles to come and sing 'Hosanna' in order that there be peace on earth. You are not saying here is a war of liberation and the enemy is waging a violent war on us. And call on our people to defend themselves. But we must make it possible for people to defend themselves.[14]

Gwala was calling on the ANC leadership to authorise MK to make weapons available for its branches in Vulindlela and other affected areas so that people could defend themselves from Inkatha warlords. The ANC leadership refused. Gwala also called on the ANC to deploy MK soldiers to the affected areas, but the ANC would not agree. The ANC felt that this would pollute the atmosphere of negotiations.

While the conference endorsed peace, initiatives undertaken by religious and business leaders, the ANC reasserted the people's right to defend themselves. The conference instructed the incoming National Executive Committee to ensure that the self-defence programme was put in place without undue delays. However, the delegates were generally not convinced that the leadership of the ANC would take seriously the issue of protecting its masses that were brutalised in the Midlands. Nzimande insisted at the plenary that the conference should come up with time frames to implement its resolutions to protect the ANC supporters who lived in areas affected by violence. Ronnie Kasrils, a leader of the ANC, bemoaned that already in December 1990 the issue of the Self-Defence Units was discussed at length with the leadership of the ANC but that all the decisions taken to form the units and support areas, such as the Natal Midlands, were not implemented. 'Here we are, six month later with many [dead] bodies lying on the road and our organisation has done nothing.'[15] Commenting on the issue, Chris Hani, who himself was unconvinced that this matter was given the attention it deserved, said:

> The problem of violence was discussed when the violence commission presented its report. There were allusions in the whole issue of the Self-Defence Units. I am not going to give any assurance . . . but it is part of our responsibility, together with the ANC and the community organisations to make sure that the Self-Defence Units are organised as soon as possible.[16]

The ANC National Conference in Durban in 1991, and the undertakings of the conference to end the violence, gave Vulindlela community members a glimmer of hope that the violence was going to end soon. However, there is no evidence that, practically, the ANC National Executive Committee carried through the instruction, but there is evidence that the violence continued and many people lost their lives in the build-up to the first democratic elections in 1994.

There is evidence that without the support of the state, the warlords would not have carried out their campaign of violence in the Natal Midlands. The state gained by watching its opponents killing one another. The state benefited from the conflict in two ways: firstly, because a large number of activists were killed, simply exterminated; and secondly, probably more importantly, because the conditions in Natal meant that no alternative or anti-apartheid organisation had been able to develop any organisational muscle.[17] If we are to believe stories about questionable polls in parts of KwaZulu-Natal in the

1994 general elections, Mangosuthu Buthelezi and the IFP gained. The ANC and the National Party leadership had to keep begging Buthelezi and the IFP to participate in the elections. As a result, Buthelezi and the IFP gained national and international attention that made them players in the elections. If the story that the Ingonyama Trust was a sweetheart deal that was reached for the IFP not boycotting the 1994 elections is a true reflection of what transpired, the Zulu king gained in the land deal. According to Hilary Lynd:

> A low-intensity civil war had simmered in the province for years. As the election date, April 27 1994, approached, it seemed KwaZulu was on the edge of catastrophic violence. Chief Minister Mangosuthu Buthelezi, King Goodwill Zwelithini and the Inkatha Freedom Party were threatening to boycott elections as they had the constitutional negotiations. The king proclaimed the 'sovereignty' of the Zulu kingdom and fears grew that a secessionist war was brewing. These fears built on the stream of information emerging about hit squads within the KwaZulu police, co-operation with the security services of the white government, stockpiling of weapons, and paramilitary training at Mlaba camp.[18]

As can be seen, the ANC blamed Inkatha for the violence, for being two-faced and reneging on peace agreements. John Aitchison argued that this was partly because Buthelezi, the leader of Inkatha, had a huge responsibility that he did not exercise in terms of action to issue a clear, publicly announced order to Inkatha key officials and commanders of troops to stop fighting. There were key Inkatha officials, chiefs, *izinduna* and town councillors who were popularly called warlords. They were heavily armed and simply seen as killers by the local community.[19] Over the years, Buthelezi had staunchly opposed strikes, boycotts and other tactics espoused by other liberation movements. This made him a favourite of Pretoria, which regarded him as a moderate black leader. This also rendered him a suspect of the liberation movement, which was then pointing a finger at him concerning the Natal Midlands bloodshed.[20]

In an interview with the Australian Broadcasting Corporation, Buthelezi was asked, 'What role should you be playing [to end the violence]?' He responded:

> Your question surprises me when you ask what role should I be playing. I am playing a role. I have been playing the role for many years. I have been going to those places. I have had prayer meetings, as a Christian, in those places where I appeal for reason among the people that are in conflict and my organisation, Inkatha, has tried to play that role as well.[21]

Some people in Vulindlela, mainly those who had been displaced from their areas and were in refugee camps in Edendale, academics and church leaders had a different view. All were adamant that it had been Inkatha *impis* who had caused the violence. When the journalist asked him about *impis*, Buthelezi could not hide his anger. He responded irately and impatiently, 'What is *impis*, what rubbish is that?'[22]

> Zulu men, I mean, if you went to any Zulu wedding here Zulu men would be having their sticks and shields. While I abhor violence and regret very much that so many lives were lost and so many people lost their property whilst our people are so poor, one must really put things in perspective and put it in that context and understanding that there are many members of Inkatha that suffered similar fate.[23]

Since his release from prison, Mandela, who had extended a hand of peace to Buthelezi, had been strongly forbidden by the ANC leadership in the Natal Midlands to meet Buthelezi. The leadership of the ANC vehemently opposed this meeting between Mandela and Buthelezi because of the violence in the Natal Midlands. Delegates from the Midlands region, who were clearly troubled by the relationship that was developing between Mandela and Buthelezi, accentuated the point that Inkatha was not a fraternal organisation of the ANC, as it sometimes presented itself. Top leaders of the ANC, who intended to hold talks with representatives of such a 'counter-revolutionary' organisation, were instructed to handle the meetings in such a manner that showed that the Natal Midlands ANC region did not regard 'the instigator of violence' as their ally.[24] For a long time, Mandela had refused to be drawn into a public spat with Buthelezi. However, when asked whether he had 'withdrawn the hand of peace to Buthelezi', he responded:

> Well, unfortunately Chief Buthelezi has not responded in the way I would have expected. He has done a lot of things which have alarmed the masses of the people. At the present moment there is such a hostility towards him that all my effort to sit down and talk to him peacefully have been frustrated. That is the reality.[25]

Some scholars believe that the turmoil that erupted in the country, including Vulindlela during the CODESA negotiations period, which left thousands of people dead, was caused by Inkatha trying to show its muscle. Aitchison argued that for Inkatha to have any significant role on the national scene, it had to be able to demonstrate that it had the most support in Natal.[26] In reality, Buthelezi was trying to win a seat at the negotiation table.

For many victims of this violence, and those who were born into the violence, the political ambitions of a man who had an irrepressible 'appetite for power' and 'double-agenda', a leader who talked peace but whose actions were totally opposite – and whose supporters brutally took part in massacres – his appetite for power was a tragedy. To a leader who thinks that apartheid was not a crime against humanity, and to a leader who thinks that the legacy of colonialism was not *that* bad, colonialism and apartheid were the reason why there was violence in South Africa. The architects and supporters of apartheid murdered thousands of black people in South Africa and neighbouring states.

This is how I experienced apartheid violence. This is how the people, who Gwala wished would have been the ones who discussed their own fate, felt. Through this book, I have given a platform to the multiplicity of voices of the people who were 'affected' and 'involved' in the violence to 'discuss their fate'.[27]

As Ryszard Kapuscinski says:

> The world contemplates the great spectacle of combat and death, which is difficult to imagine in the end, because the image of war is not communicable – not by pen, or the voice, or camera. War is a reality only to those stuck in its bloody, dreadful, filthy insides. To others, it is pages in a book, pictures on a screen, nothing more.[28]

Notes

1. M. Schuld, 'The Prevalence of Violence in Post-Conflict Societies: A Case Study of KwaZulu-Natal, South Africa', *Journal of Peacebuilding and Development* 8(1), 2013: 60.
2. A. Curle, *Another Way: Positive Response to Contemporary Violence* (Charlbury: Jon Carpenter Publishing, 1995).
3. This term is generally used to describe the National Party state police who killed black people, mainly in townships and rural areas. In KwaShange, they assisted Inkatha combatants to attack UDF supporters. For details on state police collaborating with Inkatha, see the Truth and Reconciliation Commission report, https://www.doj.gov.za/trc_frameset.htm.
4. For more on the subject see J. Parle, *States of Mind: Searching for Mental Health in Natal and Zululand, 1868–1918* (Pietermaritzburg: University of KwaZulu-Natal Press, 2007).
5. It has been applied in theology by Archbishop Desmond Tutu, *No Future Without Forgiveness* (New York: Doubleday, 2000), and in politics by anti-apartheid icon and former South African president, Nelson Mandela, *Long Walk to Freedom: The Autobiography of Nelson Mandela* (London: Little, Brown and Company, 1994).
6. D. Bonnin, 'Space, Place and Identity: Political Violence in Mpumalanga Township, KwaZulu-Natal, 1987–1993' (PhD thesis, University of the Witwatersrand, 2007), p. 286.
7. Mdluli quoted in Bonnin, 'Space, Place and Identity', p. 286.
8. M. Dlamuka, 'Connectedness and Disconnectedness in Thembeyakhe Harry Gwala's Biography, 1920–1995: Rethinking Political Militancy, Mass Mobilisation and Grassroots Struggles in South Africa' (PhD thesis, University of the Western Cape, 2018).
9. Blade Nzimande, leader of the ANC and SACP in the Natal Midlands in the 1980s, speaking at the Commission on Violence at the ANC 48th National Conference, University of Durban-Westville, 2–7 July 1991.
10. Nzimande, speaking at the ANC 48th National Conference.
11. See https://www.sahistory.org.za/dated-event/interim-report-allegations-third-force-goldstone-commission-published.
12. Harry Gwala, a member of the National Executive Committee of the ANC and a leader of the SACP in the Natal region in 1980s, speaking at the Commission on Violence at the ANC 48th National Conference, University of Durban-Westville, 2–7 July 1991.
13. Gwala, speaking at the ANC 48th National Conference.
14. Gwala, speaking at the ANC 48th National Conference.
15. Ronnie Kasrils, a member of the National Executive Committee of the ANC and a leader of the SACP, speaking at the Commission on Violence at the ANC 48th National Conference, University of Durban-Westville, 2–7 July 1991.
16. Chris Hani, a member of the National Executive Committee of the ANC and a leader of the SACP, speaking at the Commission on Violence at the ANC 48th National Conference, University of Durban-Westville, 2–7 July 1991.
17. Nicholas Haysom, South African Human Rights Lawyer, in George Case (producer and director), *Inside Story: South Africa's Killing Ground*, 20/20 T/Vision Pictures, US, 1990.

18. H. Lynd, 'Secret Details of the Land Deal that Brought the IFP into the 94 Poll', *Mail & Guardian,* 7 August 2019, https://mg.co.za/article/2019-08-07.
19. John Aitchison in Martin Butler (producer), *A Black Future*, Australian Broadcasting Corporation, 1990.
20. Aitchison in Butler, *A Black Future.*
21. Mangosuthu Buthelezi in Butler, *A Black Future.*
22. Buthelezi in Butler, *A Black Future.*
23. Buthelezi in Butler, *A Black Future.*
24. Delegates at the Commission on Violence at the ANC 48th National Conference, University of Durban-Westville, 2–7 July 1991.
25. Nelson Mandela in Butler, *A Black Future.*
26. Aitchison in Butler, *A Black Future.*
27. Gwala, speaking at the ANC 48th National Conference.
28. Ryszard Kapuscinski quoted in M. Kentridge, *The Unofficial War: Inside the Conflict in Pietermaritzburg* (Cape Town: David Philip, 1990), p. i.

2

Reasoned Arguments

IN THE LATE 1940s to mid-1960s, many people moved from farms, where they were tenants, into KwaShange.[1] They moved because of the proximity of the area to the city of Pietermaritzburg, where work was obtainable. Their lifestyles reflected all that traditionalist Zulu backgrounds imply in terms of beliefs and value systems. KwaShange was typified by faction fights from the 1940s to the 1970s,[2] but during the late 1980s to 1990s these intensified into political factionalism and resistance against the National Party apartheid regime.[3] This conflict expressed itself locally as civil war between the Inkatha Freedom Party (IFP) and the United Democratic Front (UDF).[4]

Media, academia and the Truth and Reconciliation Commission have dealt with the history of the struggles of the apartheid era extensively, but the history of this period is limited with regard to the experiences of members of the affected communities after the violence. How are the survivors of the turmoil coping or failing to cope? How have the affected communities reconstructed themselves?

Scenario of the unrest

It is difficult to identify the exact date of the beginning of violence in Vulindlela. Tension became perceptible in 1983 after the formation of the UDF as some community members began to organise and align themselves with this movement. A number of incidents occurred in 1985 that could be regarded as contributory factors. In February 1985, there were a series of incidents that resulted in deaths, injuries and destruction of property.

Records of this period were not kept as effectively as they were after 1990. From 1985, violence monitors and media in the Natal

Midlands focused primarily on the Edendale complex, including Edendale itself, Imbali, Ashdown, Sobantu and Slangspruit. While the focus was on townships, violence in the rural areas of Vulindlela was escalating.[5] When attention was eventually turned to Vulindlela, much had already happened that was not recorded. As a result, the genesis of the violence in Vulindlela was not explored.

One report that deserves special mention was written by John Battersby for the *New York Times*. On a visit to KwaShange he recorded his observations. His report sets the scene:

> In the dim light, the young man's face radiated a youthful zest for life as he spoke of death, revenge and warfare.
>
> 'We want to fight them until it is the end of them or the end of us,' Rodney said to the approval of his 'comrades,' as the young militant opponents of the Zulu tribal authorities here are known.
>
> About 20 'comrades,' some as young as 12 and 13, huddled in the iron-and-mortar dwelling and brandished homemade weapons as they discussed military tactics and chanted freedom slogans in hushed tones. Outside, other teenagers kept a night watch for the township police and conservative Zulu vigilantes . . .
>
> Rodney left home three weeks ago and is afraid to return. 'I know that if I do, I will die,' he said.
>
> The conflict among Zulus has already claimed more than 170 lives this year. At least 80 people have died in the last seven weeks . . .
>
> Last month, in the KwaShange district, 13 young members of Inkatha were killed when opposition militants set fire to the house where they were meeting. Those who tried to escape were beaten to death.
>
> In another incident, vigilantes, enraged that they could not find a man they were hunting, decapitated his 10-year-old son instead.
>
> A Pietermaritzburg court this week issued a preliminary injunction restraining two of the Inkatha leaders [Chief Shayabantu and David Ntombela] from further attacks on their opponents after two girls, 11 and 12 years old, described

> in affidavits how they watched their 11-year-old sister shot in cold blood . . .
>
> Both sides say they resort to violence only in self-defense, although some Inkatha leaders have endorsed revenge killings. Chief Gatsha Buthelezi, the paramount Zulu leader, said this week he could not be held responsible for the conduct of every member in an organization with more than a million adherents.
>
> He accused the African National Congress, an outlawed anti-apartheid organization, of fomenting violence to make South Africa 'ungovernable.'
>
> Chief Shayabantu Zondi, an Inkatha leader in KwaShange, an area that overlaps with part of Edendale, said the civil strife could be resolved by making Zulus responsible for their own law and order. 'We no longer trust the South African police,' he said. 'Some of them try to kill us. If we can get a police force of our own in this area which would not take sides – as we have in others – we could quickly solve the problem.'
>
> But Chief Zondi made clear that he would not tolerate members of the three million-strong United Democratic Front, another anti-apartheid umbrella organization, or the trade unions operating in his area.[6]
>
> Civil rights workers say most of those killed and wounded have belonged to youth organizations affiliated with the United Democratic Front. Recently, however, there has been evidence of its members striking back, they say.[7]

This quotation paints a picture of the violence that engulfed KwaShange. The KwaShange massacre in September 1987 marked the beginning of the end of 'normal' life in KwaShange,[8] Vulindlela and the province in general.[9] There were visible divisions in families and communities. Friends and neighbours became enemies because of their political affiliations or non-alignment to any party.

Even though much of this turmoil has not been recorded, it is alive in people's memories. Memories about the history of the area reflect KwaShange before and after it was turned into 'a place of pain'.[10] According to MaZamisa Shange:

> [Ironically] this place is indeed a place of peace; yes, we had violence that left many people devastated. We were all devastated. Many people lost their lives and others lost their loved ones but still there is no place like this area – this is still a place of peace. When my folks left Richmond because of faction fights, they chose this area because of the peace I am talking about . . . violence that took place was everywhere and it was just caused by the devil. It is something that was meant to be for that particular period and it really never shocked me that much because it is something written in the Word of God. It had to happen . . . it happened really to serve a purpose. Only those that do not read and understand the Word of God, who thought that the violence was forever and they moved from KwaShange permanently. Look at us now, we are living peacefully. Our children go to schools, we go to church, and people go to work. We are just leading normal lives. Those that left . . . in fact maybe God wanted them to leave us, so He allowed the devil to cause people to fight for no reason. Those who were violent and caused unhappiness in this village were displaced forever and others died – I suspect that the whole violence was meant to 'clean up dirt' [evil-doers] in the area.[11]

MaKhonza Ntusi's memories of KwaShange are different. She says:

> We arrived in KwaShange from a farm near Vryheid in the early 1960s. I cannot remember the exact year but it was early in the sixties. This area has never been what we thought it would be. When we arrived here, there were lots of tensions between people of different clans. The faction fight that comes to mind is that of the Zondi clan fighting with the Dlamini clan. When we came here, the fight had already started and that animosity continued until the 1990s. There was another one between Zondi and Ndawonde clans in the 1970s, even though it did not last long, but its consequences were devastating. Mchunu and Ndaba clans also fought. All these fights happened one after the other – sometimes they happen concurrently. The political violence of the 1980s to 1990s came to an [already] violent community. Had the KwaShange community been peaceful, the results of the violence would not

> have been as atrocious as it turned out to be. If the community members were united, they would easily avoid killings and solve differences in a disciplined manner. The results of the violence are still felt today and there is no peace yet – one small disagreement can lead to violence because people have not yet forgotten what happened to them and they have not forgiven the perpetrators of evil [violence].[12]

Sources of information about the violence in KwaShange

The political violence in South Africa during the 1970s, 1980s and 1990s attracted the attention of the international community, as well as local and international media houses and researchers. These records present divergent explanations and interpretations of the violence – how it started and why people sought to resolve their disputes through arms, arson, killing and other atrocities of civil war. Some of these documents claim that there was no single cause but 'clearly multiple causes of the violence: socio-economic deprivation, urban-rural tensions, conflict between traditional and modern forms of governance [and generational tensions], as well as political rivalry between the IFP and the ANC. A crucial factor was state backing, both overt and covert, for the IFP before 1994.'[13]

Most of the documents about the KwaZulu-Natal Midlands violence are newspaper articles or research reports that were not published in peer-reviewed journals or books. The very limited unpublished documentation was written with a political rather than an academic underlying principle.[14] Debby Bonnin states that the documentation and descriptions were to alert the public to the horror of what was happening and to shame the state into an impartial intervention to end the violence.[15]

Some of the KwaShange events were covered by the Unrest Monitoring Project. Of the authors who focused on the political violence in Vulindlela and the Natal Midlands in general, some provided 'raw information', or information that is not yet analysed, which was collected by the monitoring groups concurrently with the violence. They paint a clear picture of what was happening in Vulindlela and the Natal Midlands, in general. These sources, however, do not provide much analysis, since the objective of these publications was to provide factual information, rather than commentary.[16]

John Aitchison, who was from the Centre for Adult Education at the University of Natal, Pietermaritzburg, headed the Unrest Monitoring Project. Aitchison, Wendy Leeb and Vaughn John produced a number of unpublished articles based on this project, which presented statistics on political violence and unrest in the Natal Midlands. Members of the project even went into cemeteries and recorded names of the dead people from tombstones. This information, however, is incomplete. There are a number of fatalities that were not recorded.[17]

Leeb's articles deal with the destruction of families and communities: 'Families have been decimated, destroyed, separated, rendered parentless, childless, homeless and hopeless.'[18] She discusses the psychological effect the violence had on the generations that were involved in the infighting and on generations to come: 'This damage manifests in life-long psychological disturbances, amongst which are the inability to form long-term relationships, problems with parenting, alcoholism and/or drug abuse, criminality, neurotic behaviour, lack of motivation and lack of self-esteem.'[19]

Other projects that performed similar tasks in the province and in the country include the Natal Monitor, the Institute for a Democratic Alternative for South Africa, the Indicator Project, the Black Sash, and Peace in Natal (PIN), led by Radley Keys, which was linked to the Democratic Party and various Christian ministries. They all monitored and provided data on the trends of violence, indicators and conflict chronologies. All 'hot spots' in the province were monitored. The Indicator Project claimed that at least 4 012 people were killed in political violence in South Africa (including 1 113 by the police and army) from September 1984 to the end of December 1988. There was evidence of the decrease of death tolls from 1987 to 1988 in the country, but there was an increase in fatalities in the Midlands during the same period.[20] The Black Sash provided some invaluable data on human rights violations,[21] and much information was published in a periodical bulletin of events.[22] The works of these violence monitors predominantly consist of statistics of deaths and injuries, locate the incidents in context and sometimes describe them, at least in rough terms. Later in the 1990s, the Human Rights Commission took over the work initially carried out by the violence monitors. The Natal Monitor, however, continued its work, including the publication of reports.[23]

The work of the monitoring groups has been critiqued by Anthea Jeffery as engaging in disinformation about violence in South Africa. Jeffery states that these reports were biased; they overlook the violence committed by the UDF or ANC allies, such as Congress of South African Trade Union (COSATU) supporters, and instead focused only on the collusion between Inkatha and the South African security forces in perpetrating violence. She notes that 'the ANC's strategy of fostering "ungovernability," which has led to widespread intimidation', and 'the refusal to disband Umkhonto [weSizwe] or ANC "self-defence units" is often ignored in reports about township anarchy'.[24] Jeffery says:

> These human rights organizations not only distort the causes of violence, but also set the stage for increased confrontation and undermine attempts to generate lasting solutions to the conflict. In the politicized atmosphere of South Africa, however, it can hardly be expected that the members of the South African Human Rights Commission, who are also ANC members, would criticize their own party. Even the reporting and monitoring of the political violence is inevitably politicized.[25]

Origins of the violence

COSATU/UDF vs Inkatha

A detailed account of the Vulindlela violence is provided by Matthew Kentridge, who states that the Midlands war pitted people against people of the same region, along party political lines. Kentridge believes that the war emanated from the different political movements that existed in Natal and Zululand. He attributes the genesis of enmity in the Natal Midlands to the alliance between COSATU and the UDF, which posed a serious threat to the power of Inkatha in the region. According to Kentridge, it was from this challenge that the unofficial war between Inkatha and the alliance started.[26]

Aitchison makes the point that the UDF, which was formed in 1983, opposed the National Party government proposals for a tricameral parliament, which would constitutionally enshrine the exclusion of Africans from the government of South Africa. He states: 'At the opening rally of the UDF in Edendale, a wounded student from the University of Zululand reported to the UDF leadership that he had been assaulted at the University residence and many other students who were alleged to be from UDF-aligned communities were assaulted and others were killed.' According to Aitchison, this event was one of the precipitating causes for violence in the Natal Midlands and Durban.[27]

Father Tim Smith, a Roman Catholic priest in Elandskop, claims that the bias displayed by the police was the cause of the violence. He frequently 'called in the riot police to stop an attack in Elandskop. However, when the police arrived, it was alleged that they continued assisting the attackers to hunt down UDF supporters, either to arrest them or make them disappear from society.'[28]

Fatima Meer records that the South African Police were often accused of playing political games in deciding which areas of violence they had to attend to first. In the IFP-controlled territories, it was alleged that the police brought expensive equipment from Pretoria to assist the IFP supporters. The political games that the police were playing in the name of combating political violence in KwaZulu-Natal was costly to the government and thus also to society.[29]

The conditions in the townships and vigilantism

Other causes of the violence in the Natal Midlands, according to Aitchison, included the high cost of housing, the shortage of houses and increasing transport costs; the discontent of residents in Imbali and Ashdown townships about the excision of their townships from the Pietermaritzburg Municipality so that they came under direct KwaZulu government control; the role of Inkatha-supporting town councillors in black local authorities; the rise of vigilante groups associated with Inkatha; conflict between Inkatha and the trade union movements; and the lack of tolerance of any opposition by KwaZulu/ Inkatha authorities.[30]

UDF supporters also played their part in the violence. Khaba Mkhize, a seasoned journalist who resided in Edendale, observed and reported widely that 'crime and troublesome activities' angered local leaders and senior men aligned to the Inkatha movement.[31] Richard Carver agrees with Mkhize. He states that 'there have undoubtedly been criminal elements, *comtsotsis*, who have exploited the political struggle on the UDF/ANC side'.[32]

Others joined the vigilantes due to 'mob psychology, with the belief that it was nice being part of the vigilantes. Some others joined vigilante activities because they had no choice, in the sense that their families and next-of-kin's lives were in danger if they refused to be part of the vigilantes.'[33]

According to Anthony Minnaar:

> Vigilantism was just one side of an often-violent struggle for power. Vigilantism had its own distinction, which, according to those who were engaged in it, was a way of defending themselves in the way they thought was best. The most important distinction can be identified through the different 'styles' of violence of the two sides. Since the fury of 1985–1986 abated, opposition violence usually involved small groups of lightly armed youths, striking at specific people in minority segments of the community. It was alleged that vigilantes had generally enjoyed loyal support from the KwaZulu-Natal Legislature and in some cases the SAP [South African Police] and SADF [South African Defence Force] were alleged to have aided vigilantes, while also acting vigorously to restrain the opponents of the vigilantes.[34]

The Goldstone Commission believed that the nature and characteristics of vigilantes in KwaZulu-Natal were mainly due to the economic, social and political imbalances, which had resulted from apartheid, and a police force and army that were instruments of oppression and therefore perceived as unfair and biased. 'The Commission attributed the forming of vigilantes to a way of fighting a system that was not favourable to them. Surprisingly, the Commission said nothing about the vigilantes who operated together with the security forces in thwarting the efforts of democratic forces in the KwaZulu-Natal Midlands.'[35]

Anne Truluck notes that competition for land among clans constituted another basis for vigilantism in KwaZulu-Natal. In this form of factional organisation, men who received land from a chief traditionally owed him military loyalty.[36] In rural KwaZulu-Natal, this obligation was the source of vigilante activities, and it was another issue that the IFP exploited. In urban townships and informal settlements, particular leaders, who were appointed by the chief himself, controlled men. The best organised but rarest form of vigilantism was the private army. To finance it, a levy was imposed on all the households of a shanty town. The Lindelani settlement on the northern fringes of Durban offers a useful case study. It sprang up around 1985, and by 1986 it had 120 000 inhabitants. From the start, it fell under the control of an IFP warlord, Thomas Shabalala. Land was annexed in a violent way. In 1987, an attack was launched from Lindelani into neighbouring Ntuzuma, driving people from their homes and burning them down to acquire new land for settlement. Those who received the land in the neighbouring Ntuzuma owed military loyalty to Shabalala.[37]

Violence in surrounding areas

According to Keesing's Record of World Events, the violence in the Pietermaritzburg region was exacerbated by what was happening in the neighbouring areas. For example, in September 1992, there was a large Inkatha rally in KwaMakhutha, near Amanzimtoti. This rally caused violence to flare up anew in Pietermaritzburg when a large group of Inkatha supporters attacked the ANC-controlled townships outside the city, damaging property and assaulting residents. The conflict in Pietermaritzburg was a bitter one because the issues at stake were bigger than simply the control of several townships. The main issue that led to the attack was the deep-rooted hatred that existed among Inkatha members for members of the UDF.[38]

During October 1992, conflict in the Pietermaritzburg region seemed to escalate. Violence became an almost everyday occurrence. Regular skirmishes between IFP gunmen and ANC supporters took place. It was believed that Chief Mangosuthu Buthelezi knew about the violence and that he was the cause of the violence, as he refused to take part in the upcoming 1994 elections, at least until international observers were allowed into KwaZulu-Natal.[39]

Karl von Holdt gives more details concerning the sequence of spiralling violence in Pietermaritzburg and surrounding areas. He states that in August and September 1986 things turned violent when IFP supporters embarked on forced recruitment campaigns in a number of townships around Pietermaritzburg.[40] Violence had simmered in the area since 5 and 6 August, when township residents heeded the UDF/COSATU call for a stay-away to protest against the all-white parliamentary elections in the province, which supported and favoured the IFP. A number of bus drivers, members of the COSATU-affiliated Transport and General Workers' Union, were allegedly attacked by IFP-supporting vigilantes.[41] This was followed by sporadic attacks on UDF and COSATU members throughout the rest of the year.

In 1987, the conflict escalated into a full-scale struggle for control of the Pietermaritzburg townships. There were numerous allegations that the recruitment by the IFP was accompanied by force and demands for money. As vigilante violence increased and adversely affected the communities, they swung their support to the UDF and COSATU alliance. Defence committees were set up in many areas and the balance of power turned against the IFP supporters.[42]

Warlordism

Some authors attributed the intensity of the violence in the Natal Midlands to 'warlordism'.[43] Aitchison defines warlords as 'powerful local leaders who rely on the force of arms to maintain their power. They tend to gather a group of professional strong-arm men around them and they pay for their services by screwing [extorting] the local populace'.[44]

The United Nations High Commissioner for Refugees asserted that warlords and gang leaders were similar. The only difference was that they were 'not motivated exclusively by the acquisition of personal wealth and power, but in addition they owe allegiance to a central power, namely Inkatha. Warlords were champions for a political cause.'[45]

The UDF had its own warlords. The actions of some of the leaders of the UDF and ANC were similar to those of Inkatha leaders. The 'Lion of the Natal Midlands', Harry Gwala, and Sifiso Nkabinde, the ANC leader who later joined the United Democratic Movement, were warlords. To date, there is no warlord in the Midlands who has accepted blame for violence committed by their supporters. Minnaar, however, believes that all those who were instigators of violence (warlords) and vigilante activities were involved in one way or another. He describes and discusses violence between hostel dwellers, UDF and Inkatha supporters in Bruntville township outside Mooi River when

Inkatha undertook a vigorous recruitment drive.[46] The *Daily News* regarded it as evidence of another form of the strong ties between the IFP and the vigilantes.[47]

Senzosenkosi Mkhize describes the formation of Self-Defence Units and Self-Protection Units as the reason why violence escalated in Richmond. It was established at the time when the police were perceived as part of the problem.[48]

Political ambitions and a third force

Some attribute the violence to political movements' leaders, such as Chief Buthelezi. Meer claims that Buthelezi engineered the violence due to his ambitions to play a leading role in the new government. A reason that has been put forward by some authors is that of a third force of right-wing elements in the security establishment, bent on derailing the government's negotiation agenda. Another suggestion was that the Inkatha/ANC rivalry was engineered by an ambitious Buthelezi, who feared being sidelined rather than treated as an equal third party.[49] Meer says:

> In 1987, Buthelezi made a miscalculated comment, that should any member of the IFP be attacked, then the IFP would have no option but to retaliate, since it would be assumed as the deeds of the ANC and the UDF. This further contributed to the hostile political situation in KwaZulu-Natal. After this comment, daggers were all out for both ANC and IFP supporters in the KwaZulu-Natal Midlands. The comment was regarded by many that Buthelezi was calling for vigilantism against the ANC and UDF, should any member of his party be attacked. It implied that UDF and ANC supporters were the masterminds behind the killing of IFP supporters.[50]

Meer also mentions Gwala's speeches for inciting violence and the ANC's campaign of armed struggle, ungovernability and revolutionary intolerance, as well as ingrained tribalism, unleashed by the lessening of white repression that resulted in so-called black-on-black violence.[51]

David Everatt examines the nature and causes of the pre-election period violence. He concludes that, on the basis of a close analysis of monitoring data, the commonly held view that the violence was multi-causal, involving elements of poverty, ethnicity and political contestation, is wrong. He says that although the violence did draw on a range of socio-economic and political factors, it was deliberately fomented; that the security forces played a key role, beyond that of favouring Inkatha in trying to affect the negotiation process and protect their own futures.[52]

Hein Marais points out that the state-sponsored violence of the late 1980s and early 1990s, at most, exacerbated emerging fault lines and encouraged existing conflicts that arose as much from structural (political, economic, social and ideological) trends in society as they did from the acts and omissions of individuals, organisations and state institutions.[53]

Apartheid

Rupert Taylor fingers the system of apartheid as the cause of the conflict: 'Apartheid has succeeded in engineering group divisions among the oppressed.'[54] Heribert Adam and Kogila Moodley concur with Taylor that the conflict 'is not of some essential ethnic forces'.[55] They argue, however, that to blame it solely on the manipulations of apartheid is an oversimplification:

> Ethnic antagonisms exist in societies that do not have apartheid. Above all, in demystifying ethnicity, the analyst needs to show why the manipulators are so successful in constructing and exploiting ethnic cleavages. Apartheid did not invent all ethnic divisions; it skilfully utilised collective memories and distinct histories. Analysts who deny this historical reality invoke magic formulas to wish away deep-rooted perceptions that can be mobilised for progressive as well as retrogressive ends.[56]

To attribute all violence to a state-directed third force does not explain the attacks against Inkatha office holders and the police. Among the fatalities are equal numbers of ANC and Inkatha members or sympathisers. There is also evidence that both movements had their own third forces that were not under the direct control of the national leadership.[57]

Feuds

John Argyle is of the opinion that much of the Natal conflict was motivated principally by the desire for revenge and therefore resembles centuries-old blood feuds. He notes: 'In the past, such feuds originated not only over land but also over insults to honour or violations of women. Both sides cite provocation as a defence.'[58] According to Kentridge, 'In a war there are no aggressors; ostensibly no side ever initiates an attack . . . if an attack is made, it is always retaliatory.'[59] And yet, 'while it is wise "to believe neither side" until independent conclusive evidence is available', Argyle cautions, 'one cannot simply blame the conflict on long-standing cultural traditions of habitual feuding. The waxing and waning of the feuds can be traced to the changing conditions that precipitate or repress intergroup and interpersonal violence.'[60]

Generational differences

My interviews with residents of KwaShange revealed that clashes between generations were also responsible for the Midland's violence. Older men were absent at migrant jobs, communities had moved in from elsewhere and the youth were perceived as ill-disciplined. The two factions then aligned themselves politically on opposing sides, often with fathers against sons and vice versa. Social change was also a contributing factor. To critique such a strong view one needs to have a detailed understanding of the KwaShange milieu pre-dating the start of the violence in the 1980s.[61]

Both Kentridge and Jeffery write about the KwaShange massacre of 25 September 1987. This was the first KwaShange incident of violence to be documented, despite the fact that there were many other incidents before it. Jeffery writes:

> Twelve people, including three black policemen, were arrested in connection with the KwaShange massacre killings . . . The evidence showed that at about 11 pm on 25 September 1987 a group led by Mr Nkosinathi Hlengwa, a policeman, attacked the house in which the youngsters were gathered. The house was encircled by Hlengwa's men and stones were thrown, breaking windows. Shots were fired and a door smashed in. When the youth tried to barricade the doorway fire was

> started. More shots were fired into the house. Those who sought to escape from the blazing house were struck down one by one. The screams of those that remained in the house ceased only when a gas bottle exploded, 'producing the final holocaust'.[62]

Jeffery also discusses the KwaShange ambush of 10 February 1991:

> Two buses returning from the Inkatha and ANC peace talks were ambushed in KwaShange (near Pietermaritzburg). Some 18 Inkatha supporters were killed and 11 injured . . . They were spread out within a one kilometre radius spot, suggesting desperate attempts to escape. Automatic weapons had been used to rake the vehicles and to dispatch those who, frantic to escape the bullets, jumped from the buses only to be cornered and slaughtered by an ANC ambush party. Many of the bodies were stabbed repeatedly and some had their heads crushed or beaten in so they were almost unrecognizable.[63]

Jeffery and Kentridge rely heavily on media reports in their discussion of these two major incidents in KwaShange, and they both interpret these incidents as exclusively political violence.

As a member of the community in KwaShange when these incidents occurred, I find it difficult to commit to this sentiment. I believe that generational differences were at the bottom of both incidents.

Owing to the state of emergency in operation at this time, media reports were not free to explore either the political ramifications or the links between these two incidents. Nevertheless, Judge N.S. Page, in the court summation of the first incident, warned of the dire consequences for generational interactions that would surely result from the first incident.[64] Local IFP member, Velaphi Ndlovu (commenting at the time of the second incident in 1991), recorded that the two incidents had taken place at the exact same location.[65] At the time, the media failed to make the link, which points to a generational skirmish. This was possibly because of the confusing and complex nature of the two incidents. The older men who were responsible for the first incident were, in fact, UDF-aligned. This contrasts with the conventional media view of political allegiances and age, which regarded the UDF as an organisation with a popular youth base. Thus, it was assumed that the youth belonged to this movement and Inkatha was assumed to have the support of the older men.

However, the situation was more complex because the political allegiances of younger and older men appeared to shift from the one incident to the other. The explanation for this may be found in the political opportunism of both factions, which used the politics of the time as a front to resolve other issues.[66] Most notably, this would be generational tensions, caused by socio-economic factors of change, but climaxed in the concerns of the older generation about young people's lack of discipline. Importantly, this is the common understanding of the community itself, which still bears the scars of these traumatic events.[67]

There are three factors that give substance to the assertion that the incidents were cases of generational struggle, rather than solely of political conflict:

(a) The community understanding with regard to the ill-discipline of the younger age group, such as involvement in robbery and theft, stemming from their not receiving proper fathering.
(b) The need and the actions of the older men to wrest back control by implementing 'disciplinary courts'.
(c) The political opportunism on the part of the younger men and older generations involved in the incidents.

However, it may be that what was happening was so complex that some people in KwaShange were not opportunists to the point of aligning themselves with political movements; they were conscious, fully aware and genuine.

Adam and Moodley claim that Kentridge's work on political violence in Vulindlela, 'like most other journalistic efforts, describes the impact of the war on people's lives but does not analyse the forces that have caused and sustained the conflict. Most of these are "verbal snapshots."'[68] According to them, both Kentridge's and Jeffery's works on the KwaShange violence are 'mostly of the propagandistic kind'.[69] Kentridge implicitly blames Inkatha warlords, backed by the South African state, as if their one-sided aggression was self-evident, whereas Jeffery blames the violence on the UDF supporters as if Inkatha were innocent victims.[70]

Respect and discipline are key features in constructions of traditional Zulu masculinity. In response, younger men insisted on being treated as men, asserting their claims of manhood against men of the older generation, who they believed were trying to extend their generational control.

Few authors record that this political violence had gender and generational dimensions;[71] it was not simply Inkatha and UDF supporters fighting one another. Catherine Campbell explains that the 'analysis of South African violence has failed to take explicit account of the fact that the conflict has almost always taken the form of men fighting men'.[72] Looking at the statistics provided by Aitchison's 'Numbering the Dead', Bonnin rather believes that the violence stemmed from the usurpation of the political sphere by young men.[73] She explains that the numbers 'of those killed and injured in the violence indicates that the majority were young males. In effect the political violence concealed a generational rapture.'[74] Bonnin continues: 'Politics became the domain of youth organisation and politics the sphere of young men. Older people, men in particular, were marginalised from local politics. When the young men brought their political stances into the domain of the household it unsettled the practice of [*ukuhlonipha* – respect] and consequently patriarchal relations.'[75]

The lack of discipline and *ukuhlonipha* resulted in older-generation men forcibly disciplining the youth in 'kangaroo courts'. Khabo Mkhize reported on the violence in Vulindlela: 'The comrades do not confine their disciplinary activities to their own ranks, however, residents are also punished if they infringe some newly imposed standard of decency and good behaviour.'[76]

Adam and Moodley attribute the violence of 'mob psychology to the youths who became part of vigilante activities [which] was a serious cause for concern'.[77] They blame parents in Natal and Zululand for failing to provide proper guidance to their children, and they claim that this factor played a role in the massive increase of political violence in the region.

Adam and Moodley state that people in the rural communities and the migrant hostels resented the political activism of the urban-based youth as a subversion of the traditional order, in which children are obedient and politics is left to the elders. They stress that, for the older generation, youthful activism was 'an ungrateful waste of the educational opportunities for which the parents sacrificed so much. On the other hand, youth accuse their parents of having compromised themselves with the system.'[78]

Evidently, this facet of generational conflict of the violence destroyed many families' cohesion and pitted communities against each other, particularly in the semi-urban settlements surrounding Pietermaritzburg, where rural and urban values clashed directly under conditions of dire poverty.[79]

Socio-economic factors

Like many authors writing about this period, Bill Berkeley reasons that 'there is no doubt that political violence in KwaZulu-Natal has fed upon mass poverty'.[80]

Many of the works covering this violence emphasise socio-economic factors, which resulted in migrant labour and the labour laws introduced by colonial and apartheid governments, respectively. Thomas McClendon provides data on social and economic relations within African farm-tenant families in segregation-era Natal. He explores the ways in which rural patriarchy was constructed and contested in South Africa. He believes that the South African state, in conjunction with African patriarchs, sought to further subordinate African minors (unmarried young males and females) to the labour needs of elder males and white farmers, through the use of an increasingly rigid system of 'customary' and contract law.[81]

Social and economic deprivation is the factor most often cited by Inkatha itself to explain the violence. Gavin Woods of the Inkatha Institute argues 'that reasonably contented communities have a negligible propensity for violence' and 'politics is, in itself, not enough to have caused the levels of violence experienced'.[82]

Norman Bromberger and Yusuf Bhamjee explore the high numbers of unemployed in the Natal Midlands townships, especially among the youth.[83] John Radford and Wendy Leeb investigate 'the effects of job loss on the township of Mpophomeni'.[84] People left rural areas for the townships in an attempt to seek employment. Some had been evicted from farms and many refugees from the conflict in the greater Durban area came to Pietermaritzburg in 1984 and 1985. Leeb states that 'these growing numbers of people [were] forced to share limited resources in terms of land, houses, schools [and] clinics', and, as a result of a lack of representation in the ruling system and the oppressive nature of the state, it became apparent that the frustration must give rise to expression.[85] A vast majority of vigilantes had no formal education; therefore they were illiterate and most of them joined the vigilantes as a way of survival, since they were unemployed.[86]

Effects of violence on the society

Some studies have taken a different approach to gender or generational dimensions and economic factors as a cause of the violence, and they rather focus on the effects of violence in schools and on teaching and learning.[87] Aitchison states that schools in the Midlands were 'not significant sources of violence' in the region. Schools were 'disrupted, and severely so, but this was because of the conflict outside them, usually in the form of external invasions into schools by the groups of armed men'.[88] As Bonnin puts it, these studies show the huge societal disruptions caused by violence, the destructive effects of violence; 'the breakdown of community and family life, the resulting poverty, the complete disruption of the education system, and the psychological damage to individuals'.[89]

I reason that not only the generations and communities involved in the fighting were psychologically affected, but that generations to come would be affected by the hatred and discord that was sown by those involved in the violent activities.

Most of the liberal literature and media (particularly international media) hold that Inkatha was regarded as the only cause of violence (with the assistance of the police). In fact, Inkatha and the UDF were equally vicious with each other and the state exacerbated the situation. Many English-language South African journalists, as well as most foreign correspondents writing for a liberal opinion abroad, were more favourably inclined toward the ANC's interpretations than 'tribal' Inkatha or Africanist visions.[90]

Even though the political violence in South Africa has been well documented, albeit unpublished, particularly the records of the Natal Midlands political violence, there is a lacuna on generational and masculinity tensions. I should add that any scholarly work is incomplete by definition because it does not include the subjective element.[91]

Many authors and observers were people outside the communities that were directly affected by the violence. Some who experienced the violence avoid writing their stories from an eye-witness perspective; this is probably because they consider autobiographical life stories too subjective. I have included my own and my mother's experience of the unrest despite the drawbacks of potential accusations of a lack of objectivity, as the anxieties of recall are worth recording. These details, together with those of my interviewees, many of whom were neighbours or relatives, cover a range of age groups and both sexes. They can only but enrich the understanding of the trauma caused by the violence stemming from the civil unrest.

In order to understand the trauma of the survivors, I contend that historians and social scientists must venture to approach persons who are survivors of trauma in order to be able to understand the results of a life touched by such trauma. I discuss my personal experiences of trauma and quote verbatim accounts of other interviewees' experiences of trauma. While arguably subjective, the pay-off of this auto/biographical dimension is in-depth understanding. There is also a need to have a cultural understanding and language skills in the survivors' world in order to elucidate some of the impacts of such stress in context.

Being an insider, with language skills and community and cultural background, helps to articulate the depth of the applicability of my hypothesis regarding trauma as post-traumatic stress. I have studied, in detail, the use of *muthi* in war and the healing of those men who have been doctored and have to return to their communities that they have violated during the unrest. I also focus on women's dreams and precognitions of violence. This has been ignored, often deliberately I suggest, by many political analysts, perhaps because the cultural dynamics of *muthi* and healing are associated with the IFP, in particular. But all local organisations of that time, the UDF/ANC and the Inkatha movement, used the same cultural practices. It is hoped that the role of war doctors and the importance of the *impi* (warrior) being cleansed will contribute to the African understanding of trauma and healing. This book also brings to light a new dimension on women and war and their role in the subsequent return to civilian life.

This book not only explores and records the interviews of survivors but takes the matter further by exploring the link between history and memory. History is what happened and memory is how we remember what happened. People are better able to remember an event if they have an opportunity to tell others about it.[92]

Formal interviews are my primary source so theory on memory and oral history informed my approach. Michael Frisch and Alessandro Portelli draw attention to the 'theme' and 'plot' of oral narratives.[93] According to History Matters, 'for all their considerable value, oral history interviews are not an unproblematic source. Although narrators speak for themselves, what they have to say does not.'[94] There are obvious limits to the process of collecting oral history because people may forget details and reconstitute their tales. In other words, memory is continually being reconstructed. Nevertheless, if interviews are collected within a large group, some consensus should emerge.

Although I take account of 'social history' approaches, my focus is not mainly on official histories but histories from below – the perspectives of women, children, villains and the defeated. I am also aware of the fact that many of my interlocuters conveyed a sort of nostalgic historiography. This is not necessarily a problem as I was able to treat nostalgic representations as a certain kind of data in and of itself – a form of data that tells how people today interact with and imagine the idea of their past. This is an ethnographic approach, and it was retained alongside a historiographical approach. By that I mean that I kept my deconstructive lens. History does not actually exist, as such. All that exists is present human representations of the past, and these are always interpretations, and usually political interpretations. So the important questions are not only about what happened in the past, but rather the role that stories about the past play in the present. Whose interests do they serve? Whose voices do they leave out?

This book provides a Zulu perspective on trauma and indigenous methods used to deal with trauma. How do local people define and explain the experiences they went through? How are they dealing with the aftermath of violence? Political trauma is not simply a collection of symptoms, as is sometimes claimed. In fact, symptoms may not follow all traumas.[95] Trauma associated with political conflict is largely about the destruction of individuals, families and the social and political structures of a society. The theme of psycho-social intervention has been explored by Sigmund Freud,[96] who argues that in war people do not 'sink so low as we feared, because they had never risen so high as we believed'.[97] For Freud, violence is innate in human nature and finds easy expression in times of conflict.

Beth Goldblatt and Sheila Meintjes argue that the violence of South Africa's past has contributed to a climate of violence against women and crime in the country today.[98] According to this view, violence generally continues for decades within the social fabric of societies that have emerged from conflict. Psycho-social studies stress the importance of approaching trauma from both psychological and social perspectives. The term 'psycho-social' recognises that there is a close, ongoing interaction between an individual's psychological state and his or her social environment.[99]

Some theorists focus on the influence of culture on the course of the conflict itself.[100] 'Culture of conflict' refers to the beliefs, attitudes and opinions of particular groups that see other groups who disagree politically or on any other major issue as enemies. Such beliefs understandably influence the historical outcome of any conflict. But it is possible to explain the conflict-related aspects of cultures as culturally specific, since the belief that conflict should inevitably find expression in violence is not universal.

Despite differences between cultures concerning conflict and culturally specific practices and thought patterns, there are many commonalities in the occurrence of conflict worldwide. To contribute to a more universal understanding of the subject, these commonalities may profitably be compared to see if conflict occurs in cultures that favour, or 'naturalise', conflict as a mode of settling disputes. There is no doubt that there are layers of behaviour and thought processes that form part of a culture of conflict, and these need to be recognised as causes of violent conflict. Most processes intended to resolve conflict, such as the Truth and Reconciliation Commission, do not deal with the transition from violence to peace as a process of cultural change.[101] In KwaShange, there are a number of conflicts that erupted before the political violence of the 1980s, and this book looks at the historical dimension of beliefs and behaviour concerning peace-making after conflict, such as prayer meetings and cleansing, and how these derive from Zulu culture.

Notes

1. Interview with Mancinza Zondi and MaZamisa Shange, KwaShange, 14 March 2009.
2. For more on the faction fights in the region, see J. Sithole, 'Land Disputes, Social Identities and the State in the *Izimpi Zemibango* in the Umzinto District, 1930–1935', *Journal of Natal and Zulu History* 27(1), 2009: 60–82.
3. Interview with Mancinza Zondi and MaZamisa Shange, KwaShange, 14 March 2009.
4. For a detailed literature review on political violence in Natal and Zululand, see D. Bonnin, 'Space, Place and Identity: Political Violence in Mpumalanga Township, KwaZulu-Natal, 1987–1993' (PhD thesis, University of the Witwatersrand, 2007).
5. See, for example, J. Aitchison, 'The Civil War in Natal', in *People's Courts and Popular Politics: South African Review 5*, edited by G. Moss and I. Obery (Johannesburg: Ravan Press, 1989). See also Killie Campbell Africana Library (KCAL), Black Sash Papers, Black Sash Records, Box 18: File – Miscellaneous, Affidavits 1988, 1989, 1990. Details of what happened in Vulindlela from 1986 can be viewed in John Aitchison's presentation to the Truth and Reconciliation Commission hearing in Pietermaritzburg, http://www.justice.gov.za/trc/hrvtrans/hrvpmb/pmb7_2.htm.
6. For history of labour movements and trade unions in South Africa, see J. Sithole and S. Ndlovu, 'The Revival of the Labour Movement, 1970–1980', in South African Democracy Education Trust, *The Road to Democracy in South Africa: Volume 2 (1970–1980)* (Pretoria: Unisa Press, 2006).
7. John Battersby, 'Edendale Journal; in Apartheid's Shadow, Zulu Wages War on Zulu', *New York Times*, 9 November 1987.
8. See Chapter 5. See also Pietermaritzburg Archives Repository (PAR), *State v. Hlengwa and others*, transcript of judgment by Justice N.S. Page, Natal Provincial Division of the Supreme Court, Pietermaritzburg, 11 April 1988; personal communication with the 'first accused' Chris Hlengwa, KwaShange, 2005; A. Jeffery, *The Natal Story: Sixteen Years of Conflict in Natal* (Johannesburg: South African Institute of Race Relations, 1997).
9. I say 'normal' life had turned to 'abnormality', knowing that there was never anything normal about that lifestyle. As William Beinart suggests, violence was a normalised feature of life in apartheid South Africa. Historically South African society has been structured around violence. Structural violence, suppression and compulsion were the central characteristics of the apartheid state. See W. Beinart, 'Political and Collective Violence in Southern African Historiography', *Journal of Southern African Studies* 18(3), 1992: 455–86. See also A. Altbeker, *A Country at War with Itself: South Africa's Crisis of Crime* (Johannesburg: Jonathan Ball, 2007).
10. MaZakwe Khambule, whose four children and husband were killed in two separate incidents in KwaShange, refers to KwaShange as a place of pain. She now resides in Edendale and has never gone back to KwaShange since her husband was killed in 1990 because she 'does not want to remember what happened to her family'. I interviewed her on 17 January 2008 at Edendale.
11. Interview with MaZamisa Shange, KwaShange, 14 March 2009.
12. Interview with MaKhoza Ntusi, KwaShange, 14 March 2009.

13. R. Carver, 'KwaZulu-Natal: Continued Violence and Displacement', WRITENET for UNHCR, 1 July 1996, https://www.refworld.org/docid/3ae6a6bc4.html.
14. John Aitchison states that he was a political activist in the 1980s and 1990s. Personal communication with John Aitchison, University of KwaZulu-Natal, February 2009.
15. Bonnin, 'Space, Place and Identity'.
16. Bonnin, 'Space, Place and Identity'.
17. Interview with Wendy Leeb, Pietermaritzburg, March 2012.
18. W. Leeb, 'Daily Life, Daily Death in Pietermaritzburg', in J. Aitchison, W. Leeb and V. John, *Political Violence in the Natal Midlands: The Unrest Monitoring Project Papers, 1988–1994* (Pietermaritzburg: Centre for Adult Education, 2010), p. 69.
19. Leeb, 'Daily Life, Daily Death', p. 72.
20. M. Bennett and D. Quin (eds.), *Political Conflict in South Africa: Data Trends 1984–1988* (Durban: Indicator Project South Africa, 1986).
21. KCAL, Black Sash Papers, Black Sash Records, Box 18: File – Miscellaneous, Affidavits 1988, 1989, 1990; File – Democratic Party, Information Sheets, 1989–1990 and Durban Network Funerals, 1989–1990; File – Democratic Party, Information Sheets, 1990–1991; Box 19: File – All Bulletin's Office Copy.
22. S. Bekker (ed.), *Capturing the Event: Conflict Trends in the Natal Region 1986–1992* (Durban: Indicator Project South Africa, 1992); see also Bennett and Quin, *Political Conflict in South Africa*.
23. Personal communication with John Aitchson, University of KwaZulu-Natal, February 2009.
24. Jeffery quoted in H. Adam and K. Moodley, *The Opening of the Apartheid Mind: Options for the New South Africa* (Berkeley: University of California Press, 1993), p. 124.
25. Jeffery quoted in Adam and Moodley, *The Opening of the Apartheid Mind*, p. 124.
26. Matthew Kentridge, *An Unofficial War: Inside the Conflict in Pietermaritzburg* (Cape Town: David Philip, 1990).
27. J. Aitchison, 'The Origins of the Midlands War', in *The Role of Political Violence in South Africa's Democratisation*, edited by R. Greenstein (Johannesburg: Community Agency for Social Enquiry, 2003), p. 53; see also P. Denis and G. Duncan, *The Native School That Caused All the Trouble: A History of the Federal Theology Seminary of Southern Africa* (Pietermaritzburg: Cluster Publications, 2011).
28. T. Smith, 'Experiencing the Violence', paper presented at the Centre for Adult Education Seminar on Violence, University of Natal, Pietermaritzburg, 1988. See also Carver, 'KwaZulu-Natal'.
29. F. Meer (ed.), *Resistance in Townships* (Durban: Madiba Publishers, 1989); A. Jeffery, 'Spotlight on Disinformation about Violence in South Africa', *South African Institute of Race Relations Spotlight* 8(92), 1992: 38–9.
30. Aitchison, 'The Origins of the Midlands War'. See also South African History Online (SAHO), 'The Nature and Character of Vigilantes in KwaZulu-Natal', http://www.sahistory.org.za/archive/chapter-2-nature-and-character-vigilantes-kwazulu-natal.

31. Telephonic interview with Khaba Mkhize, Pietermaritzburg, February 2009. See also Kentridge, *An Unofficial War*.
32. R. Carver, 'South Africa: After the Elections', WRITENET for UNHCR, 1 May 1994, https://www.refworld.org/docid/3ae6a6c44.html.
33. SAHO, 'The Nature and Character of Vigilantes in KwaZulu-Natal'.
34. A. Minnaar (ed.), *Patterns of Violence: Case Studies of Conflict in Natal* (Pretoria: HSRC Press, 1992), pp. 3–4. See also SAHO, 'The Nature and Character of Vigilantes in KwaZulu-Natal'.
35. SAHO, 'The Nature and Character of Vigilantes in KwaZulu-Natal'.
36. A. Truluck, *No Blood on Our Hands: Political Violence in the Natal Midlands 1987 – Mid-1992, and the Role of the State, 'White' Political Parties, and Business* (Pietermaritzburg: Natal Midlands Region of the Black Sash, 1992).
37. Truluck, *No Blood on Our Hands*.
38. SAHO, 'The Nature and Character of Vigilantes in KwaZulu-Natal'.
39. SAHO, 'The Nature and Character of Vigilantes in KwaZulu-Natal'.
40. K. von Holdt, 'Vigilantes versus Defence Committees: The Maritzburg War; A Turning Point for Inkatha?' *South African Labour Bulletin* 13(2), 1988: 16–27.
41. SAHO, 'The Nature and Character of Vigilantes in KwaZulu-Natal'.
42. Von Holdt, 'Vigilantes versus Defence Committees'.
43. See, for example, Minnaar, *Patterns of Violence*; Carver, 'KwaZulu-Natal'.
44. Quoted in Minaar, *Patterns of Violence*, p. 61.
45. Carver, 'KwaZulu-Natal'.
46. Minnaar, *Patterns of Violence*.
47. Meer, *Resistance in Townships*.
48. S. Mkhize, 'Spirals of Suffering: Political Violence in Richmond, KwaZulu-Natal, 1980 to 1999: An Autobiographical Narrative', Paper presented at a conference at the Msunduzi Museum, 2009.
49. Meer, *Resistance in Townships*.
50. Meer, *Resistance in Townships*, p. 139.
51. Meer, *Resistance in Townships*.
52. D. Everatt, 'Analysing Political Violence on the Reef, 1990 to 1994', in *The Role of Political Violence in South Africa's Democratisation*, edited by R. Greenstein (Johannesburg: Community Agency for Social Enquiry, 2003).
53. H. Marais, 'The Shattered Mould: Patterns of Violence in the Post-Apartheid Era', in *The Role of Political Violence in South Africa's Democratisation*, edited by R. Greenstein (Johannesburg: Community Agency for Social Enquiry, 2003).
54. R. Taylor, 'The Myth of Ethnic Division: Township Conflict on the Reef', *Race and Class* 33(2), 1991: 12.
55. Adam and Moodley, *The Opening of the Apartheid Mind*, p. 122.
56. Adam and Moodley, *The Opening of the Apartheid Mind*, p. 122.
57. Adam and Moodley, *The Opening of the Apartheid Mind*.
58. Quoted in Adam and Moodley, *The Opening of the Apartheid Mind*, p. 132.
59. Kentridge, *An Unofficial War*, p. 19.
60. Quoted in Adam and Moodley, *The Opening of the Apartheid Mind*, p. 132.
61. For these details see M. Mchunu, 'Discipline, Respect and Ethnicity: A Study of the Changing Patterns of Fatherhood of Three Generations of Zulu Fathers and Sons in KwaShange, Inadi, Vulindlela Area of Pietermaritzburg,

KwaZulu-Natal, from the 1930s to the 1990s' (Master's thesis, University of KwaZulu-Natal, 2005).

62. Jeffery, *The Natal Story*, pp. 162–3.
63. Jeffery, *The Natal Story*, pp. 244–5.
64. PAR, *State v. Hlengwa and others*, transcript of judgment by Justice N.S. Page, Natal Provincial Division of the Supreme Court, Pietermaritzburg, 11 April 1988.
65. Jeffery, *The Natal Story*, pp. 244–5.
66. I admit here, however, that subsequent doctoral research indicated another dimension or layer of complex origins of these political alignments; namely, the UDF and the unions versus the chiefs and Inkatha were other possible causes of the violence.
67. M. Mchunu, 'Culture Change, Zulu Masculinity and Intergenerational Conflict in the Context of Civil War in Pietermaritzburg (1987–1991)', in *From Boys to Men: Social Constructions of Masculinity in Contemporary Society*, edited by T. Shefer, K. Ratele, A. Strebel, N. Shabalala and R. Buikema (Cape Town: UCT Press, 2007).
68. Adam and Moodley, *The Opening of the Apartheid Mind*, p. 230.
69. Adam and Moodley, *The Opening of the Apartheid Mind*, p. 229.
70. Adam and Moodley, *The Opening of the Apartheid Mind*.
71. For a broader view on the generational conflict and Zulu masculinity, see, for instance, A. Sitas, 'The Making of the "Comrades" Movement in Natal, 1985–1991', *Journal of Southern African Studies* 18(3), 1992: 629–41; K. Naidoo, 'The Politics of Youth Resistance in the 1980s: The Dilemmas of a Differentiated Durban', *Journal of Southern African Studies* 18(1), 1991: 143–65; T. Waetjen and G. Maré, '"Men amongst Men": Masculinity and Zulu Nationalism in the 1980s', in *Changing Men in Southern Africa*, edited by R. Morrell (Pietermaritzburg: University of Natal Press, 2001); T. Xaba, 'Masculinity and Its Malcontents: The Confrontation between "Struggle Masculinity" and "Post-Struggle Masculinity" (1900–1997)', in *Changing Men in Southern Africa*, edited by R. Morrell (Pietermaritzburg: University of Natal Press, 2001); C. Campbell, 'Learning to Kill? Masculinity, the Family and Violence in Natal', *Journal of Southern African Studies* 18(3), 1992: 614–28.
72. Campbell, 'Learning to Kill?', p. 618.
73. Bonnin, 'Space, Place and Identity', p. 3.
74. Bonnin, 'Space, Place and Identity', p. 3.
75. Bonnin, 'Space, Place and Identity', p. 3.
76. Quoted in Kentridge, *An Unofficial War*, p. 29.
77. Adam and Moodley, *The Opening of the Apartheid Mind*, p. 141.
78. Adam and Moodley, *The Opening of the Apartheid Mind*, p. 141.
79. Adam and Moodley, *The Opening of the Apartheid Mind*.
80. Quoted in Carver, 'KwaZulu-Natal'.
81. T.V. McClendon, *Genders and Generations Apart: Labor Tenants and Customary Law in Segregation-Era South Africa, 1920s to 1940s* (Portsmouth: Heinemann, 2002).
82. Quoted in Carver, 'KwaZulu-Natal'.

83. See, for example, N. Bromberger and Y. Bhamjee, 'Unemployment in Pietermaritzburg with Special Reference to Sobantu', paper presented at the Association for Sociology in Southern Africa conference, University of the Western Cape, 1987.
84. See J. Radford and W. Leeb, 'An Investigation into the Effects of Job Loss on the Township of Mpophomeni', paper presented to the Industrial Court of Inquiry, Centre for Adult Education, Pietermaritzburg, 2010.
85. Leeb, 'Daily Life, Daily Death', p. 72.
86. SAHO, 'The Nature and Character of Vigilantes in KwaZulu-Natal'.
87. See M. Hart, 'The Impact of Violence on Schooling', paper presented at the Centre for Adult Education Seminar on Violence, University of Natal, Pietermaritzburg, 1988; M. Hart and J. Gultig, 'The Effects of Violence on Black Schooling in Edendale and Vulindlela', paper presented at the Kenton conference, Cape Town, 1988; C. Smith and F. Khumalo, 'Refugees and Disrupted Schooling in Natal', in *Patterns of Violence: Case Studies of Conflict in Natal*, edited by A. Minnaar (Pretoria: HSRC, 1992); B. Nzimande and S. Thusi, *Children of War: The Impact of Political Violence on Schooling in Natal* (Durban: Education Projects Unit, University of Natal, 1991).
88. J. Aitchison, 'Numbering the Dead: Patterns in the Midlands Violence', in J. Aitchison, W. Leeb and V. John, *Political Violence in the Natal Midlands: The Unrest Monitoring Project Papers, 1988–1994* (Pietermaritzburg: Centre for Adult Education, 2010), p. 21.
89. Bonnin, 'Space, Place and Identity', p. 24.
90. See, for example, Battersby, 'Edendale Journal'.
91. Personal communication with Philippe Denis, Pietermaritzburg, December 2012.
92. See P. Denis, *Never Too Small to Remember: Memory Work and Resilience in Times of AIDS* (Pietermaritzburg, Cluster Publications, 2005).
93. M. Frisch, *A Shared Authority: Essays on the Craft and Meaning of Oral and Public History* (Albany: State University of New York Press, 1990); A. Portelli, *The Death of Luigi Trastulli, and Other Stories: Form and Meaning in Oral History* (Albany: State University of New York Press, 1991); see also R.J. Grele, *Envelopes of Sound: The Art of Oral History*, second edition (Chicago: Precedent Publishing, 1985), which deals with the reconstruction of memories in oral history interviews.
94. 'Interpreting Oral History', History Matters, http://historymatters.gmu.edu/mse/oral/interpret.html.
95. B. Hamber, 'The Impact of Trauma: A Psychosocial Approach', keynote address to A Shared Practice: Victims' Work in Action Conference, Limavady, Northern Ireland, 7–8 April 2004.
96. See R. Ntsimane, 'Trauma, Resilience and Reconciliation: Sinomlando's Psycho-Social Interventions in KwaZulu-Natal', *Archives News* 1, 2007: 32–8.
97. S. Freud, 'Thoughts for the Times on War and Death (1915)', http://www.panarchy.org/freud/war.1915.html.
98. B. Goldblatt and S. Meintjes, 'Dealing with the Aftermath: Sexual Violence and the Truth and Reconciliation Commission', *Agenda* 36, 1997: 7–17.

99. I. Agger, 'Psychosocial Assistance during Ethnopolitical Warfare in the Former Yugoslavia', in *Ethnopolitical Warfare: Causes, Consequences and Possible Solutions*, edited by D. Chirot and M.E.P. Seligman (Washington, DC: American Psychological Association, 2001).
100. See, for instance, M. LeBaron and B. Grundison, *Conflict and Culture: Research in Five Communities in British Columbia, Canada* (Victoria, BC: University of Victoria Institute for Dispute Resolution, 1993); E.T. Hall, *Beyond Culture* (New York: Doubleday, 1976); J.P. Lederach, *Preparing for Peace: Conflict Transformation across Cultures* (New York: Syracuse University Press, 1995).
101. See, for example, R. Ntsimane, 'A Mirage Called Forgiveness: A Critique of the Truth and Reconciliation Commission', in *Orality, Memory and the Past: Listening to the Voices of Black Clergy under Colonialism and Apartheid*, edited by P. Denis (Pietermaritzburg: Cluster Publications, 2000); P. Gobodo-Madikizela, *A Human Being Died That Night: A Story of Forgiveness* (Cape Town: David Philip, 2003).

3

The Historical Roots of the Violence

I HAVE ALWAYS wondered why KwaShange, in particular, and the whole area of Vulindlela, is called *Isigodi sokuphola* (The Valley of Peace) by many older residents. The local elders say it is because clans and families fled to the area to get away from wars or faction fights, while others were escaping from farms because of the Natives Land Act of 1913.[1] The name is ironic since it was the area from which violence and civil war spread during the 1980s and 1990s and engulfed the entire district. Did refugees fleeing from unrest elsewhere bring with them their initial penchant for rebellion against conditions elsewhere? Did the violence occur because few families had long-standing ties to other families in the area?

Isigodi sokuphola, as applied to KwaShange, is an ideal, but people fleeing there were not to find the peace they desired. The history of the area includes battles that affected all Zulus nationally as well as localised tensions that only affected neighbours and kinship groups. They can be grouped as follows:

- The Mfecane or the wars between indigenous peoples in the early to mid-nineteenth century.
- The intrusion of the Voortrekkers into Natal and the Transvaal and conflicts with the British from the 1830s to the 1840s.
- The British annexation of the Colony of Natal and Theophilus Shepstone's location system and proclamation of Zwartkop in the mid-nineteenth century.
- The Natives Land Act of 1913 and the administration of 'Native' areas with chiefdoms and customary law.
- The apartheid era, from 1948 to 1994, including the establishment of the homeland of KwaZulu,[2] the formation

of the Inkatha movement, the armed struggle of the African National Congress (ANC) and the rise of the United Democratic Front (UDF).
- The first democratic elections of 1994 and the years of democracy.

Much of the history of KwaShange is unrecorded. For this account of Zwartkop Location and how the area was before 'the white men came',[3] I depend on an oral interview I had with Sungubeza Madondo, fourth-generation descendant of Nobhiyane Madondo, King Shaka's diviner,[4] and with Mancinza Zondi, the only living descendant of the section of the Zondi clan that left Ngome, near Greytown, before the Bhambatha rebellion of 1906.[5] I also depend on an interview I had with an elderly woman, MaZamisa Shange, who was married to a son of the first Shange clan, which moved to Zwartkop in the early 1900s when escaping from Ngomankulu (near Richmond) because of faction fights.[6]

I concur with Beverley Haddad,[7] when she notes about the area:

> People of Zwartkop Location have no written history. Their history remains in the hearts of those who live there and increasingly in the spirits of their ancestors! Geographically and socially it epitomises the South African context where the forces of colonialism, racism, and apartheid raged unabated until 1994. Their untold histories are one of subjugation and control and suffering as they struggled to ensure their children survived.[8]

Scholars who have explored the history of Natal and Zululand agree that there were people living in Zwartkop before the arrival of colonists. Before this area became Pietermaritzburg, it was called Mgungundlovu.[9] T.V. Bulpin described Mgungundlovu in the 1800s as full of misty hills that 'are beautiful and gentle and as full of moods as the face of a maiden'.[10]

Some accounts of the history of Mgungundlovu portray the area as if it had never been occupied. Voortrekkers penetrated a region that had been largely depopulated by the Mfecane wars in the 1820s.[11] Most historical accounts from 1837 onwards describe the dealings of the Voortrekkers with the Zulu kingdom to the north of the Thukela River and with the British hunter-traders at Port Natal.[12] A.T. Bryant lists numbers of clans coming from the Mgungundlovu area. They were pushed out by the Mfecane and the Voortrekkers moved into that vacuum.[13] When the Mfecane destabilisation had subsided, these clans returned to reclaim their land and Shepstone placed them in locations.[14]

The existing recorded history pays little attention to the interaction between the Voortrekkers and local African communities in this area or to the prior history of these communities.[15] The testimony of Mancinza Zondi, a surviving descendant of Bhambatha Zondi, the 'rebel' leader of the 1906 uprising, who lived at Engome, Greytown, confirms Bryant and John Wright's claims that there is evidence that the region that is now called Pietermaritzburg and Edendale *did* have resident African peoples 'before the white men came'.

Wright observes that the valley of the Msunduzi, where Pietermaritzburg now stands, and the area to the west and south, was occupied by a group of Nqondo chiefdoms. In about 1820, the section of the Nqondo who lived on the site of the city and in its immediate environs, such as Edendale, was under a woman chief named Machibisa kaMlithwa, or kaMlifa (according to my informant, she was a daughter of Dlaba kaNomagaga).[16] Her name survives today as the designation for part of Edendale.[17]

Around 1819, the victory of the Zulu under Shaka over the Ndwandwe of Zwide kaLanga sent large numbers of refugees spilling across the Mzinyathi (Buffalo) River into northern Natal. The Bhele and Zizi inhabitants of this region fled southwards through the Natal Midlands into East Griqualand and beyond, breaking up the chiefdoms that they encountered.

A year or so later, a large group of Thembu fled from the lower Mzinyathi River, where they escaped subjugation under the Zulu, and they forced their way through the Midlands and southern Natal across the Mzimkhulu River. Soon afterwards, their former neighbours, the Chunu, followed suit. A short while later, chiefdoms in the northern Midlands, also driven by fear of the Zulu, formed a military alliance and fled together through the already shattered communities to the south.[18]

It was not until after the death of Shaka in 1828, and the establishment of a new Zulu regime under Dingane, that a few small communities began to re-establish themselves in central and southern Natal. Predominant among them was a group of Nhlangwini people, under Fodo kaNombewu.[19] These people had originally lived between the lower Mtshezi and Mpofana rivers, but they had fled during the upheavals of the early 1820s.[20] In the course of nearly a decade of struggling for an existence in southern Natal and East Griqualand, they had managed to preserve their cohesion as a group better than most other refugee groups. By 1830, they had settled on the middle reaches of the Mkhomazi River and were trading ivory with the British hunter-traders, who had been operating from Port Natal (later Durban) since 1824.[21] In the early 1830s, the Nhlangwini came under the hegemony of the Zulu king Dingane. To avoid conflict with the British traders at Port Natal, Dingane was withdrawing his garrisons and cattle posts from the coastlands south of the Thukela, and, to compensate, he was beginning to extend Zulu authority over parts of the interior of Natal. In 1835, when Captain Allen Gardiner visited Fodo at his great place, Dumazulu, the Nhlangwini chiefdom numbered several thousand inhabitants.[22]

Two smaller groups that established themselves in the southern Midlands in the early 1830s consisted of a section of Mpumuza under the regent Yenge kaNontshiza, who acted for the young chief Nobanda kaNgwane, and a section of the related Nxamalala (Zuma) under Lugaju kaMatomela.[23] Fear of the Zulu under Dingane had led them to separate from their respective parent chiefdoms, whose territories both lay near the confluence of the Mooi and Thukela rivers, and to migrate southwards together. After many vicissitudes, they found refuge among the forests of the Zwartkop region, where they became sub-clans and tributaries of the Nhlangwini.[24] A section of the Fuze tribe, under Madlenya kaMahawule, was allocated land by Fodo near what is now Boston, after a succession dispute had impelled them to leave the Fuze territory near Greytown. Later arrivals include the Zondi (or Nadi), who moved from near the Mooi–Thukela confluence for reasons that are not recorded. Under their chief, Dlaba kaNomagaga, they were settled by Fodo in the Zwartkop region near their genealogically junior relatives, the Mpumuza. A hundred and fifty years later, all four of these groups still have a presence in Vulindlela.[25]

The area that was later to be called Vulindlela has its place in Zulu history. About 30 kilometres from Pietemaritzburg, there is a valley called Ntembeni, which is part of the original Zwartkop, and included KwaShange. In the Ntembeni valley lies the grave of King Shaka's *isangoma* (diviner), and to the west of Ntembeni there is an area called KwaMpande (the Place of Mpande), named after Shaka's half-brother, King Mpande.

Having established that Vulindlela was settled in the not very distant past by refugees from conflicts elsewhere, I shall now give a detailed account of one such refugee and his family, who settled there after a traumatic conflict and a long pursuit by enemies. His story was available to me because his descendants recounted it to me, but it may be seen as representative of the backgrounds of many present-day residents in the area.

The tale goes that King Shaka was sceptical of diviners, for whom he had developed distrust. When there was drought in Zululand, the toll of disease and death caused massive social and economic dislocation, which impelled Shaka to take a hard line against diviners who idly blamed others for natural catastrophes. According to Mpitikazi, 'Shaka took the blood of a beast and sprinkled it in the doorway in his *isigodlo* during the night, without being seen by anyone.'[26] This act was intended to put diviners to the test. The next morning, he ordered his *izinduna* (headmen) to gather all doctors and people of the land at the capital, Bulawayo. As Lunguza kaMpukane recounted, the diviners '*smell out* people in various directions'. Only a few doctors, Mleku, Mbube, Mehlo and Nkuna, led by Nobhiyane Madondo, were exceptions. In their metaphoric jargon, they concurred that the sprinklings of blood were not '*the work of a man*', but that of '*the heavens*'.[27] They were held in high repute for correctly 'smelling-out' the king as the culprit. The rest of the diviners were executed, in full view of the masses, as a deterrence.[28]

This is a common tale in the history of Shaka and the Zulu nation. It sounds more like myth than fact but it ceases to sound like pure myth once one meets the descendants of King Shaka's diviner and listens to the story of Nobhiyana Madondo, as told by his fourth-generation descendant.[29] And seeing the grave of Nobhiyana Madondo deep inside the forests on the mountain of Ntembeni in Vulindlela makes the tale seem more factual. The family tells that the former KwaZulu chief minister and champion of the Zulu language and culture, Chief Mangosuthu Buthelezi, was eager to see the grave of the 'hero', whom he had heard about from his royal family, and he unveiled the tombstone in 1983.[30]

There was anger that Nobhiyane had survived and this led to a plan to assassinate him. This was the beginning of the flight of Nobhiyane and his family. He sought refuge in Mvoti near Greytown. After a short period, his enemies found that he had settled in Mvoti, so he fled to Mtshezi, near Estcourt. His enemies again followed him, and he and his family landed up in Mgungundlovu, in an area that later became Ntembeni. When Nobhiyane and his family sought refuge in Zwartkop, he built two homesteads because he did not want his enemies to find him easily.[31] One was in the Ntembeni area, where his descendants are still living and where he is buried, and the other is in Nadi, which was later occupied by the Zondi clan from Ngome near Greytown.

In Vulindlela there is a village that is still called KwaMpande. Two versions are given by informants as to why the area was named after this king. The first is that the Zondi clan arrived in the area during Mpande's reign. The clan had had a long relationship with the Zulu royal house. The naming relates to the Zondi clan honouring Mpande at the time of settlement.[32] The second version is that Chief Langalibalele of the Hlubi clan was in hiding in what was then Zwartkop. He had refused to submit to the Zulu monarchs, thus making Mpande his adversary. The story goes that Mpande's warriors went there with the aim of attacking Langalibalele. The area was named after Mpande because his troops settled there for a short period, hiding in caves and along river banks, waiting to ambush Langalibalele and his people. I find it difficult to accept this version. There is recorded evidence, in at least four records,[33] that there was tension between the Hlubi nation under Langalibalele and the Zulu nation, caused by the strength and independence displayed by the Hlubi nation. The amaHlubi, whose historical name was imiHuhu, were historically the largest clan in south-east Africa.

In Bishop Colenso's records, Langalibalele's son, Mango, testified that 'Langalibalele said he was King, and could not obey the summons [to attend a magistrate's court]'.[34] John Wright and Andrew Manson report that 'as early as 1852, when only in his mid-thirties,

Langalibalele sent an envoy to Pietermaritzburg to remind Shepstone (administrator of Native Affairs) that he was a great and influential chief (read king) who resented having to put up with threats from the local magistrate'.[35] There were fears that Langalibalele's general defiance, his independence and possession of firearms were a security threat to the colony's white community. Rumour had it that Langalibalele was collecting guns for the purpose of planning a rebellion. Given his prominence, it was a threat the British could not take lightly. Learning of the intention of the colonial government to attack his tribe and arrest him, he planned his escape with some of his troops. This act was considered an act of treason by the colonial administration. Langalibalele was exiled to Cape Town until 1887, when he was allowed to return to Natal and resettle in the Zwartkop area under some form of house arrest. History records that Mpande was the king of the Zulu nation from 1840 to 1872. By the time Langalibalele was under house arrest in Zwartkop in 1887, Mpande was no longer king. Because of this fact, the first version of the naming of KwaMpande sounds more accurate. These were the first noted cases of the area being a refuge for peoples fleeing from elsewhere, thus getting the name of Valley of Peace. Their descendants, however, retain some of the fears and distrust of others, which they inherited from their ancestors.

KwaShange (as part of Zwartkop) in historical context

Edgar Brookes and Nathan Hurwitz say:

> Historically, the first location in Natal (Natal at this early date was a colony of Great Britain. Zululand was the area across the Tugela River toward the coast) was the 'Zwartkop' location near Pietermaritzburg, which was demarcated in November 1846 for about 8,000 Zulus, 3,000 of whom were under chiefs who were 'original occupiers of the localities'.[36]

The proclamation of the Zwartkop Location was the result of the Natal Native Commission of 1846–1847, under a policy that became known as the Shepstone policy, one that was 'criticized for having gathered the Natives together, and left them to stagnate under a re-created tribalism'.[37] Because of economic restraints, Shepstone 'made the best of things'. According to Brookes and Hurwitz:

> Having no officers to rule, he [Shepstone] rebuilt the shattered tribes and ruled through their chiefs. Inevitably he recognised Native customary law. By the 1850s the pattern of Reserve policy in Natal was fixed, the part of the 1846–7 Commission in it being the acceptance of the principle of large but scattered locations and the siting of some of the more important among them.[38]

In the 1970s, the National Party government instituted its homeland policy, and the area became known as the Vulindlela Magisterial District, under the KwaZulu administration, which was stationed in far-off Ulundi. The Zulu homeland government of the apartheid era refused to take independence, and, after South Africa's first democratic elections in 1994, the area was once again absorbed into the province of KwaZulu-Natal.

It needs to be stated that any rural area falling under a chief was, until the promulgation of the South African Constitution in 1996, and still is to an extent, subject to African customary law (formerly termed the Natal Code). African customary law governed the locations of this province. Before 1975, these areas were termed 'locations' if they fell within the borders of Natal and 'reserves' if they fell within Zululand.

N.J. van Warmelo's 1933 survey lists these initial inhabitants of Nguni or Zulu origins as the Zondi, Ximba (Mlaba), Mafunze (Ngcobo) and Nxamalala (Zuma).[39] The family surname is given in brackets after the relevant clan name.

Writing about Edendale and its surroundings, Thomas McClendon has some interesting observations:

> Just over the ridge from that relatively comfortable pocket [Edendale Mission] lie the densely packed 'township' (black suburb) areas in the Edendale valley. That area is one of many sites in the province (KwaZulu-Natal) of a decade-long war in the late 1980s and early 1990s and involving a complex mix of struggles over political allegiances, culture, gender, generation, wages and state repression.[40]

The Edendale area is vital to the understanding of politics and events in neighbouring KwaShange and greater Vulindlela. The Zondi clan, under whom the area of KwaShange falls, first resided in Edendale

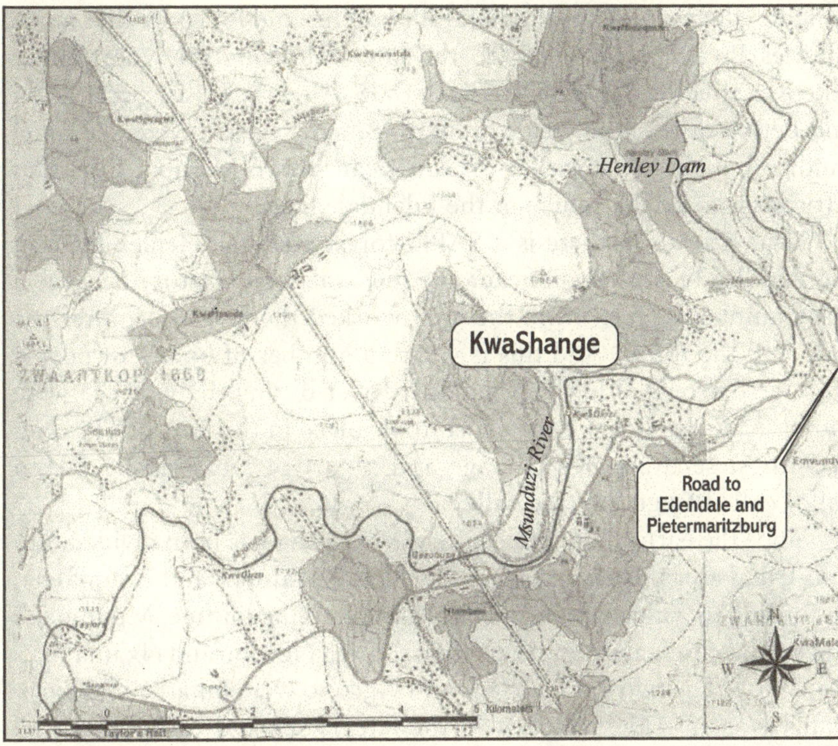

Map of Zwartkop, which shows the KwaShange area in relation to neighbouring areas, roads, railway line and the Msunduzi River (adapted from E.H. Brookes and N. Hurwitz, *The Native Reserves of Natal.* Natal Regional Survey, Volume 7 (Cape Town: Oxford University Press, 1957).

before they moved to the Crown Lands of Mgungundlovu. Some of the KwaShange people sought refuge in Edendale during the violent unrest of the 1980s and 1990s, especially during the Seven Days' War. The hospital and refugee camps served as a locus for peace monitors, politicians, church activists and aid groups.

The Edendale road forms part of the route to KwaShange from Pietermaritzburg and it passes Edendale Hospital. The hospital was founded in 1954, when the main apartheid laws were being passed. It served Africans and Indians, who, in terms of these laws, could not be cared for at Grey's Hospital, which was for whites only.

At the time of the settler occupation of the 1840s and 1850s, Edendale was known as Machibisa, named after the Zondi chief's daughter. It was perhaps the suitability of the land for cattle that made Andries Pretorius lay claim to the land following the Voortrekker takeover after the Battle of Ncome in 1838. After the British occupation and defeat of the Voortrekkers in 1842, and when Reverend Daniel Lindley bought the farm for an American Board Mission, Christian Africans also bought much of the Edendale land.

Near Edendale, there is a SAPPI forest with the Henley Dam in the middle. This is a significant site in KwaShange history because a large number of men from the area worked there, looking after the dam and the forest. And this is where a number of bodies of people who were drowned in the Msunduzi River during the violence were found. Many political battles also took place in this forest. The dam and forest separates KwaShange and a part of greater Edendale, a valley called Esigodini (the valley).

Since the early twentieth century, Vulindlela has been divided into four tribal areas (*izizwe*): Mpumuza, Inadi, Mafunze and Nxamalala. According to Zulu custom, each area has a ruling lineage. Mpumuza's and Inadi's chiefs are Zondis; Mafunze's is an Ngcobo and Nxamalala's is a Zuma. The two Zondi chiefs and Ngcobo were Inkatha members; Zuma was an ANC member. In the late 1980s and early 1990s, all four areas were under the influence of Inkatha, but included pockets of UDF affiliates in places such as KwaShange, Mphophomeni and Mthoqotho.[41]

The rule of chiefs remains influential in the present era, despite some limitations. If men wish to obtain land in KwaShange they must go to the local *induna*, who will refer the claim to the chief, who then authorises a man to place his homestead in a particular area. This applies to Zulu male homestead heads, even those that arrive from outside the area. This ground is not owned by the man himself but he has usufruct.

The history of KwaShange remains in the 'hearts' of its residents and it resides in the spirits of their ancestors, in their graves. The descendants of early residents often possess knowledge of the history of the area, which is otherwise inaccessible to the living. I had the privilege of interviewing the two most senior local residents of KwaShange from two of the most prominent clans, the Zondi and the Shange, namely Mancinza Zondi and MaZamisa Shange. Zondi is 90 years old and is illiterate and blind; his father died at the age of 105

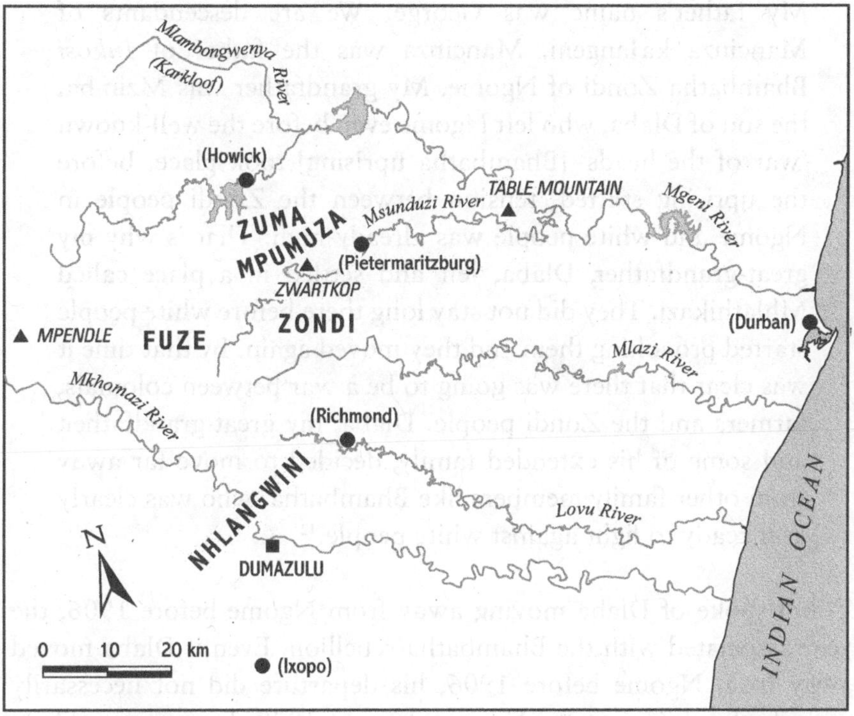

Vulindlela map showing tribal areas (adapted from Cartographic Unit, University of Natal).

in 1986. His knowledge is not based on what he read from history books; it is information that has been passed on from one generation to the next. And MaZamisa Shange is also approximately 90 years old. She married young into the Shange clan and is also illiterate. These two surnames are powerful because the Zondi people were owners of the land in the late nineteenth century and were influential in Vulindlela, even before the 'white men came'. The area of KwaShange was named after a clan, Shange, whose members were the first to occupy the small village of Inadi.

The Zondi people in Zwartkop

I quote from my interview with Zondi, discussing the relocation of the Zondi clan from Ngome near Greytown to Zwartkop:

> My father's name was George. We are descendants of Mancinza kaJangeni. Mancinza was the father of *Inkosi* Bhambatha Zondi of Ngome. My grandfather was Mzimba, the son of Dlaba, who left Ngome even before the well-known 'war of the heads' [Bhambatha uprising] took place. Before the uprising started, tension between the Zondi people in Ngome and white people was already high. That is why my great-grandfather, Dlaba, left and settled in a place called Mhlathikazi. They did not stay long there before white people started provoking them and they moved again. By that time it was clear that there was going to be a war between colonials, farmers and the Zondi people. Dlaba, my great-grandfather, and some of his extended family, decided to move far away from other family members like Bhambatha, who was clearly ever ready to fight against white people.[42]

Zondi spoke of Dlaba moving away from Ngome before 1906, the year associated with the Bhambatha rebellion. Even if Dlaba moved away from Ngome before 1906, his departure did not necessarily precede the arrival of the Voortrekkers of 1838. It was more likely that Shepstone settled the Zondi at Zwartkop. Even the naming of the area after Dlaba's daughter, Machibisa, does not indicate that his people arrived before Pretorius. Zondi makes an emotive claim, which is not necessarily supported by facts.

The Zondi people today believe that their ancestors left Ngome before the Bhambatha uprising of 1906. Prior to this, there was already tension between Bhambatha and the colonial officials. Dlaba and his household relocated, leaving Ngome for Mhlathikazi. The Zondis under Dlaba did not stay there long, since they resented the poll tax, which had to be paid in money, forcing some of the people to seek employment in the colonial economy. They left Mhlathikazi and resettled in an area today called Machibisa in Edendale. When Dlaba died, his daughter Machibisa acted as the chief of the clan. She and her warriors fought a number of battles and succeeded in defeating chiefs who wanted to take advantage of her because she was female. Later, the Zondi people under Machibisa were displaced or removed by the colonial government officials, and people of Swazi origin were settled there, which is why today you will find Msimangs, Mzolos and Smelanes in the area. Zondi people were relocated to *ngaphezulu* (higher grounds or mountainous areas, called Crown Lands). The time frame of Machibisa's reign is vague and the oral accounts of elderly people are understandably imprecise. There is almost nothing about her in literature besides the mention of her name by Wright.[43]

The names of the Nadi chiefs, who reigned from when the Zondi clan moved to *ngaphezulu*, Zwartkop, were provided by Mancinza Zondi and confirmed by other Zondi clan members who reside in KwaShange.

The first chief was Mzimba. There is a school, Mzimba Primary School, in the area on the other side of the Msunduzi River from KwaShange, named after Chief Mzimba. His son, Mhlola, succeeded him and Mhlola reigned for a long time. Upon his death, his son, Dlokwakhe, took over as chief, but he was not the legitimate heir, genealogically speaking. Apparently Zwelakhe was supposed to succeed Mhlola, but, due to the fact that he was exiled, he was overlooked. The Zondi people disputed the succession in this case, and even today the chief's homestead is called eMbangwani (Place of Dispute).[44]

There is another version of why Zwelakhe was exiled. According to an old Shange woman, MaZamisa, Zwelakhe allegedly fornicated with his sister, which was taboo. The Shange people say that the Zondi clan were ashamed to tell the truth because they would be embarrassed, while the Zondi clan say that the Shange clan discredited the Zondi clan because they were interested in the position. They wanted the chieftaincy to be given to one of them.

The Shange clan

The Shange people arrived in Zwartkop in the early 1900s. They originally came from Ngomankulu near Richmond, named after the mountain Ngomankulu across the Umlazi River. Shange was a prominent clan in the area, but there were other clans, such the Mkhizes. In 1906, there were disputes between two Mkhize factions, when *Inkosi* Skhukhukhu Mkhize fought with *Inkosi* Tilongo Mkhize. *Inkosi* Tilongo was supported by Mguquka, while Skhukhukhu was mainly supported by the Shange clan. Skhukhukhu was the loser in this conflict and the Shange clan realised that they had no future in Ngomankulu, so they fled.[45]

Three senior Shange men searched for a place where they could take refuge.[46] They approached the Zondi chief in Zwartkop at the time, Mhlola, giving him an account of their battle with the Mkhize clan. The Shange people were given land on the other side of the Msunduzi River in the Nadi area. The area thus came to be called KwaShange, which means 'the place of the Shange'.

The KwaShange headmen

I have placed the KwaShange location *izinduna* in order of succession, but I have not included the dates, as nobody knows them for certain.

- Nzwakele was the first *induna* or headman when the Shange clan initially arrived in Swartkop.
- When Nzwakele died, his son Mhlazane Shange took over the position. After his death, the Zondi chief deployed his adherent from a neighbouring area (Mvundlweni) to act as KwaShange headman. The chief trusted no one from the Shange clan to take over as headman after Mhlazane, because Shange people were ambitious and wanted to be independent from the Zondi chiefdom. This nominee, Zuma, acted for two years.
- After that period, Msane, who had come from Mafunze, was given the position of headman.
- When Msane died, Ndawonde was appointed to succeed him. Ndawonde was known to be very strict and fought with other clans. When he took over, he tried to change the name of the area from KwaShange to Ndawonde's Kraal. For many years, the area had two names, KwaShange and Ndawonde's Kraal. In this period, Chief Zondi sent some of his clan to KwaShange to reside there to ensure that the area did not become independent from the Zondi chieftainship.
- After Ndawonde's death, the position of *induna* reverted to the Shange clan. Dukuza Shange succeeded Ndawonde.
- After Dukuza's death, Masondilika Shange took over the position.
- He was succeeded by his son Mbokodo, who was a drunkard and was unceremoniously recalled from the position.
- Mbokodo's younger brother, Skhosiphi Shange, took over the position.
- Phineus Ngubane was the next *induna*. He reigned until the beginning of the political violence of the 1990s. In 1987, his

wife was stabbed to death and her mutilated body was found lying in the cattle kraal. He no longer had the power to maintain discipline and order in the area.

- After Ngubane, no one wanted the position because there was 'nothing to look after – people had gone mad and violence was rife'.[47] For a short period, a KwaShange businessman, Zondi, who owns stores in KwaShange, acted as the *induna*, but he resigned because of the violence and the position became vacant.
- In the 1990s, after the Seven Days' War, two senior men were appointed by the chief to share the duties of the *induna*: Shange and Mbanjwa.
- In 2008, Mbanjwa passed away. The current headmen, Nduna Shange and Mabhoyi Madlala, were appointed for KwaShange Number One and Number Two respectively.

My interviewees are from families who originated outside the area. Some of them settled in Inadi during the 1800s. Some moved from white-owned farms in Midlands areas, such as near New Hanover and Howick, while others came from Greytown and Vryheid. All interviewees gave as their reasons for moving that they thought they had poor economic prospects as farm-tenant labourers and hoped for an improvement in their family fortunes by obtaining work in the cities of Pietermaritzburg and Durban.

Labour tenants who lived on white farms had no land rights, worked hard, were often (but not always) brutally treated and, until recently, were frequently not paid or paid very meagre wages. Usually a tenant had rights to work some land and graze cattle in exchange for labour (his own and that of his children), but he had no security of tenure. Tenant labour was accepted by some Africans, because it allowed them to stay on the land. However, increasing demands from farmers for more and more labour was one of the reasons why young men left to seek paid labour in the cities.

Currently, unemployment rates in KwaShange are high and some members of the community have experienced retrenchment. Most older women are housewives and part-time crop farmers, leading a life that is rural and largely traditional, while some obtain work as domestic workers. Very few people in the community are professionals and those that are work as teachers, nurses and police officers. Children stay in the rural areas and attend local schools, although some attend schools outside the community and later go to tertiary institutions.

Zulu-dominated rural areas are known for faction fights between residents and neighbouring clans. In the KwaShange area, the people of neighbouring Polela, the Dlamini group, have historically been antagonistic to the Zondi from Zwartkop, and from time to time fighting has erupted. The fights relate to access to and control of land.

The more recent settler families are also subject to political conflicts and tensions. The incoming Mchunus, for instance, were in conflict with the established Ndaba families from the 1960s to the 1980s. The Ndaba, also called Mhlungwini, from the Estcourt area, mocked the Mchunu, calling them 'country bumpkins' and 'outsiders' or *amakula* (coolies). Those who were there when the area was established are referred to as *Amarashiya* (Russians) and are regarded as 'more traditional'.[48] Even today in KwaShange, there is a section called KwaMnanayi, a derogatory term for Indians. Another section is called KwaGudlintaba, named after the place the Shange clan originally came from near Richmond. This is where die-hard traditionalists are found, mainly Zondis and Shanges. In 1987, most people who were aligned to Inkatha came from this section and relocated elsewhere in fear of their lives. Most people in the KwaMnanayi section were associated with the UDF. The Mchunus were supported in these fights by the Ndlovu and Madlala, who had emigrated with them from New Hanover during the 1960s. The worst clash between the Mchunus and Ndabas took place at a shebeen (drinking spot), known as Gomorrah, in Edendale Township.

Clan faction fights were characteristic of the KwaShange area, but, during the late 1980s to 1990s, they were eclipsed by the political unrest and the struggle against the apartheid regime. The battles between the traditional clans increased the bitterness of the party political conflicts of the 1980s and 1990s. This unrest was known locally as 'civil wars' between the UDF supporters and Inkatha supporters. The ready use of weapons was characteristic of both kinds of conflict.

Violence was therefore a normal feature of life in the Midlands of Natal. Structural violence, repression and coercion were the central features of the era before colonialism and they continued under apartheid. Violence embedded itself into every facet of society and shaped the nature of state power.

According to the media and political analysts, during the unrest of the 1980s and 1990s, the UDF conducted the main struggle against the apartheid regime, while the Inkatha movement, which was associated with the ethnic grouping of the Zulu, was seen as reactionary, in collusion, to an extent, with the National Party government. There were, in fact, no clearly defined political motivations for belonging to either of these parties within the community of KwaShange, and this exacerbated the 'civil war' situation. KwaShange is known in the Pietermaritzburg area as 'Slaughter House', because people were slaughtered like animals there.

Notes

1. Interview with MaZamisa Shange, KwaShange, 14 March 2010; interview with Mancinza Zondi, KwaShange, 15 March 2010.
2. KwaZulu was a homeland or Bantustan that did not take 'independence'.
3. Phrase borrowed from A.T. Bryant, *The Zulu People, as They Were Before the White Man Came* (Pietermaritzburg: Shuter and Shooter, 1949).
4. Interview with Sungubezi Madondo, Entembeni, 11 April 2010.
5. Interview with Mancinza Zondi, KwaShange, 14 March 2010.
6. Interview with MaZamisa Shange, KwaShange, 14 March 2010; interview with Senzosenkosi Mkhize, Richmond, 10 April 2010.
7. For details of the geographical and social study of the area of Vulindlela, see B. Haddad, 'African Women's Theologies of Survival: Intersecting Faith, Feminisms and Development' (PhD thesis, University of KwaZulu-Natal, Pietermaritzburg, 2000). See also M. Mchunu, 'Discipline, Respect and Ethnicity: A Study of the Changing Patterns of Fatherhood of Three Generations of Zulu Fathers and Sons in KwaShange, Inadi, Vulindlela Area of Pietermaritzburg, KwaZulu-Natal, from the 1930s to the 1990s' (Master's thesis, University of KwaZulu-Natal, 2005).
8. Haddad, 'African Women's Theologies of Survival', p. 49.
9. T.V. Bulpin, *Natal and the Zulu Country* (Cape Town: Books of Africa, 1977), p. 341. See also J. Wright, 'Before Mgungundlovu', in *Pietermaritzburg, 1838–1988: A New Portrait of an African City*, edited by J. Laband and R. Haswell (Pietermaritzburg: University of Natal Press, 1988); Haddad, 'African Women's Theologies of Survival'.
10. Bulpin, *Natal and the Zulu Country*, p. 341.
11. L. Thompson, *A History of South Africa* (New Haven: Yale University Press, 1990).
12. M.J. de Haan, *Mission on the Margin: A Case Study on Reformed Mission Prospects in eNkumane, KwaZulu-Natal* (Pietermaritzburg: Cluster Publications, 2010). See also Wright, 'Before Mgungundlovu'.
13. The story of the Mfecane is controversial to this day. Henry Francis Fynn, who was close to Shaka, claims on no evidence that Shaka slaughtered a

million people. Such exaggeration suited colonial notions of black self-destructive violence; the idea that the region had been depopulated by Shaka gelled with settlers' desires for uncontested land. The image of a landscape littered with human bones, launched by Nathaniel Isaacs, persists as a melodramatic icon of Shaka's reign, even into the most respected of modern histories, such as Leonard Thompson. Similarly, the early historian George Theal upped the number of dead to two million. These exaggerations spawned the concept of the Mfecane (usually translated as the crushing): the notion that Shaka had been solely responsible for an explosion of aggression, which sent neighbouring tribes scattering and marauding over most of the sub-continent. The Mfecane became the historiographical sibling of the Great Trek, where the tribes displaced by Shaka had ended up providing the basis for the Bantustans (areas allocated under apartheid to black people). The issue of depopulated land has long been exploded as myth. See S. Marks, 'The Myth of the Empty Land', *History Today* 30(1), 1980: 8–12; A. Duminy and B. Guest (eds), *Natal and Zululand from the Earliest Times to 1910: A New History* (Pietermaritzburg: University of Natal Press, 1989); C. Hamilton, *The Mfecane Aftermath: Reconstructive Debates in Southern African History* (Johannesburg: Wits University Press and Pietermaritzburg: University of Natal Press, 1995). The controversy concerning the intensification of the conflict over resources is articulated in various ways by writers such as Max Gluckman, J.D. Omer-Cooper and Jeff Guy, but it remains unresolved.

14. See E.H. Brookes and N. Hurwitz, *The Native Reserves of Natal*, Natal Regional Survey, Volume 7 (Cape Town: Oxford University Press, 1957); Bryant, *The Zulu People*; C. De B. Webb and J. Wright (eds), *The James Stuart Archive of Recorded Oral Evidence Relating to the History of the Zulu and Neighbouring Peoples*, Volumes 1–5 (Durban: Killie Campbell Africana Library and Pietermaritzburg: University of Natal Press, 1975–2001).
15. Bryant, *The Zulu People*.
16. Interview with Mancinza Zondi, KwaShange, 14 March 2010.
17. Wright, 'Before Mgungundlovu'. See also Bulpin, *Natal and the Zulu Country*.
18. Wright, 'Before Mgungundlovu'.
19. Bulpin, *Natal and the Zulu Country*. See also Bryant, *The Zulu People*; Wright, 'Before Mgungundlovu'.
20. Bryant, *The Zulu People*; Wright, 'Before Mgungundlovu'; interview with Mancinza Zondi, KwaShange, 14 March 2010.
21. Bryant, *The Zulu People*.
22. S. Mkhize, *Uhlanga lwas'Embo: The History of the Embo People* (Durban: Just Done Production, 2007). See also Bryant, *The Zulu People*; Wright, 'Before Mgungundlovu'.
23. P. Denis, 'Indians versus Russians: An Oral History of the Political Violence in Nxamalala (1987–1992)', *Journal of Natal and Zulu History* 24(1), 2006: 64–93. See also Wright, 'Before Mgungundlovu'; interview with Mancinza Zondi, KwaShange, 14 March 2010.
24. Wright, 'Before Mgungundlovu'.
25. Denis, 'Indians versus Russians'. See also Wright, 'Before Mgungundlovu'.

26. Webb and Wright, *James Stuart Archive*, Volume 1, 1975, p. 9.
27. Webb and Wright, *James Stuart Archive*, Volume 1, 1975, p. 331 (original emphasis). 'Man' implied any ordinary person, including a wizard. 'Heavens' was used as an expression for Shaka.
28. Webb and Wright, *James Stuart Archive*, Volume 1, 1975, p. 195.
29. Interview with Sungubezi Madondo, 14 April 2010.
30. Interview with family members of the Madondo clan, Ntembeni, 14 April 2010.
31. Interview with Sondubezi Madondo, Ntembeni, 14 April 2010.
32. Interview with Khulekani Hadebe, KwaMpande, 24 April 2010; interview with Chief Sondelani Zondi, KwaNkosi, 25 April 2010; interview with Mancinza Zondi, KwaShange, 14 March 2010.
33. J. Bird, *The Annals of Natal: 1495 to 1845*. Pietermaritzburg: P. Davis & Sons, 1888. See also A.T. Bryant, *Olden Times in Zululand and Natal Containing Earlier Political History of the Eastern-Nguni Clans* (Cape Town: Struik, 1965); N. Herd, *The Bent Pine: The Trial of Langalibalele* (Johannesburg: Ravan Press, 1976).
34. 'Isizwe SamaHlubi', submission to the Commission on Traditional Leadership Dispute and Claims, July 2004, http://www.mkhangelingoma.co.za/heritage/history, p. 10. For more on Langalibalele's trial, see J. Guy, *The View across the River: Harriette Colenso and the Zulu Struggle against Imperialism* (Cape Town: David Philip, 2002).
35. J. Wright and A. Manson, *The Hlubi Chiefdom in Zululand-Natal: A History* (Ladysmith: Ladysmith Historical Society, 1983).
36. Brookes and Hurwitz, *The Native Reserves of Natal*, pp. 3–4.
37. Brookes and Hurwitz, *The Native Reserves of Natal*, pp. 2–3.
38. Brookes and Hurwitz, *The Native Reserves of Natal*, pp. 2–3.
39. N.J. van Warmelo, *A Preliminary Survey of the Bantu Tribes of South Africa* (Pretoria: Government Printer, 1935). See also Denis, 'Indians versus Russians'; Wright, 'Before Mgungundlovu'.
40. T.V. McClendon, *Genders and Generations Apart: Labor Tenants and Customary Law in Segregation-Era South Africa, 1920s to 1940s* (Portsmouth: Heinemann, 2002), p. xiii.
41. Denis, 'Indians versus Russians'.
42. Interview with Mbongeni Zondi, 14 March 2010, translated by me from the original Zulu.
43. Wright, 'Before Mgungundlovu'.
44. Interview with Mbongeni Zondi, 14 March 2010, translated by me from the original Zulu.
45. In 1906, Mnukwa was the leader of Chief Mguquka Mkhize's warriors. He was captured and sentenced to many years in prison for his involvement in the *Impi YaseMbo*, a war between the Embo clan and the Mabhoyi people (the Mabhoyi area comprised of different clans, including the Shange, Mchunu, Ngubane and a few Mkhize people). This war coincided with the Bhambatha rebellion of 1906. Many Mkhize warriors hid in the caves in the area called Gudlintaba, but Tilongo was imprisoned in 1906 and this ended the Embo war. The Shange clan had already left the area and they never returned after Tilongo's imprisonment.

46. My interviewee could not remember the names of these three men, except that of his father-in-law, who was one of them. His name was Mhlezane Shange. In my interviews with other people in the area, two other prominent names appear: Kufakakuceli Shange and his brother Nzwakele Shange. From this I deduce that the three men were Mhlazane Shange, his father Nzwakele and his brother Kufakakuceli. (She probably refused to mention his name because, according to the custom of *hlonipha*, or Zulu respect culture, daughters-in-law do not mention their in-laws by name.)
47. Interview with Mvunyelwa Ngubane, KwaShange, 8 March 2009.
48. Denis, 'Indians versus Russians.'

4

The Ringleaders

IN KWASHANGE, THERE were four prominent men who were instigators of the conflict. Their involvement in the struggle was wider than the KwaShange area and they participated in the broad politics of the region. The information in this chapter has been gleaned from interviews with Nunu 'Ngedlezi' Mchunu, Chris Hlengwa, Moses Ndlovu and Phillip 'Makhekhe' Thabethe and from newspaper reports.[1]

Ndlovu and Thabethe lived only a kilometre apart.[2] So did Mchunu and Hlengwa. Ndlovu and Thabethe became political rivals but were once good neighbours. They belonged to one church, played for one soccer team and exercised together as young men. They shared jokes and their children attended the same school.[3] Mchunu and Hlengwa were once friends. All these families shared and exchanged gifts, such as mealies, *amadumbe* (local potatoes) and sweet potatoes; they enjoyed each other's harvests, itself a culturally valued interdependence in a community. This chapter describes the breakdown of this community into civil war.[4]

The rivals Ndlovu and Thabethe belonged to different political groups and were also divided along union lines – the Congress of South African Trade Unions (COSATU) and the United Workers' Union of South Africa (UWUSA). Mchunu and Hlengwa represented the local factions, Inkatha and the United Democratic Front (UDF), respectively.

KwaShange was part of Inadi, which fell under the chieftainship of Shayabantu Zondi, who was aligned to Inkatha.[5] In KwaShange, UDF-aligned residents were at war with the Inkatha-aligned residents, who rallied under Chief Zondi. Inkatha received support from the

National Party government, while the UDF formed the African National Congress (ANC) in exile's internal wing in the struggle for democracy.[6]

My interviews with these four men made me realise that KwaShange was the centre of the initial clash that led to the intensified violence in the greater Vulindlela area and to the Seven Days' War in March 1990. These events were part of a conflict that reflected the politics of the country as a whole.

Moses Ndlovu

Moses Ndlovu was born on 19 June 1944 at Swayimane in the Otto's Bluff area near Pietermaritzburg.[7] His parents were farm tenants. He attended primary school in Cramond. At the age of fourteen, he was forced to work on the farm, according to the labour-tenant system of the times.[8] He was embittered by his experiences and deliberately drove the farmer's cattle onto the railway line in front of an oncoming goods train. They were killed or maimed, which led to him and his family being expelled from the farm.[9]

Ndlovu's family then relocated to KwaShange Location. He enrolled at a local school where he studied until he reached Standard 8 (Grade 6). He was forced to leave school after his father's death as he was the oldest son and he had to look after his siblings and his mother.[10] He was employed at Meadow Feeds in 1962. In 1963, he moved to a newly built industrial area in Hammarsdale, where he worked until 1972. Here he was exposed to trade unionism.[11] When he was recruited into the ANC, his initial assignment was mobilising workers into trade unions. Among the highlights of his unionist career were the well-remembered 1973 strikes in Durban.[12] He worked closely with Barney Dladla and Alec Erwin in the Trade Union Advisory Co-ordinating Council. In 1975, he was tasked to do the underground work of identifying suitable young men and women within the trade union structures who could be sent abroad for military training.[13] Ndlovu worked in KwaShange and in other places in Natal and Zululand, recruiting mainly young males.[14] This brought him close to seasoned unionists and ANC leaders, such as Harry Gwala, Matthews Meyiwa, Alpheus Mdlalose and William Khanyile.[15]

During his work as an underground operative he evaded the dragnet of the apartheid security police but he was arrested in 1976 while co-ordinating transport for families of his comrades who were standing trial in Pietermaritzburg. He was banned from 1977 to 1981 and prohibited from being in the company of more than three people at one time.[16]

When his banning order expired in 1985, Ndlovu had an opportunity to contribute to the formation of COSATU structures in the Natal Midlands region. He joined forces with Jay Naidoo, Johnny Makhathini, Kenneth Dladla, Theo Nene and Pat Horn, and he began to organise workers into unions under COSATU. When the executive decision had been taken to establish sector-based affiliates of the Federation of South African Trade Unions (FOSATU), Ndlovu and Makhathini contributed to the formation of almost all the Pietermaritzburg-based trade unions that subsequently became affiliates of COSATU. He organised workers as far away as Ladysmith and Cato Ridge.[17]

At the height of violence in Natal, Ndlovu led the formation and co-ordination of Self-Defence Units in the greater Vulindlela area. As a result, he was subjected to constant harassment by the national security police and Inkatha vigilantes.[18] Nunu Mchunu of Inkatha said Ndlovu was regarded as troublesome, which is why KwaShange received so much attention from state security police and the Inkatha leadership, locally and provincially.[19] Ndlovu not only witnessed the killing of his friends, he also experienced the pain of the murder of his daughter by vigilantes in KwaShange.[20]

Nunu Mchunu, commonly known as 'Ngedlezi'

Mchunu was instrumental in the conflict in the KwaShange area;[21] he was connected with Inkatha and participated in national strife, as well as in KwaShange conflicts.[22] He represented more than 3 000 members of the Natal Provincial Administration union.[23] He was imprisoned in 1987 under the state of emergency on the grounds that he was the source of the turmoil of KwaShange, which spread to neighbouring areas.[24]

Mchunu was born in 1942 on a farm near New Hanover in Mshwathi.[25] He left the farm when he was very young because the enforced labour tenancy stifled his ambitions. Standard 5 (Grade 7) was the highest grade available at the Melville Primary farm school. When farm dwellers' children completed Standard 5, they were expected to work full-time on the farm. Mchunu sought employment off the farm, first in Greytown and then in Pietermaritzburg. The younger Mchunu, despite being banned from the farm, nevertheless kept visiting the farm at night to see his parents and siblings. The relationship between Mchunu's father and the farmer became intolerable in 1964 and in 1965 the entire Mchunu family moved to KwaShange.[26] Mchunu was working in Pietermaritzburg for the Natal Provincial Administration when he joined the workers' union and began to be politically active.[27] He remembers that he met with many 'highly educated' people who had read leftist literature. These people had a great influence on him. He also read newspapers, particularly *Ilanga lase Natal*, which 'broadened his mind' and politicised him. He remembered:

> We eventually left the farm and when we went to Pietermaritzburg, I got employment in town and I understood that there was a party that was fighting against the white men's regime. At that time, I hated white people. I began to understand politics in Pietermaritzburg and I became part of the organisation that was fighting against black men's oppression. That was the ANC. I joined the African National Congress because it was fighting for black people. We used to attend meetings in Pietermaritzburg Town Hall – and police would come and harass us. I remember the day [Nelson] Mandela was caught by the police. We had a meeting with him in a place known today as Retief Street. We had gathered on that day to burn our passes. Police came and they asked where our passes were and they sjambokked [whipped] us. I will never ever forget that day in my life.[28]

Mchunu had difficulty in remembering details of this period of his life: the hall he mistakenly called the Town Hall was probably a ramshackle hall called 'People's Hall'. This was where the early ANC had their meetings. Nearby this 'People's Hall' in Retief Street there was a bookshop and restaurant where the 'highly educated' people who influenced Mchunu bought 'leftist literature' and had discussions, which introduced Mchunu to politics.

Mchunu recalls the names of prominent people who attended these meetings: Moses Mabhida, Harry Gwala, Agrippa Ngcobo, 'Mfenendala' Xaba, Mtimkulu, Nhlangulela and Sithole. Mchunu recalls that sometimes the South African Police would come and beat them during these meetings. As the situation intensified, some people left the country and went into exile.

Both Moses Ndlovu and Mchunu attended these meetings; they knew each other because they came from the same area, but they were not close. Both alluded to the fact that discussions at the 'People's Hall' were mainly about mobilising people in their local areas and educating them about the struggle against the National Party government.[29] There were meetings where they had to appoint leaders for the ANC, and they recalled that sometimes there was infighting and battles for positions.

Mchunu and Ndlovu noted that in their meetings at the 'People's Hall' discussions were about the significance of a national movement and engaging in the class struggle, and the trade unions were concerned with shop-floor programmes.[30]

Both Mchunu and Ndlovu recalled the last meeting addressed by Mandela in Pietermaritzburg in the 1960s, before he was captured by the South African Police near Howick. The National Party regime was harsh on people who participated in these kinds of gatherings, and in 1960 the ANC and the Pan-Africanist Congress (PAC) were banned. Mchunu recalls that many people he knew, who used to attend meetings at the 'People's Hall', disappeared, perhaps jailed or exiled:

> Many people who were members of the ANC faced a difficult time. Many went into exile in places like Mozambique, Lusaka, Angola and Swaziland, because the state police were looking for them. The government had decided to ban organisations that challenged the state. Many people I met and got to know when I first arrived in Pietermaritzburg went into exile. I contemplated escaping the country, but it was still difficult for me. I had a farm mentality. I feared for my life; I decided to withdraw myself and not associate with political groups.[31]

Some of those who remained in the country heard that there was another organisation that was going to be an 'internal wing' of the ANC. Mchunu recalls that Sithole and Nhlangulela came to him and told him about the movement that '*uMntwana wakwa Phindangene*'

(Mangosuthu Buthelezi, often called 'the Prince of Phindangene') had started and it was going to fight for black people's rights like the ANC. In other words, Inkatha was going to be 'the internal wing of the ANC' and it was going to negotiate with the National Party government. 'The Inkatha National Cultural Liberation Movement did not claim to be the sole and authentic representative of the Black people of South Africa,' Mchunu stated.[32] It claimed that its aim was to use a multi-strategy approach for a united, non-racial democratic country. Its formation was a result of a need for a black democratic force to pick up the gauntlet of the black liberation struggle.[33] From the commencement of the first state of emergency, and the bannings after the Sharpeville massacre in 1960, there had been no significant organised black political activity.

Wave after wave of repression by the South African government had, by 1975, left black politics in disarray. At the time of Inkatha's launch in 1975 the names of ANC leaders Nelson Mandela, Walter Sisulu, Govan Mbeki, Moses Mabhida and others, including PAC leader Robert Sobukwe, were being whispered in quiet corners. Dr Buthelezi, from the beginning, spoke of them in his speeches and even quoted them, which was a punishable offence. He raised questions about their release and made their release conditional to any dialogue with the white racist National Party regime.[34]

Mchunu joined Inkatha because it was the ANC's suggestion that Chief Buthelezi start the movement. It was the kind of movement that he sought because he did not want to go into exile or to prison. Some of the men he had recruited for the ANC in KwaShange were already in prison because of the state of emergency; men such as Amon Kubheka, known as 'Brahman', who later became an Inkatha warlord in KwaShange. When Khubeka was freed from prison, Mchunu persuaded him to join Inkatha and to assist him to mobilise members of the community to join. In 1975, Buthelezi set up the Inkatha National Cultural Liberation Movement after receiving the consent of the ANC in exile.

Inkatha articulated its mission through the language of Black Consciousness and black identity, in such a way that it avoided open conflict with the National Party government.[35] Inkatha challenged the government in a less radical manner than other parties. Buthelezi claimed:

> I wanted democratic forces emerging in South Africa to accept a multi-strategic approach and offer to work in harmony with the ANC Mission in Exile. In 1974, when I set about gathering leaders together to establish Inkatha in 1975, I set about doing so with the clear intention NOT of subverting the ANC Mission in Exile – but of proving to them that democratic opposition to apartheid and non-violent tactics and strategies were still possible.[36]

Mzala and Gerhard Maré and Georgina Hamilton argue against Buthelezi's claim to have participated in the official structures of apartheid only to oppose the system from within and by virtue of popular support. In contrast, he was demonstrated to have been intimately and collaboratively engaged in the erection and working of oppressive structures and machinery in KwaZulu for decades, notwithstanding his rejection of Bantustan independence.[37]

John Aitchison notes that Inkatha legitimised itself as an authentic expression of the (largely ANC) tradition of inclusive black nationalism through negotiations carried out with the ANC and the Zambian president, Kenneth Kaunda, as well as through Buthelezi's connections with the ANC and Mandela. Its language of non-violence was aimed at business interests and foreign powers intent on constructive engagement.[38] Aitchison says:

> Black Consciousness, in spite of its positive, identity-building character that did much for psychological liberation, contained within it a wellspring of resentment that later was to develop within Inkatha into a distrust of leftist white, Indian and any black radicals associating with them in either group. Cultural liberation as a means of raising political awareness within a repressive apartheid environment lost its discrimination once Inkatha and its leader Chief Buthelezi had established its strong identity as 'at one' with the traditional tribal chiefdoms long used by the apartheid regime's 'divide and rule' policies.[39]

Nunu Mchunu, Nhlangulela, Sithole and Amon Kubheka became staunch Inkatha members and attended meetings in Ulundi. To the question of what Inkatha leaders discussed in Ulundi, Mchunu answered:

> In Ulundi we discussed nothing but how to strengthen the struggle in the country and to ensure that those who were in exile be allowed to come back. We called these people by names: Mandela, Mbeki, Sobukwe, Oliver Tambo, Mabhida and others. All of what was discussed was that Chief Buthelezi should talk and reason with the white government of the time to treat black people with respect. We discussed that we needed to embark on a constructive and passive struggle for freedom and we would encourage each other to mobilise support in our areas so that the government could see that all black people were concerned and not just a few people who were in leadership.[40]

Mchunu confirmed that Buthelezi refused to negotiate with the National Party government or to accept homeland 'independence':

> I can tell you, we discussed nothing but how to get the government of the Nationalists to listen to the majority of people of South Africa and release ANC leaders who had been jailed and to unban the organisations that were banned. That is why Mangosuthu Buthelezi refused to enter into talks with the Nationalist government unless the political prisoners were released. Later, as there was tension between Buthelezi and ANC leaders in exile, we [as Inkatha] were then attacked in our areas [by the UDF, the new 'internal wing']. It became the subject of our discussions; all leaders, including myself, reported that we were being attacked either verbally or physically by young people, in particular, and those who believed that Buthelezi had betrayed the African National Congress. We agreed that we are not going to 'fold our arms' but we were going to defend ourselves from the attacks. That is how this violence problem started in many areas, including this one in KwaShange.[41]

Mchunu mentioned that he attended Inkatha meetings in Ulundi before the relationship between Buthelezi and the ANC in exile became bitter. Mchunu was annoyed by what the ANC leaders in exile were doing to promote the struggle, and more so by proposed sanctions. He agreed to strengthen the Inkatha movement in KwaShange, in preparation for complete independence from the ANC. He had connections with Inkatha leaders in other areas, who met frequently in Ulundi.[42]

Some people who were recruited by the ANC, and who had participated in the meetings at the 'People's Hall', did not go into exile but there are no records that they joined Inkatha. I asked Mchunu why they did not join. He replied that some people decided not to get themselves involved in politics because their lives were in danger. They believed that the government would turn against Inkatha as the ANC was already banned.[43]

Moses Ndlovu's responsibilities, however, at the time of the formation of Inkatha, suggest that he had either been conscientised to the leftist view of the armed struggle or had no time to actively participate in Inkatha activities because he was tasked to do underground work for the ANC. He had been given the responsibility of identifying young people within the trade unions who could be recruited and sent abroad for armed force training. Soon after the formation of Inkatha in 1977, he was banned.[44] Clearly, however, there was no tension between Ndlovu and Mchunu at that time.

Chris Hlengwa

Chris Hlengwa was born in KwaShange. His grandparents were originally from Bishopstowe, but they left for Zwartkop (later called KwaShange) in 1929 due to bad living conditions. Hlengwa grew up in KwaShange and went to school at the nearby KwaMpande Maria Memorial Primary School. Later he went to Mpande High School, where he completed his Junior Certificate. He was then employed by the South African Railways Police, which, in the mid-1980s, were incorporated into the South African Police.

Hlengwa played an important role in preventing the violence in KwaShange from escalating. He said:

> As police, we were called to many areas in Vulindlela and other parts of the Natal Midlands to mediate between UDF and Inkatha people who were fighting. I used to get disconcerted by Inkatha members who mercilessly killed UDF supporters. I used to be annoyed by some of my white colleagues but more so by black police who killed black people in townships like Hammarsdale and Imbali.[45]

Some UDF people, such as Moses Ndlovu and Harry Gwala, knew Hlengwa's feelings about the situation and his relationship with them strengthened. Within the South African Police, he took it upon himself to defend the UDF from Inkatha assault. Chief Shayabantu Zondi of Vulindlela, an Inkatha leader, became aware of Hlengwa's anger towards Inkatha. In 1987, in the widely publicised KwaShange massacre court case, Hlengwa and eleven other men in KwaShange were found guilty of killing thirteen Inkatha members, who were allegedly planning to attack UDF-supporting families. Hlengwa and his co-accused were represented by Pius Langa, a human rights lawyer and an ANC activist, who later became the Chief Justice of the Constitutional Court of South Africa after 1994.

Phillip Thabethe, commonly known as 'Makhekhe'

Thabethe was interviewed by the *New York Times* in January 1988. Here is an extract:

> One man with a bitter grievance against the front [UDF] is Phillip Thabethe, a 40-year-old driver for the bus company that serves many of the 300,000 blacks living in the Edendale region. Mr Thabethe said front militants had mounted an all-out assault on him and his family after he began organizing at the bus depot on behalf of the United Workers Union of South Africa. The union is an Inkatha affiliate that is a rival of the more powerful labor affiliate of the front, the Congress of South African Trade Unions.[46]

Thabethe claimed he was on his bus in September 1987 when a man in the line at the door opened fire on him. He showed monitors of the violence scars on his chest from eight bullets from a Soviet-made Tokarev automatic pistol. His driver's licence, in his shirt pocket at the time, had four holes in it where bullets had passed through. Thabethe underwent weeks of surgery before returning home to KwaShange. While he was recuperating, ten days before Christmas 1987, gunmen killed his twenty-year-old son as he walked to a local store. Six days later, while Thabethe was at the hospital, about 50 youths surrounded his home and set it on fire. His wife, his mother and another son were killed.[47]

The *New York Times* article continues:

> At the offices of the Pietermaritzburg Association for Christian Social Awareness, a white-run agency that has tried to mitigate suffering in the townships, a black welfare worker described the bus driver as 'one of the top Inkatha killers' and said he had been involved in many slayings of people with front [UDF] affiliations. But when the accusation was repeated to Mr. Thabethe, he smiled, saying: 'I cannot be a killer. I do not have a gun.'
>
> Inkatha's chief representative in the region, Vusumuzi Mvelase, produced a sheaf of affidavits that the Zulu group has presented in court, seeking injunctions against further attacks. The applications dealt with fire-bombings and shootings directed at Inkatha officials in the Pietermaritzburg and Durban areas, attacks that Mr. Mvelase said arose from attempts by the front, dating from 1985, to supplant Inkatha as Natal's pre-eminent black group.[48]

Two bulls in one kraal: The breach between Mchunu and Ndlovu

Nunu Mchunu was one of Chief Shayabantu Zondi's councillors from 1980 and was responsible for peace and order.[49] He instilled discipline mainly in young people who were 'disrespectful' in their behaviour within the community. As he remembered it:

> As much as I was doing my job – assigned to me by the community, there were people who hated me for working for the community. Some would deliberately do things which were really out of order in my presence – because they wanted to provoke me; they knew that I would not keep quiet. But from 1983, I was undermined, and it looked as though there was a campaign to challenge my authority. One of the people who were causing me trouble was Moses Ndlovu and many young people who were in one way or the other connected to him.[50]

During our interview in 2003, Ndlovu commented on Mchunu as a community leader:

> Mchunu was using his authority as a community leader to campaign for a political movement. He was very cruel to those people he deemed were not interested in his movement. Mchunu and I were in a war, so I was not ashamed to tell people not to take him seriously. It would have been better if he did justice, but he was biased.[51]

Mchunu joined a large Zionist church because he wanted to influence people, and many people who belonged to the Zionist church were members of Inkatha.[52] Ndlovu followed suit and took a senior position in the Presbyterian church in KwaShange.[53] He said:

> As I said, there was a war between myself and Mchunu. This was triggered by the fact that Inkatha leadership and supporters in other areas were treating UDF supporters unfairly; in fact, our members were being brutally killed in Johannesburg, in Transvaal and many other areas. Arrogance and attitude displayed by Inkatha leadership nationally compelled us to prevent Inkatha from spreading to every corner of our society. In our UDF and COSATU meetings it was agreed that we needed to stop Inkatha's influence and do anything that would counteract them . . . Can you imagine if I allowed him [Mchunu] to do as he pleased? This area would not be what it is today.[54]

In 1986, Mchunu was appointed as the first chairperson of the first secondary school in KwaShange (Mtholangqondo School). Some people were unhappy about this appointment, but his influence was irrefutable in the community.[55] In 1987, schoolchildren, influenced by Ndlovu's canvassing among the youth in the UDF, began to be ill-disciplined and insolent towards teachers. There was tension among the learners: some wanted Mchunu to be on the school committee, while others wanted him removed because he was an Inkatha leader and because he was very harsh on undisciplined youths.[56]

Ndlovu said:

> That was the only strategy we could use to stop Mchunu. He was very influential in the community. I, together with my

> team, mobilised a few boys and told them to cause chaos and make sure that they made school ungovernable. By that time Mchunu had won [over] many teachers in all our local schools to join Inkatha.[57]

One day in 1987, there was a serious fight at the school, where children from UDF-supporting homes fought with children whose families were Inkatha supporters. The latter were chased away and told to go home and tell their parents to pack their possessions and leave KwaShange. The UDF learners refused to attend classes, and the school principal, Clement Mathonsi, sent some children to call the chairperson of the school, Mchunu, to address students. He said:

> I refused. I said they must tell the principal that I am not coming; I feared that the children were going to kill me. I had heard that the plan was to kill me. Because one of my daughters was a learner in the same school, she heard from friends of hers that it was the day to kill me. Instead, I went to KwaZondi store (where there was a public telephone) and I phoned the police.[58]

Ndlovu commented:

> I was not at home that day, I was at work, but one of my boys [UDF supporters] phoned me at work and he told me that a police helicopter came to the school and it was the first time in our area a helicopter landed. Nobody knew who had informed the police – but we suspected that Mchunu had called the police. It was a shock because we had hoped that he was going to go to the school to talk. Mchunu was a person who never feared anyone – he had unbelievable bravery. We were sure that he would go to school and try to stop the chaos and my boys would 'deal' with him then.[59]

On 25 September 1987, thirteen youths from KwaShange, mainly learners from the Inkatha-supporting families, were attacked by UDF supporters and killed. They were buried in a mass grave in the school yard. In 1988, Mchunu resigned from the board of the school and Ndlovu succeeded him.

Philippe Denis, drawing on his personal collection of recorded interviews in his submission to Amnesty International, noted that the local spark for conflict between the two camps was the strike at the BTR Sarmcol factory in Howick, which started on 30 April 1985. There had been an earlier stoppage in March over management's prolonged delays in recognising the Metal and Allied Workers' Union. In contrast, UWUSA was recognised immediately after its formation in May 1986 at the same factory. In retaliation for the strike of 1985, the entire African workforce was dismissed. The factory management started to recruit 'scab' labour soon after the strike started. This inevitably led to conflict. A successful stay-away was called on behalf of the strikers on 18 July 1985, endorsed by FOSATU and the UDF, and it was followed by a consumer boycott of white-owned shops. A survey conducted by the Pietermaritzburg Chamber of Commerce at the end of August showed an average fall-off in black trade of between 60 and 70 per cent. The boycott was denounced by the Inkatha-supporting Inyanda Chamber of Commerce. On 12 January 1986, Buthelezi instructed all Inkatha members and supporters to be prepared to mobilise workers against the newly formed COSATU. Mchunu and Makhekhe Thabethe made public announcements in KwaShange and neighbouring areas that people should dissociate themselves from COSATU.

A 200-strong Inkatha group was bussed into Mpophomeni Township (the home of the Sarmcol strikers) on the evening of 5 December 1986. Some KwaShange Inkatha leaders were among them. Mchunu recalled this incident, but never admitted that some KwaShange Inkatha leaders were part of the group. They abducted and assaulted four COSATU members in Mpophomeni and executed three of them; while one managed to escape. The Inkatha group was then escorted out of the township by the police. Within a day or two, at least three of the perpetrators were arrested by the Howick police but they were ordered by a high-ranking police officer to release the accused. The inquest in March 1988 found that nine Inkatha members (against whom there have as yet been no prosecutions) were responsible for the murders. One of those named was Vela Mchunu, who, together with about 200 other Inkatha men, had received South African Defence Force Special Forces military training.[60] Vela Mchunu was arrested in the early 1990s and tried under another name for a taxi-related double murder, but he was acquitted. The Attorney

General of Natal, Tim McNally, refused to bring him to court for the Mpophomeni killings.[61]

Police were present throughout Mpophomeni and KwaShange, searching for guns in the homes of known UDF supporters, including Hlengwa, Ndaba and Zondi. The police confiscated weapons they found in these households, leaving them vulnerable to attack by Inkatha supporters. During the Truth and Reconciliation Commission hearings in Pietermaritzburg in 1996, Eugene de Kock from the government security police admitted the role the police played in exacerbating the situation. They were to become known as the 'third force'.[62]

August 1987: D-Day for Moses Ndlovu

At a meeting in August 1987, everyone in KwaShange, including children as young as ten years old, was forced to join Inkatha. Chief Shayabantu Zondi was the chairperson at the meeting; on stage were the local top Inkatha leadership: Guvaza Khanyile (the local *induna*), Nunu Mchunu, Phillip Thabethe, Amon Kubheka and Mlungisi Ngubane (a youth activist).

Moses Ndlovu had been summoned to the meeting to explain why he had acted as a 'traitor' and been 'disrespectful' to Chief Buthelezi and the KwaZulu government. Despite the pressure, Ndlovu did not answer the questions. He was being bullied, and in another room in the school community members were being forced to pay R5 for Inkatha membership cards.

Aitchison writes:

> There were now daily reports of a heavy Inkatha recruitment drive backed by threats and coercion. Apparently in many Vulindlela areas a final date of 4 October was proclaimed, by which time everyone had to have joined Inkatha. Conventionally, it is here that the Midlands war can be said to have begun.[63]

I had been informed that this was the day that Inkatha had planned to publicly kill Ndlovu.[64] They wanted to show the community members who were reluctant to join Inkatha what was 'coming to them'. Ndlovu was asked why he worked for COSATU and he was instructed to resign.

Hlengwa's account of the meeting is as follows:

> I arrived late to that meeting because I had been working night shift. I remember well that day; it had been raining the day before [Saturday] so it was muddy. The school hall was packed and the road to the school was full, almost every community member was there; it was indeed a sad day. People were scared. We were all terrified. When I arrived at the school hall, Moses Ndlovu was standing in the front [*kwakungadlalwa*], the man was crying literally. Moses Ndlovu had been forced by a group of men to attend the meeting. And he was being forced to 'lead by example' and take membership of Inkatha. And there was a heated debate where many were questioning Chief Zondi and Ngendlezi [Mchunu] as to why they were forcing them to join Inkatha, and others were asking what they are going to gain by joining Inkatha. Phakathi, a senior KwaShange man, upon my arrival, raised a hand and asked me 'as a policeman – a person who understands law' to answer some of their questions. The question was: is it correct for Nkosi Zondi and Ngedlezi Mchunu to compel them to join Inkatha? What does the law say? My answer was, 'No, nobody should be forced to join any organisation.'[65]

From then onwards, Chief Zondi and Chris Hlengwa were arch enemies. The following day, Chief Zondi saw Hlengwa in KwaShange and threatened him. Hlengwa took out his gun and Chief Zondi ran away. Hlengwa requested and received protection from the police for about a month, but when the white station manager heard that Hlengwa was UDF, he withdrew the police that were looking after Hlengwa's home and children.

State police started harassing UDF supporters in KwaShange and some UDF supporters were taken away by the police and beaten. Police in plain clothes used to come in a white taxi, with the sign 'Dambuza' in the window. Some white police would wear brown make-up so as not to be recognised by people in KwaShange. In the same year, Inkatha youths started recruiting people, 'toyi toying' in KwaShange, forcing people to join Inkatha and going to surrounding areas such as Vulisaka.

In August 1987, Inkatha youths met at Mzamweni High School, across the Msunduzi River, to plan one of their attacks. The UDF leaders in KwaShange were aware of this meeting and, with the assistance of Harry Gwala, they managed to get uMkhonto weSizwe (MK) soldiers to defend homes that were going to be attacked. An anonymous source said:

> We realised that waiting for them would make it difficult for us to prevent them. The best thing was to corner them where they met because we were sure that they had some weapons. Inkatha-trained police were going to accompany them, so we decided to go to the school and we shot them.[66]

Aitchison's version of the story is that the COSATU leader, Alfred Ndlovu, borrowed an AK-47 from an MK member and attacked an Inkatha group in Vulindlela, wounding several people.[67] Seven youths were permanently paralysed as a result of this attack. Others were killed later in similar political violence.

The *Daily News* reported:

> About 12 complainants and potential court witnesses had been killed, or their houses burned down, in the past year in Pietermaritzburg police district, the regional court was told yesterday. The witness, Captain A. Upton, of the Unrest Unit here, said that intimidation was so bad that even bereaved people were scared to be seen near the police. Other potential witnesses who had made a statement to lawyers later denied having made it. This fear of reprisal made it very difficult to prosecute perpetrators of political crimes here. Captain Upton was testifying at the regional court trail of Mr Alfred Ndlovu (38), second national vice-president of the Transport and General Workers' Union and regional chairman of COSATU. He faces a charge of terrorism and two of attempted murder, one arising out of the wounding of 13 youths aged from 10 to 17, and a 22-year-old man, at Vulisaka [KwaShange] in August last year.[68]

The National Party government was guilty of aggravating and even engineering the confrontation between black people. The rupture between the ANC and the Inkatha movement in 1979 provided a useful occasion for the government to aggravate the conflict. Much publicity was given to what was described by the government, and portrayed by the state media, as 'black-on-black violence'.[69] One of the established strategies of the regime was to use divisions to maintain its rule. Inkatha was seen as relatively pro-National Party government, with Buthelezi opposing sanctions and receiving funding for military and police training.[70] The UDF was formed in 1983 to oppose the tricameral system that was being imposed on South Africa.[71] It identified all participants in a National Party government structure as enemies.

During 1986, the UDF, as the ANC internal wing, had started boycotts of businesses and used intimidation to compel unwilling black participants to observe them. Municipal transport in Pietermaritzburg was targeted. Strikes and labour actions were used to increase pressure on the government. In his interview, Moses Ndlovu said, 'We were instrumental in organising the strikes; many young men from my area [KwaShange] would participate in the strikes, but when we came back, we would face challenges, anger, hatred from our neighbours who were anti-UDF and COSATU.'[72] Chief Zondi and the Inkatha leaders in KwaShange, Mchunu and Amon Kubheka, attended Inkatha meetings in Ulundi, and reported that Moses Ndlovu and his supporters were a bad influence in Vulindlela.[73]

During 1984 and 1985, the spectre of 'necklace' killing came into its own. Many people identified as being in the opposition camp or informers were killed by means of necklacing – a car tyre was placed around the neck of a victim, it was doused in petrol and the victim was set alight. The intention was to terrorise those who supported the National Party government. Particular areas were targeted to be used to test the necklacing system. It was agreed at a meeting that took place in Durban that KwaShange was one of the places that was going to be a 'testing ground', simply because it was the only area under a chief that had a large UDF following. All those who opposed the UDF were perceived to be informers in the area and would be targeted. Ndlovu, however, cautioned that Inkatha leaders in KwaShange were very strong and feared. The UDF/COSATU supporters could not face Inkatha leaders there, particularly not Mchunu, who had a track record of 'slaughtering' his opponents. The idea of testing necklacing in KwaShange was thus not a success.[74]

News reached Mchunu that he was going to be necklaced:

> When I heard that, at first I did not believe that my neighbours would want to do such a cruel thing to me. One senior woman came to me at night and told me that I must go, because I was going to be burnt. She had heard a plan being made to attack me. I started hunting those people she mentioned. I went to Moses [Ndlovu] and I told him: *Ngizokuninyisa, ngizonibamba nonke* [a deliberate insult]; one by one. I then started looking for them, even in town in Pietermaritzburg. Every time they saw me, they would run away and I would chase them and they failed to kill me but we heard that they killed a lot of Inkatha people in Hammarsdale using a similar method.[75]

The regional government structures in Natal were the Natal Provincial Administration and the KwaZulu homeland government. The South African government imposed order in the provincial administration section of Natal through the South African Police, but left the maintenance of law and order in the homeland of KwaZulu to Buthelezi, who was then chief minister and minister of police. The uprisings that took place in 1985 and 1986 in the Cape, the Free State and the Transvaal were easily identified as an attempted UDF or ANC-in-exile revolution; this was termed 'the armed struggle'. In Natal and KwaZulu, the police force, in which Inkatha was influential, was the legitimate authority. The UDF uprising was interpreted as an insurgency against the authority of KwaZulu, and the person of Mangosuthu Buthelezi, and not a struggle against the South African government regime, with all its oppressive apartheid laws. Ndlovu commented (and Hlengwa concurred with him): 'What confused us as members of the UDF is that Inkatha members saw UDF as their enemies, but in fact our struggle was directed towards the Nationalist government. We had no intention to fight with our fellow blacks.'[76]

Aitchison alludes to this when saying that the UDF and the ANC were depicted as 'terrorists' and communists rather than the freedom fighters they were later seen as.[77]

Mchunu said:

> The terrorism activities of the UDF and ANC supporters, especially in areas in northern Zululand, where they used to cross the borders and . . . put bombs and kill people, we [Inkatha] realised that we had to wage a war against these people. In fact, we saw this as contempt towards *umntwana wakwaPhindangeni*. It would have been a cowardly act to remain silent while 'terrorists' undermined our leader. At that time, my people and I were crazy; I hated [the] smell of *iqabane* [comrades]. I used to fight them; to me fighting became my daily activity in KwaShange. I could not control what was happening in other areas, but it angered me to hear about our people [Inkatha supporters] in other areas being killed by the terrorists [UDF/ANC] and I made it my mission to avenge them in KwaShange.[78]

In all these attacks, police would come into KwaShange, but instead of taking Inkatha supporters to prison, they would enter UDF-supporting homes, taking weapons and arresting people. This would open doors for Inkatha supporters to attack UDF people.[79]

Aitchison claims:

> The Nationalists thus evidently engineered a state of 'low-intensity warfare', the intention of which was to keep the atmosphere between the UDF and Inkatha tense, but at the same time they were concerned about the economy of the region and the country as a whole. It was not intense enough to destroy the economy of the region.[80]

From 1987 to 1990, this 'low-intensity warfare' was maintained. The leadership of the UDF and Inkatha was drawn into this divide-and-rule strategy.[81] The followers, on the whole, were unaware that they were being used as pawns in the political struggle for power.[82] Allegations of a third force proliferated. Aitchison argues that there were three third forces:

> The government had its police and military, which operated clandestinely to undermine its opponents and the De Kock and Malan trials have exposed these elements. The second of the three forces was the ANC in exile, with its training camps

> inside and outside the country, and their public proclamation to make the country ungovernable. The third of the three forces was that of the Inkatha Freedom Party, where camps were established inside the country and on the borders. Here, with the collusion of the South African Defence Force, their members were trained in insurgency and counter-insurgency. All three of these third forces were well armed and trained to destabilise, kill and destroy their opponents. The South African Police, especially in Pietermaritzburg, particularly the Riot Unit, under the command of Major Terreblanche, who was then in charge, were used as a tool to implement the National Party's policy of divide-and-rule.[83]

Police measures were primarily intended to undermine the UDF, as it was a front for the ANC. Government powers under the state of emergency from 1986 to 1990 legalised murder and abuses. Detention without trial was used widely against UDF members, whereas only a few Inkatha members were imprisoned.[84]

Notes

1. These names were mentioned by all interviewees who participated in this study and appear here with the consent of the individuals.
2. Interview with Moses Ndlovu, KwaShange, 10 August 2003.
3. Interview with Moses Ndlovu, KwaShange, 10 August 2003. See also interview with Nunu Mchunu, KwaShange, 14 March 2008; interview with Chris Hlengwa, KwaShange, 15 March 2008.
4. The theme of division in communities as a result of political violence in the 1980s to 1990s has been dealt with in a number of studies. See, for example, D. Bonnin, 'Space, Place and Identity: Political Violence in Mpumalanga Township, KwaZulu-Natal, 1987–1993' (PhD thesis, University of the Witwatersrand, 2007); A. Jeffery, *The Natal Story: Sixteen Years of Conflict* (Johannesburg: South African Institute of Race Relations, 1997); P. Denis, R. Ntsimane and T. Cannell, *Indians versus Russians: An Oral History of Political Violence in Nxamalala (1987–1993)* (Pietermaritzburg: Cluster Publications, 2010).
5. Interview with Nunu Mchunu, KwaShange, 14 March 2008; interview with Moses Ndlovu, KwaShange, 10 August 2003; interview with Chris Hlengwa, KwaShange, 15 March 2008. These men confirmed that Chief Shayabantu Zondi of Inadi was a leader of Inkatha in Vulindlela; other authors called the chief the 'staunch supporter of Inkatha' – see Denis, Ntsimane and Cannell, *Indians versus Russians*, p. 10. Nunu Mchunu, who was an ally of the late chief, mentioned that 'Ulundi [capital of Zululand] expected chiefs

and *izinduna* (headmen) to comply with the Act that stated that they had to be leaders of Inkatha in their respective places: Chief Shayabantu Zondi had no option (but to lead Inkatha in Vulindlela)'. See also G. Maré and G. Hamilton, *An Appetite for Power: Buthelezi's Inkatha and the Politics of Loyal Resistance* (Johannesburg: Ravan Press, 1987).

6. Many authors have written on the state of emergency of 1987 and the bias shown by the National Party government towards Inkatha supporters. See J. Aitchison, 'The Origins of the Midlands War', in *The Role of Political Violence in South Africa's Democratisation*, edited by R. Greenstein (Johannesburg: Community Agency for Social Enquiry, 2003); Detainees Aid Committee, *Detention under Three Emergencies: A Report on the Natal Midlands, 1986–1989* (Pietermaritzburg: Detainees Aid Committee, 1989).
7. For details on Moses Ndlovu's experiences and involvement in political violence in the Midlands, see L. Levine (ed.), *Faith in Turmoil: The Seven Days War* (Pietermaritzburg: PACSA, 1999).
8. Interview with Moses Ndlovu, KwaShange, 11 August 2003. Jabulani Sithole has conducted interviews with many older ANC and COSATU leaders in KwaZulu-Natal. He mentioned that many young men of his age joined unions later because of their experiences on farms. Personal communication with Jabulani Sithole, University of KwaZulu-Natal, Pietermaritzburg, 11 June 2010.
9. Levine, *Faith in Turmoil*. See also http://www.anc.org.za.
10. Interview with Moses Ndlovu, KwaShange, 11 August 2003.
11. Interview with Moses Ndlovu, KwaShange, 11 August 2003.
12. Interview with Moses Ndlovu, KwaShange, 11 August 2003.
13. Interview with Moses Ndlovu, KwaShange, 11 August 2003.
14. Interview with ten men who were recruited by Moses Ndlovu in KwaShange, 13 September 2008; interview with Moses Ndlovu, KwaShange, 11 August 2003; interview with Chris Hlengwa, KwaShange, 15 March 2008.
15. Interview with Moses Ndlovu, KwaShange, 11 August 2003.
16. Interview with Moses Ndlovu, KwaShange, 11 August 2003; interview with Dumisani Lushazi, former ANC Ward 4 Councillor, KwaShange, 21 January 2008; interview with Chris Hlengwa, KwaShange, 11 March 2008.
17. Interview with Moses Ndlovu, KwaShange, 11 August 2003.
18. Interview with Moses Ndlovu, KwaShange, 11 August 2003.
19. Interview with Nunu Mchunu, KwaShange, 14 March 2008.
20. Interview with Moses Ndlovu, KwaShange, 17 October 2003. See also J. Sithole, 'The African National Congress in Natal, 1990–1995', in South African Democracy Education Trust, *The Road to Democracy in South Africa: Volume 6 (1990–1996): Part 1* (Pretoria: Unisa Press, 2013); Levine, *Faith in Turmoil*.
21. For a brief history of the Mchunu family in KwaShange, see M. Mchunu, 'Discipline, Respect and Ethnicity: A Study of the Changing Patterns of Fatherhood of Three Generations of Zulu Fathers and Sons in KwaShange, Inadi, Vulindlela Area of Pietermaritzburg, KwaZulu-Natal, from the 1930s to the 1990s', Master's thesis, University of KwaZulu-Natal, 2005.
22. Interview with Nunu Mchunu, KwaShange, 14 March 2008; interview with Moses Ndlovu, KwaShange, 11 August 2003; interview with Chris Hlengwa, KwaShange, 11 March 2008.

23. Interview with Nunu Mchunu, KwaShange, 14 March 2008.
24. Interview with Nunu Mchunu, KwaShange, 14 March 2008; interview with Moses Ndlovu, KwaShange, 11 August 2003; interview with Chris Hlengwa, KwaShange, 11 March 2008.
25. For details on the history of uMshwathi, see K. Bhengu, *Uphuya waseMshwathi* [Poor/Pauper Man from Shwathi] (Johannesburg: Educum, 1983).
26. Interview with Nunu Mchunu, KwaShange, 14 March 2008.
27. Interview with Nunu Mchunu, KwaShange, 14 March 2008.
28. Interview with Nunu Mchunu, KwaShange, 11 March 2008.
29. Interview with Nunu Mchunu, 14 March 2008; interview with Moses Ndlovu, 11 August 2003.
30. Interview with Nunu Mchunu, KwaShange, 11 March 2008; interview with Moses Ndlovu, KwaShange, 26 October 2003. See also T. Karon, 'An Interview with Harry Gwala', Dambuza, Pietermaritzburg, 8 January 1989, https://disa.ukzn.ac.za/int19890108043049.
31. Interview with Nunu Mchunu, KwaShange, 11 March 2008.
32. Interview with Nunu Mchunu, KwaShange, 11 March 2008.
33. See Maré and Hamilton, *An Appetite for Power.*
34. Interview with Nunu Mchunu, KwaShange, 11 March 2008.
35. See Aitchison, 'The Origins of the Midlands War'; M. de Haas, 'Violence in Natal and Zululand: The 1980s', in South African Democracy Education Trust, *The Road to Democracy in South Africa: Volume 6 (1990–1996): Part 1* (Pretoria: Unisa Press, 2013); Maré and Hamilton, *An Appetite for Power.*
36. M. Buthelezi, 'Policy Speech', KwaZulu Legislative Assembly, 1993, p. 56.
37. Maré and Hamilton, *An Appetite for Power*; Mzala, *Gatsha Buthelezi: Chief with a Double Agenda* (London: Zed Books, 1988). See also R. Southall, 'An Appetite for Power: Buthelezi's Inkatha and South Africa', *African Affairs* 87(349), 1988: 635–6.
38. Aitchison, 'The Origins of the Midlands War'.
39. Aitchison, 'The Origins of the Midlands War', p. 48.
40. Interview with Nunu Mchunu, KwaShange, 11 March 2008.
41. Interview with Nunu Mchunu, KwaShange, 11 March 2008.
42. Interview with Nunu Mchunu, KwaShange, 11 March 2008.
43. Interview with Nunu Mchunu, KwaShange, 11 March 2008.
44. Interview with Moses Ndlovu, KwaShange, 26 October 2003.
45. Interview with Chris Hlengwa, KwaShange, 12 March 2008.
46. J.F. Burns, 'Black versus Black in South Africa', *New York Times*, 21 January, 1988, http://www.nytimes.com/1988/01/21/world/black-vs-black-in-south-africa p5.
47. Burns, 'Black versus Black in South Africa'.
48. Burns, 'Black versus Black in South Africa'.
49. '*Izinkunzi ezimbili esibayeni esisodwa*' (Two bulls in one kraal) is a Zulu saying that was used by some of my interviewees in KwaShange, who observed tension that was going on between Mchunu and Ndlovu. They were regarded as peers who were equally intelligent, strong and influential. One elderly woman felt that it was not right for both Mchunu and Ndlovu to be residents of KwaShange; she felt that one should have been elsewhere.
50. Interview with Nunu Mchunu, KwaShange, 15 March 2008.

51. Interview with Moses Ndlovu, KwaShange, 26 October 2003.
52. Interview with MaZamisa Shange, KwaShange, 11 April 2010.
53. Interview with MaZamisa Shange, KwaShange, 11 April 2010.
54. Interview with Moses Ndlovu, KwaShange, 26 October 2003.
55. Interview with Moses Ndlovu, KwaShange, 26 October 2003; interview with Nunu Mchunu, KwaShange, 15 March 2008.
56. Interview with MaZamisa Shange, KwaShange, 11 April 2010.
57. Interview with Moses Ndlovu, 26 October 2003.
58. Interview with Nunu Mchunu, KwaShange, 14 March 2008.
59. Interview with Moses Ndlovu, 26 October 2003.
60. Interview with four KwaShange former policemen who followed and observed what was happening in Howick/Mpophomeni: C. Hlengwa, S. Zondi, M. Goge and N. Msane, KwaShange, 25 September 2008. See also Aitchison, 'The Origins of the Midlands War'.
61. J. Aitchison, 'KwaZulu-Natal: The Pre-election Wars of the 1990s', in *The Role of Political Violence in South Africa's Democratisation*, edited by R. Greenstein (Johannesburg: Community Agency for Social Enquiry, 2003).
62. John Aitchison's presentation to the Truth and Reconciliation Commission hearing in Pietermaritzburg, http://www.justice.gov.za/trc/hrvtrans/hrvpmb/pmb7_2.htm.
63. Aitchison, 'The Origins of the Midlands War', p. 59.
64. Interview with anonymous former leader of Inkatha, KwaShange, 17 February 2009.
65. Interview with Chris Hlengwa, KwaShange, 11 March 2008.
66. Interview with anonymous, KwaShange, 11 March 2008.
67. See Aitchison, 'The Origins of the Midlands War'; Aitchison, 'KwaZulu-Natal'.
68. *Daily News*, 23 August 1988.
69. Burns, 'Black versus Black in South Africa'.
70. Aitchison, 'The Origins of the Midlands War'; Aitchison, 'KwaZulu-Natal'. See also Maré and Hamilton, *An Appetite for Power*; Mzala, *Gatsha Buthelezi*.
71. Maré and Hamilton, *An Appetite for Power*. See also Aitchison, 'The Origins of the Midlands War'.
72. Interview with Moses Ndlovu, Ashdown, 2003.
73. Interview with Moses Ndlovu, Ashdown, 2003. Nunu Mchunu confirmed this in an interview with him in 2008.
74. Interview with Moses Ndlovu who attended the UDF/COSATU secret meeting in Durban in 1986, where the national leadership of the UDF and COSATU recognised KwaShange as their base in rural Vulindlela and agreed to offer all support needed to sabotage rivals, Inkatha, in particular, and the state.
75. Interview with Nunu Mchunu, KwaShange, 11 March 2008.
76. Interview with Moses Ndlovu, KwaShange, 11 August 2003.
77. Aitchison, 'The Origins of the Midlands War'; Aitchison, 'KwaZulu-Natal'.
78. Interview with Nunu Mchunu, KwaShange, 14 March 2008.
79. Interview with Chris Hlengwa, KwaShange, 15 March 2003; interview with Moses Ndlovu, KwaShange, 11 August 2003. See also Aitchison, 'The Origins of the Midlands War'; Aitchison, 'KwaZulu-Natal'.

80. John Aitchison's presentation to the Truth and Reconciliation Commission hearing in Pietermaritzburg, http://www.justice.gov.za/trc/hrvtrans/hrvpmb/pmb7_2.htm.
81. Interview with Moses Ndlovu, KwaShange, 11 August 2003.
82. In retrospect, Moses Ndlovu, Nunu Mchunu and Chris Hlengwa agreed that supporters of the UDF and Inkatha at the grassroot level knew very little about violence. Leaders of the movements were fighting for power using their followers. Interview, Moses Ndlovu, KwaShange, 11 August 2003; interview with Nunu Mchunu, KwaShange, 14 March 2008; interview with Chris Hlengwa, KwaShange, 11 March 2008.
83. John Aitchison's presentation to the Truth and Reconciliation Commission hearing in Pietermaritzburg, http://www.justice.gov.za/trc/hrvtrans/hrvpmb/pmb7_2.htm.
84. Personal communication with John Aitchison, University of KwaZulu-Natal, 2009; interview with Nunu Mchunu, KwaShange, 14 March 2008; interview with Chris Hlengwa, KwaShange, 11 March 2008; interview with Moses Ndlovu, Ashdown, 2003. See also G. Maré, *Ethnicity and Politics in South Africa* (London: Zed Books, 1993); Mzala, *Gatsha Buthelezi*.

5

A Turning Point

MUCH INFORMATION RELATED to violence in KwaZulu-Natal in the 1980s and 1990s, and South Africa in general, has not been recorded. This was probably one of the largest and longest 'black-on-black' conflicts of the twentieth century. It was full of paradoxes; for example, the struggle was by blacks against white domination, but the violence became 'blacks against blacks', and, for the first time in the history of 'blacks fighting against blacks', machine guns and petrol bombs were used. Old-fashioned methods of fighting battles were also used, such as the use of *muthi*, even though it was not generally known and is still a taboo subject.

Political analysts reviewing the political violence in Natal and Zululand accept that 1987 was a turning point in the struggle for liberation. Writing about this period, John Aitchison states that the beginning of 1987 saw a hardening of the confrontation between Inkatha vigilantes and United Democratic Front (UDF) youth organisations.[1]

The KwaShange massacre, known locally, even today, as *Ulwesihlanu Lwezibhelu* (Friday of Killings), took place on 25 September 1987. It marked the start of organised and large-scale violence in KwaShange and the Natal Midlands.[2] Thirteen Inkatha Youth Brigade members attending a meeting were killed. This incident was to precipitate the wider fighting in the region.

KwaShange was once a very dangerous area – even journalists were afraid of going there to report what was happening, so very little information is publicly available. KwaShange had a number of policemen among their community members, who fought to defend their area, and this made other policemen fear for their lives. There were many instances where police were called into KwaShange, but failed to respond for fear of going into the area.

A former Inkatha leader in KwaShange (who wishes to remain anonymous) has a notebook in which his daughter recorded much of what was discussed in meetings, especially in 1987. I was privileged to get some specific dates from these notes.

January 1987

Nunu Mchunu and Innocent Dlamini, as Inkatha leaders in KwaShange, called a general meeting of Inkatha members in the area. Members had to bring their children with them. Mchunu also invited Chief Shayabantu Zondi, explaining in an interview, 'Our intention was to show the chief that we had recruited a lot of people in the area.'[3] The chief gave Mchunu and Dlamini a goat from his kraal, thanking them for 'a job well done' and encouraged them to work harder to get everybody in the area to join the movement.[4]

February 1987

At a meeting for Inkatha leadership in Vulindlela at Henley Combined School in KwaShange, which 'was well attended by leaders from all structures of Inkatha, it was agreed that before the end of the year, everybody (from the age of seven upwards) in KwaVulindlela must have joined Inkatha – we set a date that before the end the year everybody would be expected to have been a card-carrying member of the movement.'[5]

Aitchison records that there was a final date set of 4 October in many Vulindlela sub-areas, by which time everyone had to have joined Inkatha. The date of 4 October vies with 25 September as the start of the Midlands civil war.[6]

KwaShange was the first area in Vulindlela to launch the recruitment campaign. Every Friday after school, KwaShange youths met at the Henley Combined School hall and discussed Inkatha issues, encouraging each other to recruit family members. They used to march in KwaShange, chanting Inkatha slogans and singing struggle songs and forcing everybody they met to join them. About 52 youths who refused to join were severely beaten.[7] Many who were injured and hospitalised mentioned the harsh treatment they received at Edendale Hospital. They were told by nurses that if they continued 'rejecting' Inkatha, they would not be helped at Edendale Hospital.[8]

Inkatha youths began a door-to-door recruitment campaign. They beat those who refused to join Inkatha. Taking an Inkatha membership card became mandatory,[9] and the Inkatha motto was 'if you are not for us or with us you are our enemy'.[10] A significant number of homesteads were identified by Inkatha youth members as needing attention from Inkatha to enforce membership. Among these were the Hlengwa family, the Mchunu family (relatives of Mchunu, who was the Inkatha leader in the area) and the Ndlovu family.[11]

Towards the end of April 1987

Latu Ngubane, who was a Standard 8 (Grade 10) learner, went home and told his parents that he had been forced to accept the position of Inkatha Youth Brigade secretary. When his parents reprimanded him and declined the appointment, he was stabbed to death in front of them.[12]

The Hlengwa family members were wanted by Inkatha warlords and Chris Hlengwa, a policeman, asked for police protection.[13] 'I asked for protection; when they asked me why, I said I am a member of Inkatha and UDF youths are threatening to attack my family . . .'[14] Hlengwa knew that if he said that he was associated with the UDF, they would not give him a police guard.[15]

May 1987

A Sizanani MaZulu Transport bus driver came to collect other bus drivers in KwaShange to report for work. At about 09h30, children saw the bus at a bus stop – the engine was still running and blood was dripping from the doors of the bus. Killing bus drivers was an Inkatha campaign that took place thoughout Vulindlela.[16] Aitchison associated these killings with the Pietermaritzburg workers' stay-away called by the Congress of South African Trade Unions (COSATU) and the UDF in 1987 to protest against the whites-only elections. Many people heeded the call from COSATU and the UDF and did not go to work, which was a considerable defeat for Inkatha and Chief Mangosuthu Buthelezi, who had urged his supporters to campaign against a stay-away. Inkatha blamed the success of the stay-away on the Transport and General Workers' Union, whose striking bus drivers effectively made it impossible for many workers to get to work, even if they wanted to. Many bus drivers, including the one who died in KwaShange, were killed because of this.[17]

Also in May, Chief Shayabantu Zondi noticed that the Hlengwa homestead was under police protection. He went to the police station in Plessislaer, where Hlengwa worked, and challenged the police decision to protect Hlengwa's homestead. He told them that Hlengwa had lied when he said he was a member of Inkatha and threatened by the UDF. On 15 May, police protection was withdrawn from the Hlengwa family. Chris Hlengwa threatened to kill the youth activist who had come with Chief Zondi to tell the policeman who was guarding Hlengwa's homestead to leave.

At the end of May, Chris Hlengwa was threatened by Chief Zondi and his KwaZulu Police bodyguards. Hlengwa drew the official gun he was carrying and Zondi ran back to his car and drove away.

August 1987

In August an important meeting took place at Henley Combined School in KwaShange. Chief Zondi threatened that anyone who did not come to the meeting would be forced to leave the area of KwaShange. Children would be beaten and the families' houses burnt.[18]

Moses Ndlovu was instructed to come to the meeting, as he was a member of the KwaShange community. He was present when Chris Hlengwa arrived at the meeting; Inkatha leaders were questioning him as to why he was working for COSATU. Seated on the stage of the hall were Shayabantu Zondi, Guvaza Khanyile (headman), Nunu Mchunu, Innocent Dlamini, Phillip 'Makhekhe' Thabethe and Amon Kubheka. Moses Ndlovu was in tears as the leaders were trying to force him to resign from COSATU. He refused, saying COSATU was paying him; if he resigned how would he support his family? The chief and his Inkatha men promised Ndlovu that if he resigned Inkatha would support his family. He asked about his other benefits, such as his pension. The chief stood up and said he must resign no matter what and all these other needs would be taken care of by Inkatha.[19]

A KwaShange senior man by the name of Phakathi asked Chris Hlengwa as a policeman to explain to the delegates if it was legal for Chief Zondi to compel people to join Inkatha. Chris Hlengwa said that 'legally speaking, people should not be coerced to join any political movements, but it should be a choice of individuals'. Phakathi stood up and lifted up his stick and said, 'If my son was still alive, we'd start fighting now.' He then left the meeting, along with many other people, including Chris Hlengwa and Chairperson Madlala.[20]

KwaShange, 26 September 1987 (courtesy Pietermaritzburg Archives Repository).

Crime scene: KwaShange massacre, 25 September 1987 (courtesy Pietermaritzburg Archives Repository).

Victims of the KwaShange massacre, burnt beyond recognition. This photo was taken by a police forensic expert on 26 September 1987. It shows the homestead where thirteen Inkatha youth were attacked and killed by UDF supporters (courtesy Pietermaritzburg Archives Repository).

Mass funeral of victims of the KwaShange massacre, 25 September 1987 (courtesy of KwaZulu-Natal Museum).

KwaShange houses burning during the first day of the Seven Days' War, 27 March 1990 (courtesy of KwaZulu-Natal Museum).

A mother and her son mourning a victim of the Seven Days' War in the Natal Midlands (courtesy of KwaZulu-Natal Museum).

The body of one of the victims of the Seven Days' War who was trying to escape to the refugee camp in Edendale (courtesy of KwaZulu-Natal Museum).

A friend standing guard over a dead boy, 28 March 1990, KwaShange (courtesy of KwaZulu-Natal Museum).

Women mourning the death of their loved ones in the Natal Midlands violence (courtesy of KwaZulu-Natal Museum).

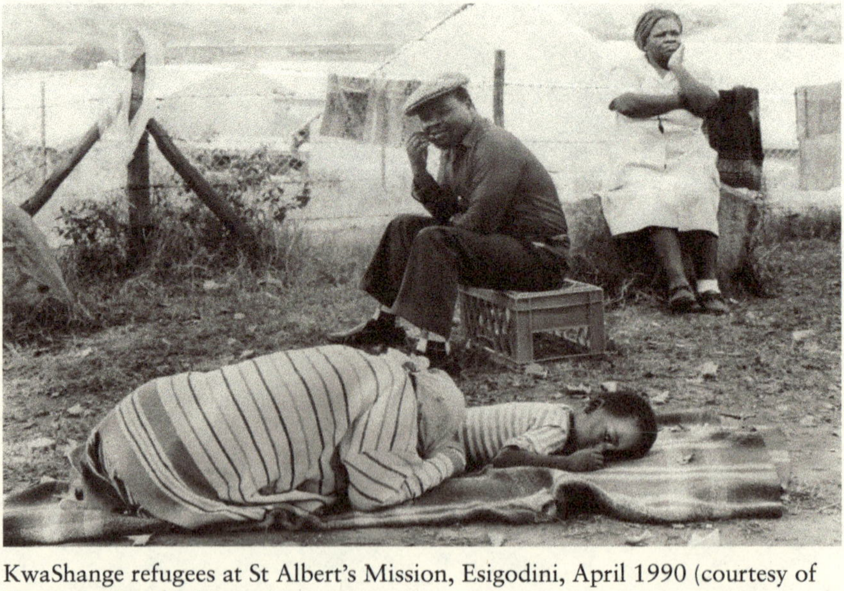

KwaShange refugees at St Albert's Mission, Esigodini, April 1990 (courtesy of KwaZulu-Natal Museum).

A woman with her baby looks hopelessly at her petrol-bombed house (courtesy of KwaZulu-Natal Museum).

Inkatha *impis* at Elandskop launching an attack, 27 March 1990 (courtesy of KwaZulu-Natal Museum).

Women mourning the death of a loved one – a victim of political violence in Vulindlela, 27 March 1990 (courtesy of KwaZulu-Natal Museum).

Also in August 1987, Inkatha youths were on a recruitment campaign in KwaShange and other neighbouring areas. They were mandated by Chief Zondi and the KwaShange leader, Nunu Mchunu.[21] This KwaShange Inkatha Youth Brigade went across the river to meet at Mzamweni High School.[22] UDF supporters in KwaShange were 'fed-up with this nonsense' and organised 'somebody to sort out Inkatha youth that were troublesome in the area'.[23] The Inkatha Youth Brigade was attacked at Mzamweni School. Aitchison recorded that on the same occasion, a COSATU leader, Alfred Ndlovu, borrowed an AK-47 from an uMkhonto weSizwe (MK) member and attacked an Inkatha group in Vulindlela, wounding several people. He was later arrested and convicted for the offence.[24] The *Daily News* reported:

> A man had fired short bursts with an AK-47 rifle into a group of singing school children, it was said in a witness's statement handed into court yesterday. The children began screaming and running in all directions, the statement said. The gunman had told the witness that he had 'come here to help supporters of the United Democratic Front in the fight against Inkatha'. The statement, made to a policeman by a witness, was handed in during the Regional Court trial of Mr Alfred Ndlovu (38), second national vice-president of the Transport and General Workers' Union and regional chairperson of COSATU. Ndlovu is charged with the attempted murder of the children, and attempted murder of a bus driver colleague. He had pleaded not guilty to all the charges. The witness said in a statement that Mr Ndlovu had driven a gunman and two others to and from the Emzamweni School where the shooting occurred, to shoot Mr Joseph Mabaso, an Inkatha Youth organiser, and others who were having an Inkatha meeting at the school.[25]

One informant said, 'The KwaShange I had known for many decades came to an end [with this attack].'[26] Many people who were suspected Inkatha supporters and who might be witnesses in court were killed. In August, more than 50 homesteads or families aligned to Inkatha 'packed and left the area at night; they came back accompanied by police to demolish their mud-built houses; most families who fled were descendants of the Zondi clan who had originally been sent to "oversee" KwaShange area in the early 1900s'.[27]

The *Daily News* reported on the court case:

> About 12 complainants and potential court witnesses had been killed, or their houses had been burned in the past year in Pietermaritzburg police district, the regional court was told. The witness, Captain A. Upton, of the Unrest Unit [in Pietermaritzburg], said intimidation was so bad that even bereaved people were scared to be seen near the police. Other potential witnesses who had made a statement to lawyers later denied having made it. This fear of reprisal made it very difficult to prosecute perpetrators of political crimes . . . Captain Upton was testifying at the regional court trial of Mr Alfred Muntu Ndlovu (38), second national vice-president of the Transport and General Workers' Union and regional chairman of COSATU. He faces a charge of terrorism and two of attempted murder, one arising out of wounding 13 youths, aged from 10 to 17, and a 22-year-old man, at KwaVulisaka (KwaShange) in [August 1987].[28]

In this case, many families from KwaShange whose children attended the school that was attacked were present at the court case and some were witnesses. They feared for their lives, because UDF supporters had already started killing all potential witnesses. Every day at least one person was killed. Captain Upton testified in support of an application made by state counsel, Peter Blomkamp, that a witness should be allowed to give evidence in camera. The witness said he wanted to give evidence in camera because the 'UDF and COSATU have said that if one of us betrays another he will be killed. By betray I understand any person who informs or testifies in a case . . . If one of a group is arrested he must not testify. If people know I am testifying my family will be placed in danger.'[29]

September 1987

September was the most stressful month in Natal and KwaZulu in 1987, and even more so in KwaShange. The month of September is associated with Cyclone Demoina.[30]

These floods damaged houses in Vulindlela and Edendale and were seen as a sign of the beginning of the period of crisis. Ndlovu alleged that Inkatha was making offers of assistance to flood victims conditionally on their joining the movement. Mchunu denied these allegations. Matthew Kentridge says in *An Unofficial War* that even the mayor of Pietermaritzburg, Mark Cornell, criticised Inkatha for making political capital out of the floods.

The flood relief was undermined by the recruitment drive for the D-Day of 4 October, when all inhabitants had to either join Inkatha or leave the area. The UDF reported the recruitment drive was encountering strong resistance.

> It was in the Pietermaritzburg region that the many early tussles between the Inkatha movement and the rising power of the United Democratic Front (UDF) and the Congress of South African Trade Union (COSATU) took place and where open warfare broke out in September 1987. It was also in this region that some of the subterranean activities of agents and surrogates of the South African state came to their most deadly fruition as they attempted to reverse or neutralise the democratisation of South Africa.[31]

3 September 1987

Mtungani Mbanjwa worked in Johannesburg and seldom came home. The family used to sell basic foodstuffs, including sorghum and other types of beer to supplement Mbanjwa's salary, and many KwaShange men used to gather in this home to drink. One of the Inkatha warlords, Mlungisi Ngubane, who was a close relative of the Mbanjwa family, visited the family and asked the two sons to join Inkatha. They refused, on the basis that they did not understand what Inkatha was going to do for them and they were scared that their parents would punish them if they participated in political activities.

After a week, Mlungisi Ngubane went back and demanded that Mbanjwa's family home fly the Inkatha flag; Mbanjwa's sons would be responsible for unfurling the flag every morning and taking it down at night. He told them that if they did not do this, it would mean that they were UDF supporters. The Mbanjwa family refused to do as Ngubane had instructed them.[32] On 18 September, the Mbanjwa family was attacked by Inkatha vigilantes, who burnt the house and shot Bhekithemba Mbanjwa in the leg.[33]

Also on 18 September, the Zibula family was attacked; a six-month-old baby was stabbed,[34] and the father of the baby survived with burn wounds.[35]

19 September

Some of those involved in the attacks were caught by UDF supporters. They took them to headman Zakhele Makhathini and instructed him to take them to the police station. They also gave evidence to the headman that the young men had been involved in the attack. The headman obeyed and the attackers were kept in custody for one night but were released from Plessislaer Police Station the following day.

20 September

UDF leaders in KwaShange went to the police station and enquired as to why the youths were released. They claimed that they did not receive an answer. They vowed in front of the police that they were going to take the law into their own hands.

22 September 1987

On 22 September, the Thusi family was attacked by Inkatha vigilantes, who burnt their house and injured the children. The family was attacked because this homestead was close to the bus stop and many Sizanani MaZulu Transport bus drivers used to have lunch there.

24 September

Hlengwa's niece, Nobuhle Ngubane, who was a member of the Inkatha Youth Brigade in KwaShange, visited her uncle Chris Hlengwa. She told him of the meeting of the Inkatha Youth Brigade in KwaShange where a plan for attacking his homestead (and those of three other prominent community members) was discussed. His house was to be burnt with everybody inside. She warned him to run for his life with his family and pleaded with him not to mention that she had disclosed this information to him. Hlengwa did not run, he prepared himself for a fight and organised some older men to camp at his home.

25 September 1987

At approximately 22h00, another well-known member of the Inkatha Youth Brigade in KwaShange, Ndoda Ndlovu, went to Hlengwa's homestead. He went to tell him that he had just left a meeting about the Youth Brigade planning to attack Hlengwa's home and other targeted homes that day. Ndlovu told Hlengwa that Guvaza Khanyile and other prominent Inkatha leaders were to be part of the planned attack. Guvaza Khanyile had gone to get more guns and reinforcements from Bhobhonono and Sweetwaters.[36]

Hlengwa's men decided that they were not going to wait for Inkatha to attack because they might not be able to protect themselves them as they had powerful machine guns. They decided to attack first. Hlengwa's men divided into three groups: two groups went with Ndoda Ndlovu to the homestead where the Inkatha youths had gathered. One group remained in Hlengwa's homestead to protect Hlengwa's family and the others that had been targeted.

At 23h00, Hlengwa's men arrived at the Ngubane homestead, where the Inkatha youths had gathered. There was no electricity in KwaShange in the 1980s, but there was a gas light on in the house. One of Hlengwa's men locked the door of the house from the outside and started shooting and throwing stones. One of the bullets hit the gas cylinder and it exploded.

Just after 12h00, Mchunu arrived:

> I will never forget what I saw that night. I arrived at the scene; many were already dead, but one was hanging out the window of a burning house, he had been shot, the bottom part of his body was burning, and he was crying. Phetha, his father, who was a policeman, arrived just after me. I asked him to help me to help his son but Phetha refused, asking what was he doing there at night because he was supposed to be home? That boy died before he reached hospital.[37]

The Citizen reported:

> The house was encircled by Hlengwa's men and stones were thrown, breaking windows. Shots were fired, and a door was smashed in. When the youth[s] tried to barricade the doorway, a fire was started. More shots were fired into the house. Those who sought to escape from the blazing house were struck down one by one. The screaming of those that remained in the

> house ceased only when a gas bottle exploded, producing the final holocaust. Five of the youths died from severe burns, six [died of] burn and stab wounds, one of pneumonia associated with burns, and one of head and stab wounds. Most of the bodies were unrecognisably scorched, with shin bones and skulls showing through their skin.[38]

In his book, Kentridge claims that the KwaShange massacre took place on 16 September 1987 and that the youths were ambushed.[39] In fact, the youths died on 25 September 1987 – this was corroborated by Nunu Mchunu and Chris Hlengwa.

26 September 1987

The next day, a number of South African Police (SAP) vehicles went to the scene where the killing had taken place. Bullets found were identified as being from a gun issued to Hlengwa as a policeman. Hlengwa's homestead was surrounded by more than 100 policemen, mainly white, all fully armed and with guns cocked to fire. The police arrested Hlengwa and went to look for other people who were suspects, such as Sakha Ndaba and Babayi Ndlovu.

When police arrived at Sakha Ndaba's house in the morning, they asked him to get his assegai and shield. He brought it, blood-stained from use at the massacre the night before, which was enough evidence that he was indeed involved in the attack. This was a shock to his wife, who later (in 2008) said, 'When he arrived home around 02h00 that night, he never mentioned a thing to me. He just joined me and slept as if nothing had happened. I only knew what had happened when police came to fetch him in the morning.'[40]

28 September 1987

On 28 September, Nunu Mchunu was imprisoned under the Public Safety Act. A gun had been found in his home and he was accused of being the instigator of violence. He was put in the same cell as his UDF and trade unionist arch enemies from KwaShange.

> I remember how they insulted me that night, eleven people against me. They showed me a very sharp, glittering knife and they said that night was my last night; they were going to kill

> me . . . I said to them I was not going to die alone, at least one of them was going to die with me. They waited for me to go to sleep but I refused. I stayed awake until morning when the police came to check us. The policeman was shocked to see that I was put in the same cell with UDF people. He took me to another cell with AZAPO [Azanian People's Organisation] prisoners.[41]

Also on 28 September, Makhekhe Thabethe, a member of the Inkatha-aligned United Workers' Union of South Africa and a bus driver, was shot (allegedly by another KwaShange bus driver who belonged to COSATU). The *New York Times* reported:

> Mr Thabethe, an Inkatha loyalist, said he was on his bus in September when a man in the line at the door opened fire on him. Pulling up his shirt, he showed visitors a tattoo of scars where he was struck by eight bullets from a Soviet-made Tokarev automatic pistol. His driver's license, in his shirt pocket at the time, has four holes where the bullets passed through.[42]

2 October 1987

On 2 October, the funeral of the thirteen Inkatha Youth Brigade members killed in the massacre took place at Mtholangqondo Secondary School. Mangosuthu Buthelezi, Velaphi Ndlovu and many other leaders of Inkatha were present.

The local Inkatha leadership invited every KwaShange community member to take part in the funeral. They said everybody should come to the funeral whether they belonged to the UDF or Inkatha. The provincial Inkatha leadership (including Sichizo Zuma, the chairperson of the Harewood branch of the Inkatha Youth Brigade, and Jerome Mncwabe and Abdul Awetha, both Inkatha town councillors in Imbali) claimed that they wanted to discuss 'peace and how to prevent similar deaths in the future'. They mentioned that the national leadership of the movement would be present. Many UDF supporters had gone into hiding for that weekend, but a significant number of people who were not Inkatha members, but sympathised with the bereaved families, attended the funeral.

After the funeral, some Inkatha leaders in KwaShange called community members aside, as if they were going to have a separate meeting. Inkatha started encircling all these members, particularly those that had not joined Inkatha.[43] A voice was heard shouting '*baphakathi*'. Historically, when the first trekkers arrived in the territory of the Zulu King Dingane, he invited them to his headquarters in Umgungundlovu and called upon his *amabutho* (warriors) to kill them, crying '*Babulaleni abathakathi*' ('Kill the witches').

The UDF leadership in the Midlands had warned its members in KwaShange and Vulindlela generally to leave the area during the funeral weekend. Those who had no plans to flee had to be careful that Inkatha '(did) not invite us to the funeral to smash us'. Fortunately, on this occasion the police intervened and no one was hurt inside the school premises.[44] Inkatha waited for the police to leave and then attacked UDF supporters outside the school premises. More Inkatha attacks and burning of houses followed, especially houses of those people who were known to have taken part in the massacre.

Ndlovu's house was burnt and everyone who had attended the funeral, but had not joined Inkatha, was beaten. Some were stabbed in the presence of the Inkatha national leadership. Among those who suffered gunshot wounds were Babayi Ndlovu and S'thayi Ndlovu.[45]

3 October 1987

The UDF leadership in KwaShange had a secret meeting at Makhura's Tuck Shop, which had been closed from Friday, 1 October. The following issues were discussed:

- How to support those who had been imprisoned for killing the thirteen Inkatha Youth Brigade members and how to protect and financially support their families.
- How to 'clean-up' KwaShange (by chasing away all Inkatha-supporting families).
- A list was drawn up of all the Inkatha 'ring leaders' who were to be killed in the following four weeks. Top of the list were Nunu Mchunu, Innocent Dlamini, Phillip 'Makhekhe' Thabethe, Chief Zondi and Guvaza Khanyile.

Present at the meeting were Mathi Ngcobo, Cija Ngcobo, Ntaksi Ngcobo, Khabza Ngcobo, Thulani Ndlovu, Sayi Zondi (policeman), Shosa Zondi and three 'comrades' sent by Mhlabunzima Maphumulo from Table Mountain, and three representatives from Nxamalala and Mthoqotho. Three MK soldiers were deployed to KwaShange and could be expected to be on the UDF side. Thobani Shazi claimed that support from the MK soldiers had been sought in order to counter-attack state police who supported Inkatha attacks on UDF people.[46]

October 1987

In October, fighting intensified in KwaShange. Some Inkatha supporters were being 'forcibly removed' within 48 hours, while others were given a maximum of three hours to pack and leave the area. About 80 Inkatha-supporting homesteads left the area in two days. Those who tried to resist were killed.

In revenge for the imprisonment of Chris Hlengwa and other UDF men, the KwaShange UDF began to attack Inkatha supporters in KwaShange and neighbouring areas, who had given refuge to people forced to leave KwaShange. UDF militants tried to recruit youths in all these areas to the UDF. The whole area of Vulindlela was affected and people from KwaShange became the arch enemies of all those in surrounding areas.[47]

According to Moses Ndlovu, the leader of COSATU in KwaShange and the Midlands, these attacks in KwaShange's neighbouring Inkatha-aligned areas prompted the UDF and COSATU to form a de facto alliance. The two groups consulted one another about policy and strategy but maintained separate organisational structures. This alliance co-ordinated a 'peace talks' strategy and contacted the Pietermaritzburg Chamber of Commerce, which offered to play the role of 'honest broker'.

Ndlovu admitted that it was just pretence. 'We wanted peace during the day but used machine guns at night.'[48] Kentridge recorded that Inkatha contacted the Chamber with a similar request. The Chamber tried to set up a meeting with both parties. COSATU, meanwhile, sent a legal team to Pietermaritzburg to investigate complaints against the Inkatha warlords for assault, intimidation and murder.[49]

In the same month, Innocent Dlamini was attacked and stoned to death by a group of fifteen young men. One of my UDF interviewees, who wished to remain anonymous, explained:

> We knew that he had a gun and there was no way we could have killed him by stabbing or shooting because he was known to be using *muthi*. Many attempts had been made before [to kill him] but all failed because he would just disappear. We sent strong young men who were prepared to lose their lives. It took them about ten minutes to knock him down, and then they finished him when he had fallen. They had to cut his throat just to make sure that he was dead because anything could happen [in regard to dealing] with him – because of the kind of *muthi* he used, he could rise and kill us![50]

Local informants reported that in late October 1987 a white Nissan E20 kombi with the name 'Dambuza' emblazoned on it was seen around KwaShange. This kombi was full of white passengers and was seen watching Innocent Dlamini and Nunu Mchunu's homesteads. In the following days, weeks and months the same kombi came back to arrest people who were regarded as strong UDF supporters (and, for the most part, those who were involved in killing Dlamini). Later, it became clear that these were plain-clothes policemen, known to be killing UDF supporters.

Late in October, during the day, police shot and killed Khabza Ngcobo. On that occasion, they were reported to have come in a private car with darkened windows. It is believed that there was someone (presumably an Inkatha supporter) in the car who knew Ngcobo and asked the policemen to shoot him.[51]

The situation in Vulindlela and Edendale prompted the National Party government to send the SAP there to 'bring about peace'. Pretoria-based riot policemen were despatched to Pietermaritzburg and stationed at Oribi. Brigadier Kotze, divisional commander of the SAP, said that there was no need to worry as the situation was normal and under control. This was the response of the government, despite the numbers of refugees who began fleeing from rural areas into urban townships and 'white' Pietermaritzburg.[52]

November 1987

More than 100 policemen (black and white) were present to monitor the situation at Khabza Ngcobo's funeral. Chief Zondi arrived at the funeral with his bodyguards. UDF supporters attempted to grab him at the funeral, intending to kill him with their bare hands like in traditional cattle killing. For *muthi* use, people had to be killed by hand, not with a gun or knife. The SAP protected the chief. The crowd started insulting him, telling him that he was thin and extremely dark in complexion, because they were no longer giving him their monies. They told him that he was banned from KwaShange.[53] Chief Zondi and Nunu Mchunu were taken to jail for inciting violence in Vulindlela, but the next day they were released.

The KwaShange UDF leaders attended a gathering in which people prayed for peace in Pietermaritzburg in an attempt to end the violence in the Vulindlela area. Speakers at the service emphasised that there was no need for black people to fight one another and stressed that they should be fighting against the real enemy, namely the racist regime. Inkatha leaders were not present at the service.[54]

Inkatha warlords from Imbali, David Ntombela and Chief Zondi, with some of the Inkatha Youth Brigade, severely beat learners at Mtholangqondo Secondary School in KwaShange. Moses Ndlovu, through the COSATU legal team, launched a strategy aimed at forcing the police to investigate complaints against Inkatha warlords.[55] Kentridge records that on 2 November three applications were made for restraining interdicts against Inkatha warlords – David Ntombela, *induna* and chairperson of the Vulindlela Inkatha branch, Sichizo Zuma, chairperson of the Harewood branch of the Inkatha Youth Brigade, and Jerome Mncwabe and Abdul Awetha, both Inkatha town councillors in Imbali. All of them denied the allegations against them. Interim restraining interdicts were granted, and the cases were referred for oral evidence.[56]

December 1987

In December, about 10 000 people attended a peace rally at Wadley Stadium convened by the UDF and COSATU. Moses Ndlovu and others reported back on peace talks that were taking place between the UDF and Inkatha in KwaShange, and other areas in the Midlands. Activists called on people to stop fighting. However, the bus transporting KwaShange people back from the peace rally was stoned in Mvundlweni and two people were killed.

The corresponding Inkatha rally in KwaMkhulu (Chief Zondi's homestead) was poorly attended. KwaShange UDF members were blamed, even by Buthelezi, for intimidating people and blocking roads leading to Chief Zondi's place. A second round of peace talks was held, but Inkatha refused to proceed unless the UDF and COSATU repudiated an article calling for the destruction of Inkatha, which appeared in *Inqaba yaBasebenzi: Journal of the Marxist Workers' Tendency of the ANC*. David Ntombela claimed that KwaShange COSATU leader, Moses Ndlovu, was behind the article, and therefore implicated provincial COSATU leaders. Although the UDF and COSATU distanced themselves from the article, Inkatha refused to accept that they had had nothing to do with it, and peace talks broke down. In KwaShange and other UDF-supporting areas in Vulindlela, traditional leaders lost what little respect they still commanded.

In KwaShange, UDF supporters appeared to have gained the upper hand as a significant number of their members had had military training with the ANC in exile. Ties between KwaShange and Nxamalala, a neighbouring area, were very strong at this stage and the residents there began to support the UDF. Inkatha supporters and leaders who were driven out of KwaShange fled into neighbouring areas, such as KwaMpande, Bhobhonono, Mvundlweni, Elandskop and Mpumuza.

At about the same time, Kentridge reports, the authority of the chiefs in rural Vulindlela was undermined and Inkatha was forced onto the defensive. This was a reversal of traditional patterns of political control in the area. The police deployed a squad of 150 kitskonstabels in the area.[57] Two further interdict applications were brought by COSATU against Inkatha. Aitchison's figures for the year show that in 1987 altogether 397 people died, of whom 126 were known to be UDF supporters and 62 were known to be Inkatha supporters. There were 895 occurrences of political unrest in Edendale and Vulindlela, although the death rate was also high in Imbali, Slangspruit, Ashdown and Mpumalanga.

An informant who wished to remain anonymous recalled: 'Makhekhe Thabethe's homestead was attacked in December. The intention was to capture Thabethe himself, because he had been on night shift (as a bus driver), so we believed that he would be home sleeping, but we missed him; he had just left with Mchunu.'

In this attack about six people, including Thabethe's wife and children, were burnt to death in their house. Of this attack, the *New York Times* reported:

> Mr Thabethe underwent weeks of surgery before going home to KwaShange township . . . While he was recuperating, 10 days before Christmas, gunmen killed his 20-year-old son as he walked to a local store. Six days later . . . about 50 youths surrounded his home and set it afire. His wife, his mother and another son, were killed.[58]

January 1988

On 31 January, Inkatha had a prayer rally at Mbangweni, Chief Zondi's homestead, 3 kilometres from KwaShange. This meeting was called by the chief himself, who was distressed that 'some of his people had turned against him'. He said that KwaShange was the first area to 'complain about him' and they had tried several times to kill him, often showing no respect for him. He claimed this included the Inkatha leader, Mangosuthu Buthelezi. On this day, provincial Inkatha launched 'Operation Clean Up'. Inkatha leaders were commanded to drive non-Inkatha members out of KwaShange or kill them. After the rally, vigilantes escorted by the police attacked KwaShange and killed two people. The UDF, with the help of Harry Gwala's Edendale supporters, managed to fight back and Inkatha and the SAP gave way. Their attempt to 'clean up' KwaShange was thus a failure.[59]

After this event, there were reports of police collusion with Inkatha against the KwaShange UDF and COSATU. Moses Ndlovu and his two sons escaped after they were attacked in daylight by uniformed police, who were escorted by Inkatha warlords. Police collusion with Inkatha was also reported in other areas: Nxamalala, Tafuleni and Gezubuso. Commenting on this, Kentridge says that police were authorised by the National Party government minister of law and order, Adrian Vlok, who said that police will face the future with moderates and fight against radical groups.

The Inkatha Institute, a sociological research unit based in Durban, released a report that claimed that unemployment, rather than political antagonism, was the real cause of the conflict. The report was endorsed by Buthelezi, who blamed the violence on apartheid.[60] After the attack on Ndlovu and his sons in KwaShange, the president of the UDF, Archie Gumede, again called for peace. Buthelezi responded by saying Gumede supported the ANC and that peace talks would therefore be futile. Buthelezi also declared that he wanted talks to be held among national rather than local leaders.[61]

February 1988

In February 1988, a group of Inkatha people, led by Mlungisi Ngubane, who had been displaced from KwaShange,[62] attacked and injured KwaShange people at a bus stop in Retief Street in downtown Pietermaritzburg. They were arrested and charged with public violence. This was later altered to the lesser charge of constituting an illegal gathering. They received light and suspended sentences.

Further interdict applications were brought against Inkatha warlords, but these were hampered by the murder of some of the applicants and witnesses on the eve of the hearing of the applications. Some interim interdicts were granted and cases were deferred until August 1988 for oral evidence to be heard. Supreme Court judges became concerned about the situation and called in the Attorney General, demanding to know what was being done about prosecuting the perpetrators of violence. Other judges complained that the interdict applications were wasting the court's time. David Ntombela, an Inkatha warlord cited as one of the respondents in several of the interdict applications, threatened to shoot the COSATU official, Moses Ndlovu, after a court hearing and he received a warning from Justice Booysen.[63]

A delegation of women from KwaShange, Mnyandu, Vulisaka and Nxamalala joined another group of women from Greater Edendale and visited the offices of the Progressive Federal Party (PFP) in Pietermaritzburg to complain about police involvement in an attack on 31 January. After further allegations of police collusion with Inkatha, a police spokesman, Brigadier Leon Mellet, said that it was not the duty or the policy of the police to side with political groupings. The mayor of Pietermaritzburg, Mark Cornell, called on the South African Defence Force to send troops to halt the violence, but was told by the minister of police that the SAP was up to the task.[64]

According to Moses Ndlovu, the Chamber of Commerce in Pietermaritzburg was assisting in facilitating peace between Inkatha and the UDF but because of the 31 January incident (in which police and warlords attacked KwaShange), the Chamber of Commerce peace facilitators were sceptical about Inkatha's commitment to peace and told the media that Inkatha was not committed to non-violence in the Midlands, quoting what had happened in KwaShange as an example.[65]

Kentridge records that Buthelezi demanded an explanation from the Chamber of Commerce for remarks attributed to the managing director of the Chamber, Paul van Uytrecht, who had told a reporter on the *New York Times* that he was not convinced of Inkatha's commitment to the peace process. Even though the Chamber repudiated these comments, Buthelezi was dissatisfied. The Chamber continued to push for another round of peace talks, but on 10 February, UDF activists were detained, including the UDF regional secretaries, Skhumbuzo Ngwenya Mbatha and Martin Wittenberg. The detentions scuppered any hopes of further talks. The police were accused of undermining the peace process and the deputy minister of law and order, Roelf Meyer, declared that the Chamber of Commerce and church were wasting their time with peace talks.[66]

March 1988

Severe conflicts took place between KwaShange and neighbouring areas, where people who had been displaced from KwaShange were living. Almost every day KwaShange was attacked. A SAP mobile station was placed in KwaShange in March 1988. The attacks intensified despite the police presence in the area. Four police searches took place in March, in which police confiscated ammunition, guns and any other kind of weaponry. In March alone, about 150 youths were imprisoned for being in possession of homemade firearms. After each search and confiscation of weapons by the SAP, Inkatha would attack the area of KwaShange the following day and the police would do nothing. Chief Zondi was seen several times openly having meetings with the SAP stationed in KwaShange.

It is recorded that 300 kitskonstabels were deployed in KwaShange at the beginning of March. The men had been recruited in Natal and trained in Cape Town, but some were from KwaShange: Tana Zuma, Mlungisi Ngubane, Mzi Zuma and others. There was dismay among township residents, who said that the kitskonstabels were simply Inkatha vigilantes in police uniforms.

A group of women from KwaShange joined women from various Pietermaritzburg areas affected by the kitskonstabels' activities and went to see the Attorney General of Natal to express fears that these men would use their newly acquired rank to exact vengeance. The Attorney General was non-committal. The police declared that recruits were not screened as to their political affiliation, but while Inkatha members could be policemen, supporters of the UDF could not, as it was described as an 'extremist organisation'. Activists claimed that many of the kitskonstabels were known criminals and some even had cases pending against them (such as Mlungisi Ngubane, who had criminal and murder charges brought against him).

In mid-March, interim interdicts were granted against various Inkatha warlords, including Chief Zondi. At the inquiry into the assaults on KwaShange, on UDF members who had participated in the Sarmcol strike and in the deaths of the three COSATU supporters killed in Mpophomeni in December 1986 the examining magistrate found that a number of Inkatha members were responsible for the murders. The matter was referred to the Attorney General for prosecution. David Ntombela arrived at the inquest armed. His firearm was confiscated during the course of the proceedings. On 21 March, the police rounded up all the UDF supporters they could find in KwaShange, Mnyandu, Gezubuso and other UDF strongholds in Nadi and detained them briefly. On the same day, the minister of defence and his deputy, as well as the minister of police and his deputy, were taken on a tour of Vulindlela, including KwaShange.

April 1988

April was yet another 'black month' in KwaShange. The Durban Supreme Court found two former policemen guilty of the murder of thirteen Inkatha Youth Brigade members in September 1987. The judge found mitigating circumstances in that the men had feared an attack by the group and had pre-empted this by attacking first. They were sentenced to twelve years' imprisonment. Of Hlengwa's trial it was reported: 'In the KwaShange killings, policemen worked together with UDF supporters to attack Inkatha. In the massacre that ensued, thirteen community Inkatha members were "methodically executed without a shred of mercy".'[67]

The UDF young people recommitted themselves to fighting Inkatha. Zakhele Makhathini was attacked and was stoned to death and his throat was cut in front his wife and mentally disabled daughter. His wife was also killed after telling his assailants that she would inform the police.

May 1988

After Buthelezi was refused a visa by the Austrian authorities, who were concerned about his role in South African politics,[68] he met Inkatha leaders in the Midlands and instructed them to stop the violence. He threatened to dismiss Inkatha members who continued violent activities. The Inkatha Central Committee suspended three KwaShange Inkatha members (Tleko Ndlovu, Tito Nxele and Tozama Magubane) who were accused of using violence for political ends.

An Inkatha member, Mlungisi Shabalala, was sentenced to death for the murder of Mgayo Miya, a UDF member. Jerome Mncwabe, also of Inkatha, appeared in the Pietermaritzburg Supreme Court on three charges of murder. Although the victims were shot in the back, the judge accepted Mncwabe's claim that he acted in self-defence, and he was acquitted. His co-accused, Nkosinathi Mncwabe, was found guilty of culpable homicide and sentenced to five strokes and one year imprisonment, suspended for four years. UDF supporters were furious, more fighting ensued and two KwaShange Inkatha members were killed in Pietermaritzburg at the East Street bus rank.

June 1988

Two stay-aways were called by COSATU. KwaShange, Mnyandu and Vulisaka UDF supporters marched to Edendale but were attacked in Mvundlweni by Inkatha supporters, who were accompanied by police. Nevertheless, both these strikes were well supported by workers. KwaShange and Edendale youths waited near Georgetown for buses transporting Inkatha commuters and stoned the buses. The PFP called on the police to prohibit a rally in Sweetwaters organised by the Inkatha Youth Brigade, alleging that Inkatha youth intended to attack Nxamalala, Mthoqotho and KwaShange. Inkatha claimed it was merely a meeting to discuss strategy and dismissed residents' fears that anyone who failed to attend would have to 'face the consequences'. There was intense fighting in Slangspruit and KwaShange and Nxamalala UDF members were called to assist there.

July 1988

School protests took place in many schools in Edendale and Ashdown. Kitskonstabels had been deployed in several schools. A number of schoolchildren at Mzamweni and Mtholangqondo schools in

KwaShange were shot and injured by kitskonstabels. The pupils had protested against the presence of the police on the school grounds. A delegation of women went to the PFP offices to ask for a meeting to be set up with the police, and the kitskonstabels were subsequently almost entirely withdrawn from KwaShange schools.

The police released a number of detainees from Vulindlela; some of whom had been taken from KwaShange, allegedly for causing violence. Many of them had severe restrictions placed on them, designed to prevent them from engaging in any further political activity. Residents fled from their homes in Vulisaka and Gezubuso to KwaShange to escape fresh outbreaks of violence in these areas.

August 1988

The violence in Vulindlela intensified. Brigadier Buchner attributed this to the reinfiltration of the area by youths and activists who had previously been kept in custody by the police. Moses Ndlovu, the KwaShange COSATU leader, ascribed the upsurge of violence to another forced recruitment drive by Inkatha in Vulindlela. An army of 300 Inkatha vigilantes killed five people and burnt a bus carrying KwaShange UDF supporters to a funeral in Mpumalanga.

September 1988

Fifteen KwaShange women who had been victims of Inkatha warlords' attacks participated in the hearings of oral evidence against Inkatha in Pietermaritzburg. Among these women were Ntongo Thusi, Nana Thusi, Sibongile Mdlalose, Thulisile Khanyile and Nomaswazi Ngubane. A Complaints Adjudication Board, under the presidency of a retired judge, was established to monitor the situation. All those found responsible for acts of violence by the board would be referred to their organisation (the UDF or Inkatha) for discipline. Moses Ndlovu says that before the process of hearing oral evidence against Inkatha warlords could be completed COSATU and Inkatha signed a peace accord. The accord led to tension between COSATU and UDF comrades in the Midlands, as the latter were not signatories of the agreement because of the restrictions placed on the UDF by the government in February. UDF comrades also complained that they had not been consulted by COSATU before signing.

October 1988

By October, there were reports of over 20 000 refugees in the greater Pietermaritzburg area. There were also reports of fighting in and around Retief Street in Pietermaritzburg, where KwaShange commuters were fighting with Elandskop Inkatha members. Most deaths were caused by fighting in Mpumalanga Township in the Midlands.[69]

November 1988

Three UDF supporters – Mathi Ngcobo, Thulani Zondo and Duka Makhathini – were wanted dead by Chief Zondi and Inkatha warlords because they had attacked and killed Inkatha members in Ezibomvini and attempted to kill the chief's headman, Guvaza Khanyile. The young men were given refuge by Chief Mhlabunzima Maphumulo of Maqongqo. Late in November, Chief Maphumulo was summoned to Ulundi to answer an inquiry into the administration of his area, following complaints from Inkatha members that Maphumulo's policy of non-alignment in the war meant that UDF refugees were settling in the Table Mountain area and living among Inkatha members. They also claimed that he had sent people to support the UDF in KwaShange.[70] Maphumulo refused to attend the inquiry, as he claimed that the directive he had received was vague and ambiguous. There were reports that Inkatha had embarked on a new forced recruitment campaign at Trust Feed near New Hanover.

December 1988

Fighting between KwaShange UDF supporters and Inkatha at Retief Street, East Street and West Street bus stops in Pietermaritzburg intensified after fifteen people were killed at a vigil in a house at Trust Feed, New Hanover. The UDF accused Inkatha members at Trust Feed of this killing and of attempting to kill two young men from KwaShange, who had been sent to assist the UDF at Trust Feed. Buthelezi threatened to sue anyone who suggested that Inkatha members were responsible for the murders. He claimed that the dead people were in fact Inkatha members, although survivors and relations of the dead people denied this.

Also in December, shopkeepers in Retief Street, Pietermaritzburg, complained that the continued fighting at the bus and taxi depots was bad for the Christmas trade.

January 1989

There was further fighting between residents of KwaShange and Mvundlweni. The police continued to harass KwaShange residents. A number of people were found dead in the area and police stationed in KwaShange were always suspects, but nothing was done to investigate these cases. Inkatha members attacked and killed four KwaShange women at a bus stop near Gezubuso. A deputation of KwaShange women, joined by Nxamalala, Gezubuso and Mnyandu women, went to the PFP offices to complain about police handling of the incidents.

February to March 1989

Clashes occurred between UDF and Inkatha vigilantes under the command of different warlords throughout Vulindlela. The regional director of the PFP in Pietermaritzburg, Radley Keys, accused an Inkatha warlord of having murdered up to 25 people between February and March. The KwaZulu Police in KwaShange and Inkatha denied this. The police released several detainees, including UDF secretary, Skhumbuzo Ngwenya Mbatha, following a hunger strike. The regional secretary of the Transport and General Workers' Union, Alfred Ndlovu, was, however, found guilty of terrorism and sentenced to eight years' imprisonment for killing KwaShange Inkatha youth in 1988.

April to May 1989

Winnie Mandela visited KwaShange at the behest of Moses Ndlovu and Harry Gwala. She paid a secret visit to young men who had been conducting surveillance in KwaShange and told them never to allow traitors and government agents and spies to use KwaShange as their 'playground'.

Later in April, Nelson Mandela sent a cordial letter from Victor Verster Prison, near Paarl, to Mangosuthu Buthelezi. Mandela called for national unity in the struggle and peace in Vulindlela and in the Pietermaritzburg townships. Chief Maphumulo, a strong ally of the KwaShange UDF, also called for peace and petitioned the state president to appoint a judicial commission of inquiry into the causes of violence. Buthelezi condemned the petition and opposed the idea of a judicial commission. The minister of law and order, Vlok, also dismissed the call.[71]

Towards the end of April, 30 people were killed in one weekend in the Vulindlela area. The escalating killings galvanised fresh calls for peace. COSATU and the UDF said that they shared a 'common view and commitment to a mass movement for peace' with Inkatha and called for a peace conference to be convened by church and community leaders.[72] Buthelezi proposed a peace plan involving a massive media campaign in the townships. Vlok reiterated his view that UDF and COSATU were responsible for all the violence in the region and announced an increase in police personnel and equipment, a move that he had already discussed with Buthelezi.

The peace talks were bogged down before they could begin because Buthelezi insisted that the talks be held at Ulundi, while COSATU and the UDF wanted a neutral venue, such as Durban. Although Buthelezi had said to Archbishop Denis Hurley of the Catholic Church that he would be prepared to 'go to the ends of the earth if needs be' to stop the violence, he now declared he had no intention of going to Durban or anywhere other than Ulundi to hold peace talks.[73]

June to July 1989

Several high-ranking UDF and COSATU officials in the Midlands and Vulindlela, including Archie Gumede and Moses Ndlovu, were under virtual house arrest, thereby making it almost impossible for them to attend the talks. This undermined the planned peace talks.

August to September 1989

The peace negotiators agreed on an agenda for a top-level peace conference to be held at an overseas venue and attended by the presidents of Inkatha, the UDF, COSATU and the ANC. The plan was endorsed by all parties but did not get off the ground as Inkatha accused the ANC of dragging its feet over the proposals.[74]

A hit squad consisting of policemen operating from a red mini-van was seen in many UDF-aligned areas, such as Nxamalala, KwaShange, Mthoqotho and Edendale. The hit squad was responsible for assaulting and abducting UDF comrades. In KwaShange, they abducted three boys between the ages of eighteen and twenty-one, shot them and threw their bodies into the nearby Msunduzi River. From September to October, peace talks between Inkatha and the UDF and COSATU in the Midlands failed.

October to November 1989

An interim interdict was granted to KwaShange activists, restraining the police hit squad from further assaulting or abducting them. On the same day, one of the activists, Thulani Ngcamu, was briefly detained by the squad and interrogated. In November, there was sporadic violence in KwaShange, as small groups of UDF comrades and Inkatha supporters clashed with each other, but the worst fighting occurred in Mpumalanga and Hammarsdale.

December 1989

Two unofficial commissions of inquiry into the Pietermaritzburg violence were convened: one under the auspices of Chief Maphumulo, and the other under the auspices of local church groups. A number of people, some from KwaShange, gave testimony to the commissions. The most significant feature of December was the intensity of fighting in the squatter camps of Inanda near Durban, giving rise to the (temporary) impression that the focus of the war had shifted from the Midlands to the coast.

January 1990

Violence between KwaShange people and KwaMpande Inkatha warlords continued. These attacks were worsened by the massacre of ten people at Wartburg, among whom were a number of Inkatha warlords. Inkatha supporters from KwaMpande then began to attack Nxamalala and KwaShange communities, probably to show solidarity with their Wartburg counterparts.

February 1990

In his speech at the opening of parliament, the state president, F.W. de Klerk, unbanned the ANC. A few days later, Nelson Mandela was released after 27 years in prison. The ANC stated that the resolution of the conflict in Natal was a priority for all parties. Walter Sisulu, leader of the internal wing of the ANC, toured Pietermaritzburg towards the end of the month and met the Inkatha secretary general, Oscar Dhlomo. On 25 February, Mandela addressed a rally of 125 000 people at King's Park Stadium in Durban and made conciliatory remarks about Inkatha and Buthelezi, praising their opposition to apartheid over the years. Mandela also called on his followers to throw their weapons into the sea and 'close down the death factories now'.[75]

There was an immediate upsurge in violence between the UDF in KwaShange and Inkatha in neighbouring areas. Towards the end of the month, the focus of the violence was on Vulindlela and Chief Maphumulo's chieftaincy, Table Mountain. UDF authority was slipping and Inkatha was becoming increasingly powerful in the area. Many refugees, including some KwaShange youths who had fled to Table Mountain in the early months of the war, moved out again to seek refuge elsewhere.

March 1990

March 1990 was the high-water point of the war in terms of deaths, with its death tally of 162, despite Mandela's call for peace. In contrast to the conciliatory tone of Mandela's speech, Buthelezi, in his opening speech to the KwaZulu Legislative Assembly, verbally attacked the ANC and the UDF, explicitly blaming the latter for starting the war and keeping it going over the years.

Inkatha held a rally on 25 March at King's Park Stadium, attended by 8 000 people. A few days later, Inkatha launched a sustained attack in the Pietermaritzburg region, which amounted to a full-scale invasion of UDF strongholds in Edendale and Vulindlela. A feature of the attack was the size of the armies (up to 3 000 *impis* were reported) and the large number of guns in evidence. Fatalities were high, with 35 people killed in a single day and over 80 in a week.

Within days, 11 500 refugees were accommodated in makeshift camps in Pietermaritzburg. Eyewitnesses claimed that David Ntombela was pivotal in co-ordinating the Inkatha offensive.

This upsurge in violence dominated local media for over two weeks and received much coverage overseas. Buthelezi repeated his claim that the instigators of violence were the UDF, COSATU and the ANC. Inkatha also claimed that the current attack was in retaliation for the stoning of Inkatha buses by UDF comrades. The UDF responded by saying that the retaliation was out of proportion to the stoning and that the scale of the invasion was so large that it must have been prepared well in advance.

There were many reports of the SAP colluding with the Inkatha attackers, and police dispersed a peaceful march of unarmed women to the Plessislaer Police Station in protest at police involvement in the attacks.

At the height of the fighting, Buthelezi announced that he and Mandela would address a joint rally in Taylor's Halt, the heart of the war zone. However, Mandela said that he had never agreed to this and he argued that a joint rally at such a time could lead to a bloodbath.

The Black Sash called for the deployment of troops in the Natal townships, saying that the police had lost all credibility and that only the army could restore control.

These complex antagonisms on both sides led to the Seven Days' War of 25 to 31 March 1990.[76] The balance of the war kept changing in favour of one side or the other and ordinary people were caught up in it, not being allowed to stay neutral.

Notes

1. J. Aitchison, 'The Origins of the Midlands War', in *The Role of Political Violence in South Africa's Democratisation*, edited by R. Greenstein (Johannesburg: Community Agency for Social Enquiry, 2003).
2. See interview with Moses Ndlovu, KwaShange, 24 June 2003; interview with Nunu Mchunu, KwaShange, 13 August 2008; interview with Chris Hlengwa, KwaShange, 14 August 2008; interview with Bhekithemba Mbanjwa and group interviews I had with a significant number of informants, KwaShange, 12 March 2010. These interviewees confirmed what is documented in the body of literature that deals with the history of violence in KwaZulu-Natal. See, for example, A. Minnaar, *Conflict and Violence in Natal/KwaZulu: Historical Perspectives* (Pretoria: HSRC, 1990); R. Taylor and M. Shaw, 'The Natal Conflict', in *Restructuring South Africa*, edited by J.D. Brewer (London: St Martin's Press, 1994); A. Johnston, 'Politics and Violence in KwaZulu-Natal', in *Violence in Southern Africa*, edited by W. Gutteridge and J. Spence (London: Frank Cass, 1997); Aitchison, 'The Origins of the Midlands War'; J. Aitchison, 'Numbering the Dead: The Course and Pattern of Political Violence in the Natal Midlands, 1987–1989' (Master's thesis, University of Natal, 1993); M. Kentridge, *An Unofficial War: Inside the Conflict in Pietermaritzburg* (Cape Town: David Philip, 1990).
3. Interview with Nunu Mchunu, KwaShange, 14 August 2008.
4. Interview with group of informants in KwaShange, and this information was confirmed by Nunu Mchunu, 12 March 2010.
5. Interview with Tana Zuma and Mzi Zuma, KwaShange, 13 October 2008.
6. Aitchson, 'The Origins of the Midlands War'.
7. These figures were given by informants who admitted having forgotten some events; some caution is advised in the interpretation.

8. Interview with a group of informants in KwaShange. Dr May Mashego-Mkhize confirmed that staff at Edendale Hospital swore that they would not 'undermine *uMntwana wakwa Phindangene (Inkosi* Buthelezi)', but Dr Mashego-Mkhize refused to take that oath when she started working in Edendale as a doctor.
9. Taken from Nsizwa Makhaye's notes, Chief Zondi told Inkatha leaders in Vulindlela that it was not optional to be a member of Inkatha for people living under his leadership. Chief Zondi said this repeatedly, even in compulsory Inkatha meetings in KwaShange; see interview with Chris Hlengwa, KwaShange, 14 August 2008.
10. This was confirmed by Nduduzo Ndlovu, who was a member of the Youth Brigade but later became a member of the UDF in KwaShange.
11. Interview with Chris Hlengwa, KwaShange, 14 August 2008. This was also confirmed by group of informants in KwaShange, 12 March 2010. Ndoda Ndlovu was part of Inkatha Youth Brigade, which listed these homesteads that had to be attacked. He later went to spy on Inkatha and mentioned that Inkatha was preparing itself to attack these homesteads.
12. Interview with Khonzi Ngubane and Donda Ngubane, KwaShange, 12 March 2010. This was confirmed by Nunu Mchunu and a group of informants in KwaShange, 12 March 2010.
13. Interview with Chris Hlengwa, Bhekithemba Mbanjwa, Mancinza Zondi and Sizwe Ndlovu, KwaShange, 12 March 2010.
14. Interview with Chris Hlengwa, KwaShange, 14 August 2008.
15. There is an important body of literature on state police colluding with Inkatha.
16. See Kentridge, *An Unofficial War*. Kentridge records in detail the tension among bus drivers in Pietermaritzburg.
17. Aitchison, 'The Origins of the Midlands War'.
18. Interview with a group of informants in KwaShange, 12 March 2010. This was confirmed by Nunu Mchunu and Chris Hlengwa.
19. Interview with Chris Hlengwa, KwaShange, 14 August 2008; interview with Nunu Mchunu, KwaShange, 13 August 2008; interview with Moses Ndlovu, KwaShange, 24 June 2003.
20. Interview with Chris Hlengwa, Zama Phakathi and a group of informants in KwaShange, 13 March 2010.
21. Interview with Nunu Mchunu, KwaShange, 13 August 2008.
22. Interview with Nunu Mchunu, KwaShange, 13 August 2008; interview with Chris Hlengwa, KwaShange, 14 August 2008. Many other informants in KwaShange remembered this event. It still exists in many people's minds because it was the first emotionally and psychologically disturbing major incident that left a number of youth in KwaShange permanently paralysed.
23. Interview with group of informants in KwaShange, 12 March 2010.
24. Aitchison, 'The Origins of the Midlands War'.
25. *Daily News*, 16 April 1988. The newspaper only reported the court case but not the event. As mentioned, KwaShange was not a 'user-friendly' area for journalists, police and researchers.
26. This informant wanted to remain anonymous because she still fears for her life today, twenty years after the violence.

27. Interview with Mancinza Zondi, Chris Hlengwa and group informants in KwaShange, 10 March 2009.
28. *Daily News*, 16 April 1988.
29. *Daily News*, 16 April 1988.
30. Torrential rains, which caused floods that left a number of families in Natal and KwaZulu without homes: their houses, bridges and roads were washed away and a significant number of people lost their lives.
31. Aitchison, 'The Origins of the Midlands War', p. 47.
32. This family harassment was quoted by all men who were involved in the 25 September KwaShange massacre as one of the reasons why they were very upset with Inkatha.
33. Interview with Bhekithemba Mbanjwa, KwaShange, 12 March 2010; interview with Nunu Mchunu, KwaShange, 13 August 2008; interview with Chris Hlengwa, KwaShange, 14 August 2008.
34. Winnie Zibula survived the violence, but she has permanent scars on her body from burning and stabbing that took place when she was only six months old. She is not in a position to talk about what she feels about it now. She has a lot of emotional scars as a result of this event.
35. Chris Hlengwa had come home late from work. As he was walking from the bus stop, 2 kilometres away, he saw flames, and as he got closer he heard people crying. He rushed home to alert the group of men from KwaShange; he had organised himself to look after his homestead after the withdrawal of police protection. He asked these men to accompany him to where there were burning houses and screaming voices. When he arrived, the Zibula and Mbanjwa homes were burning. The attackers were still on the scene. Hlengwa shot one bullet. The attackers ran away but Hlengwa and his team were able to catch one of the attackers. He named all of those who had been there burning the Mbanjwa and Zibula houses.
36. Information provided by a number of informants in KwaShange, including Chris Hlengwa, 2008, Nunu Mchunu, 2008, and Moses Ndlovu, 2003.
37. Interview with Nunu Mchunu, KwaShange, 14 March 2009.
38. *The Citizen*, 28 September 1987.
39. Kentridge, *An Unofficial War*, p. 229.
40. Interview with MaSibisi Ndaba, KwaShange, 13 June 2009.
41. Interview with Nunu Mchunu, KwaShange, 2008.
42. J.F. Burns, 'Black versus Black in South Africa', *New York Times*, 21 January 1988, http://www.nytimes.com/1988/01/21/world/black-vs-black-in-south-africa p5.
43. Bearing in mind that the Inkatha motto at that time was: 'If you are not for us, you are against us.'
44. Interview with survivors (some of whom inisisted that they remain anonymous) of this incident in KwaShange, 14 June 2009.
45. Interview with survivors (some of whom inisisted that they remain anonymous) of this incident in KwaShange, 14 June 2009.
46. Interview with Thobani Shazi and two anonymous ex-MK solders, 14 March 2008.
47. Interview with So Ndlovu and Thobani Shazi, former MK soldiers.
48. Interview with Moses Ndlovu, Kwashange, 24 June 2003.

49. Kentridge, *An Unofficial War*; Aitchison, 'The Origins of the Midlands War'. Moses Ndlovu confirmed the legal team went to KwaShange in a fact-finding mission.
50. Interview with anonymous, KwaShange, 24 August 2009.
51. Interview with a group of informants in KwaShange, 24 August 2009.
52. Interview with a group of informants in KwaShange, 2009. See also Aitchison, 'The Origins of the Midlands War'.
53. Interview with Mduduzi Mchunu, Mabhengwane Bhengu and Zibuse Madlala, who were present at the funeral, KwaShange, 2 February 2009.
54. Interview with Moses Ndlovu, KwaShange, 24 June 2003. See also Kentridge, *An Unofficial War*.
55. Interview with Nelly Ngcobo and Sipho Khanyile, confirming Moses Ndlovu's testimony, KwaShange, 14 March 2008.
56. Kentridge, *An Unofficial War*. See also J. Sithole, 'The African National Congress in Natal, 1990–1995', in South African Democracy Education Trust, *The Road to Democracy in South Africa: Volume 6 (1990–1996): Part 1* (Pretoria: Unisa Press, 2013).
57. These were Inkatha supporters, who were recruited by the apartheid state agent. They were untrained 'policemen'; rather they were alleged to be 'hitmen' who killed UDF supporters in townships and rural areas. The Truth and Reconciliation Commission report goes into detail concerning the collusion between state police and specially trained 'police' and the Inkatha attacks on UDF/ANC supporters. See testimony and public submission by General Magnus Malan before the Truth and Reconciliation Commission, 7 May 1997. See also testimonies of South African Defence Force members at Armed Forces Hearings in October 1997; A. Minnaar, 'The "Third Force": In Retrospect', in *The Hidden Hand: Covert Operations in South Africa*, edited by C. Schutte, I. Liebenberg and A. Minnaar (Pretoria: HSRC, 1998); P. Pigou, 'The State and Violence: What Has the Truth and Reconciliation Commission Found?', in *The Role of Political Violence in South Africa's Democratisation*, edited by R. Greenstein (Johannesburg: Community Agency for Social Enquiry, 2003).
58. Burns, 'Black versus Black in South Africa'.
59. Interviews with groups of informants in KwaShange and Inkatha-aligned informants in Mvundlweni.
60. Kentridge, *An Unofficial War*.
61. Kentridge, *An Unofficial War*.
62. He is the most wanted warlord to this day in KwaShange. Some families say they want him dead or alive because of suffering he caused in the 1980s.
63. Interview with Moses Ndlovu, KwaShange, 2003. See also Kentridge, *An Unofficial War*.
64. Kentridge, *An Unofficial War*.
65. Interview with Moses Ndlovu, KwaShange, 24 June 2003; interview with Nunu Mchunu, KwaShange, 13 August 2008.
66. Kentridge, *An Unofficial War*.
67. Pietermaritzburg Archives Repository (PAR), *State v. Hlengwa and others*, transcript of judgment by Justice N.S. Page, Natal Provincial Division of the Supreme Court, Pietermaritzburg, 11 April 1988.

68. Interview with Nunu Mchunu, KwaShange, 13 August 2008; interview with Moses Ndlovu, 24 June 2003.
69. Kentridge, *An Unofficial War*. See also D. Bonnin, 'Legacies of Political Violence: An Examination of Political Conflict in Mpumalanga Township, KwaZulu-Natal, South Africa', *Transformation* 62, 2006: 59–83.
70. This was probably the reason why, in 1990, during the Seven Days' War, Nyavu people assisted David Ntombela to attack KwaShange, in particular. See, J. Kelly, *To Swim with Crocodiles: Land, Violence, and Belonging in South Africa, 1800–1996* (East Lansing, MI: Michigan State University Press, 2018).
71. Kentridge, *An Unofficial War.*
72. Lindiwe Ngcobo worked for the UDF office; this was also mentioned by Moses Ndlovu of COSATU. See also Kentridge, *An Unofficial War*.
73. Aitchison, 'The Origins of the Midlands War', p. 68.
74. Aitchison, 'The Origins of the Midlands War'.
75. Kentridge, *An Unofficial War*, p. 242.
76. For details on the Seven Days' War, see L. Levine (ed.), *Faith in Turmoil: The Seven Days War* (Pietermaritzburg: PACSA, 1999); A. Jeffery, *The Natal Story: Sixteen Years of Conflict* (Johannesburg: South African Institute of Race Relations, 1997); Kentridge, *An Unofficial War.*

6

The Effects of National Politics on KwaShange

BOTH THE AFRICAN National Congress (ANC) and Inkatha were formed as a response to white colonial power and the exclusion of the indigenous African majority. When Nunu Mchunu, Moses Ndlovu and other members of the ANC attended meetings at the 'People's Hall', they were all instructed to recruit and mobilise their community members to 'resist white supremacy' and the abuse of black people. Ndlovu and Mchunu recruited members of the KwaShange community.

Inkatha was originally founded in 1923 and was revived in 1975 by Mangosuthu Buthelezi when the ANC in exile suggested the formation of an internal wing. Thabo Mbeki is credited with facilitating the establishment and drafted the first constitution of Inkatha, saying he was not worried about what the movement was to be called, as long as there was this movement that was going to mobilise people inside the country. It was Mbeki's responsibility to nurture the relationship between Buthelezi and the ANC.[1] Many people, like Mchunu, who had been active in the ANC, felt it was still appropriate that they mobilise people to join Inkatha, as it was like the ANC in disguise anyway.

Some ANC members did not participate in Inkatha activities and meetings. Ndlovu and others were deeply engaged with the ANC in exile. It is uncertain why Ndlovu was not involved in the Inkatha revival in 1975. At the time, Mchunu was recruiting people in KwaShange to join Inkatha. Mchunu and Ndlovu's agendas were not opposed as both movements shared the same constituency.

The first signs of tensions came at Robert Sobukwe's funeral in Graaff-Reinet on 11 March 1978, where *Umuntwana wakwa Phindangene* (Mangosuthu Buthelezi) was ill-treated by people who were at the funeral.[2] Buthelezi attributed his ill-treatment to 'some misguided youths who did not understand the respect and camaraderie between all those fighting in the liberation struggle [and] did not think that I should have attended the funeral'.[3]

Ndlovu concluded from this that many people, particularly the youth, felt that Buthelezi's participation in the KwaZulu government as its chief minister was hindering the struggle against apartheid. Even a well-known struggle veteran, and the most influential church leader at the time, Desmond Tutu, called those that had chased Buthelezi away from the funeral 'a new breed of young people with iron in their soul'.[4] Buthelezi characterised them as 'thugs'.[5]

One day in 1978, after one of many Ulundi meetings, Mchunu met with Ndlovu in KwaShange. He recalled, 'I went to ask him to join hands with me and explain to our people that Inkatha is working for people; it is not an enemy to our leaders in exile.' Mchunu's fear was that what had started in Graaff-Reinet would spread and they would fail to control it. Ndlovu refused, without giving his reasons to Mchunu, and continued doing what the ANC in exile had requested him to do – recruiting young men and women. Mchunu did not know whether they 'were still pulling together or they were pulling in different directions'.[6]

In 1979, the top leadership of Inkatha, particularly Buthelezi, became estranged from the leader of the ANC in exile, Oliver Tambo.[7] In their interviews, both Mchunu and Ndlovu told me that 1979 was a year during which difficulties between Inkatha and the ANC emerged. There had been a series of meetings between Buthelezi and the ANC in exile, aimed at ironing out tensions in a relationship that was slowly turning sour. In 1979, the time seemed ripe for a top-level meeting between Inkatha and the ANC. A summit conference between Inkatha and the ANC in exile took place in October 1979 in London. Tambo attended the meeting, which was chaired by Dr A.H. Zulu, the speaker of the KwaZulu Legislative Assembly.[8] Buthelezi later reflected on why he went to London:

> I went to London determined to seek reconciliation and determined to bring about a working relationship between the ANC Mission in Exile and Inkatha. I was aware of the fact that Mr Oliver Tambo was having difficulties with some elements of his organisation. Those with a firm commitment to violence did not want any evidence that non-violent strategies were viable in South Africa.[9]

This probably was the reason why Ndlovu in KwaShange never got himself involved in Inkatha activities. In all his discussions with the ANC in exile, Buthelezi insisted that Inkatha should remain Inkatha; and that it should remain committed to black popular will, reflected in Inkatha's massive membership, which had doubled in 1977 and doubled again in 1978. Inkatha interpreted this huge increase in membership as a vote of confidence in the movement and a rejection of the armed struggle by black South Africans.[10] According to John Aitchison:

> By the time the 1979 London meeting between Inkatha and the ANC Mission in Exile took place the militant elements in the ANC could no longer be controlled by Oliver Tambo. After the London meeting, for the first time in his career, Mr Tambo began criticising Buthelezi and Inkatha publicly. He had sided with those in his ranks who saw Inkatha as a threat . . . the London meeting would prove to be a pivotal point in the relationship between the two organisations.[11]

Mchunu recalls 1979 as the year in which Ndlovu started mobilising people against Inkatha. 'He went to all families and school teachers and youths I had recruited to join Inkatha and he told them that Inkatha was not the ANC and it was not fighting for black people but Inkatha was "selling" black people to the whites.'[12] Mchunu believes that the disagreement between Buthelezi and the top ANC leadership in exile led to Ndlovu's campaign against Inkatha.[13] Clearly, the tension between the ANC in exile and the Inkatha leadership spread to the lower levels of leadership. The clashes between the 'ringleaders' and the escalating violence in KwaShange was a reflection of what was happening nationally and provincially. When Inkatha met in Ulundi, these matters were on the agenda, but the leadership encouraged regional leaders to be 'calm but not to stop recruiting for Inkatha'.[14] Hostility between Mchunu and Ndlovu increased when they started to campaign against each other in one small area. This divided the community, as many people still believed Inkatha to be the internal wing of the ANC.

Among those who Mchunu recruited were Phillip 'Makhekhe' Thabethe, Amon Kubheka, who had been in the ANC, and many others. Chief Shayabantu Zondi also joined Inkatha and used to attend Inkatha meetings in Ulundi along with Mchunu.[15] Ndlovu, meanwhile, recruited Chris Hlengwa (who had been Mchunu's family friend), Sayi Zondi, Ngudla Msane and Mathuba Goge, all of whom were members of the South African Police living in KwaShange.

The ill-treatment of Buthelezi at Sobukwe's funeral in 1978, and the breach between Buthelezi and Tambo in exile, made Inkatha regional leaders realise that things were not normal. They deduced from this situation that they were all going to be treated with disrespect.[16]

Throughout this period, there were signals that Buthelezi was taking an increasingly hard line towards any black radicals who contradicted him, and by then there were many adherents of the Black Consciousness Movement coming out of universities.[17]

The behaviour of unionists also tended to give offence to Buthelezi, who did not like being manipulated by some of the intellectuals leading the independent union movement in Durban.[18] In contrast with the working-class black unionists, he got on well with white business leaders. This coincided with the formation of the United Democratic Front (UDF) in 1983, in an atmosphere saturated with suspicion between Inkatha and the left.[19] Ndlovu recalled that there were rumours that Archie Gumede, the national and Natal UDF leader, would arrange meetings with Buthelezi to come to an understanding. But political conditions made such mediation impossible and the attempts were abandoned. In the interim, Inkatha was concentrating its activities in Natal and Zululand.[20]

Mchunu's campaign in KwaShange started after the Sobukwe incident. He recalls that this event made him start manufacturing homemade guns, an activity for which he was later to be jailed. He distributed these firearms to Inkatha followers in KwaShange and neighbouring areas.[21]

In our interview, Mchunu recalled:

> I remember one night, very late, I heard a knock on my door, I did not open the door; I thought it was UDF guys who had come to kill me. I just kept quiet and waited for them to push the door by force. I had already prepared myself that I was going to kill all of them. The knock continued but I did not open. After a long time I heard voices; it was not UDF people but it was whites' voices. When they came back and knocked again, I opened the door; it was police looking for guns. They had been told that I am the one who made and distributed guns in the area. The police searched my house for more than an hour, they couldn't find anything. They cornered me with questions, coercing me to show them my guns and I refused, saying that I had no gun. When they were just about to give up, one Boer [Afrikaner] policeman kicked my small *isigqiki* (headrest). I had made my *isigqiki* and put a small hole underneath and that is where I kept the guns and many others were buried outside in my yard. The police kicked the *isigqiki* and heard that there was something in it, and that is how they got my gun and they took me [into custody]. They drove with me the whole night looking for all other people who were suspected to have guns.[22]

In 1983, Ulundi was made the capital of KwaZulu, and all people under the traditional leadership of chiefs had to contribute financially towards the building of Ulundi. Chief Zondi was tasked with collecting the funds in areas under his jurisdiction in Vulindlela. Only KwaShange refused to pay the requested contribution towards the building of Ulundi. Some people objected to the building of Ulundi and rejected Inkatha itself. 'How is Inkatha going help us?' they asked. 'Why should we pay for a building miles and miles away from us?' Ndlovu was singled out for leading the campaign to refuse.

Tensions grew between those who contributed and those who did not. This is when Chief Zondi 'lost his respect' among members of the KwaShange community. This was confirmed by Ndlovu and Mchunu. Mchunu and Inkatha, in general, were annoyed by this action, because they felt 'this was disrespect to *uMntwana wakwa Phindangene* (Buthelezi) himself', a man who was 'the hope of the blacks in South Africa'. Natal and KwaZulu were then, as they are today, essentially black areas and it is likely that some people, both blacks and whites, genuinely thought that a multiracial region, free of apartheid, was a possibility.[23]

The history of liberation struggles in Natal and Zululand

Natal and Zululand have long been associated with African liberation struggles. The Battle of Ncome River (Blood River), between the Voortrekkers and the Zulu, took place in 1838. Many battles took place in the province between the Zulu and the British in the Anglo-Zulu War of 1879. During the Bhambatha rebellion of 1906, Zulu people rose against the colonial Natal government. In 2006, former President Mbeki described Chief Bhambatha as a leader who fought for liberation and tried to change people's lives for the better.[24] The former president of the ANC and of South Africa, Jacob Zuma, has several times referred to *umlando wezimpi zakwaZulu* (the history of Zulu wars), particularly the Bhambatha rebellion, as events that inspired him to join politics.[25] The first president of the democratic South Africa, Nelson Mandela, described KwaZulu-Natal as a place where the struggle for liberation originated; hence he chose to cast his vote in 1994 in KwaZulu-Natal, at Ohlange Mission School, which was established by John Langalibalele Dube, who became the first president of the ANC. In the 1960s, when the ANC was banned, it was led by a Zulu, Chief Albert Luthuli.

KwaShange was the first rural area to strongly oppose Inkatha, and the UDF in this region took up arms against them. Later, they were followed by Chief Mhlabunzima Maphumulo's people at eMkhambathini. This was the start of the civil war of the 1980s and 1990s.

In northern Zululand, black political resistance was, to some extent, less confrontational. This can be attributed to the fact that there were two significant political movements: Inkatha, under the leadership of Buthelezi, and the independent black trade union movement. Buthelezi was the hereditary chief of the Buthelezi clan. He gained control of the KwaZulu Legislative Assembly in the 1970s and avoided any serious confrontation with the National Party government.

In the mid-1960s, the security police distrusted Buthelezi, as he had been an ANC supporter and Mandela had visited him when 'on the run'. During the late 1970s, Buthelezi and Inkatha gathered considerable support in the province. It was hoped that this would keep the region stable in the aftermath of the Soweto uprising of 1976 and inhibit the growth of radical oppositional politics.[26] This was never the case – the ANC in exile had already called for an armed struggle and the UDF was already successfully mobilising the youth. The spiral into civil strife was accelerating.[27] Inkatha was unprepared for the revival of the anti-apartheid mobilisation that occurred in 1983 with the formation of the UDF.[28]

Inkatha brutally attacked students at the University of Zululand in October 1983, which was an indication of already deteriorating relationships. The 1980s saw a consequential decline in support for Buthelezi at national level. This exposed what had always been an ambiguity between Buthelezi and his Inkatha movement, who were in essence Zulu, and the ANC, which was multi-ethnic. Inkatha's emphasis on Zulu ethnic identity showed that the regional tension had become the more powerful force.[29]

The rise of vigilante groups associated with Inkatha, conflict between the UDF and the Black Consciousness Movement, struggles between Inkatha and the trade union movements, and the lack of tolerance of any opposition by the KwaZulu/Inkatha authorities, led to conflict in the region.[30]

Tensions engendered by these factors led to skirmishes between Inkatha and the UDF-supporting youth. Congress of South African Trade Union (COSATU) members took part in rent and bus boycotts, as did members of civic associations. Conflict in Natal escalated in the Durban region, where clashes between Inkatha supporters and UDF and COSATU supporters increased from 1983 to 1985. This was as a result of the attempts to incorporate the townships of Hambanathi, Lamontville, KwaMashu and Umlazi into KwaZulu, as well as resistance to rent and transport fare increases and school boycotts.[31] During the same period, prominent self-appointed squatter settlement leaders in the areas to the north of Durban, particularly in Lindelani and Inanda, became overtly pro-Inkatha and were involved in violent attacks against UDF supporters in both squatter areas and more established townships.[32]

In 1983 and 1984, several youth organisations affiliated to the UDF in Pietermaritzburg and Hammarsdale areas were involved in fights between Inkatha and the UDF.[33] In November 1983, there was a major clash in Imbali involving nearly 1 000 people, and there was another clash in Mpumalanga, in which Inkatha Youth Brigade members clashed with UDF supporters and set a bus ablaze.[34]

In mid-1985, the pro-UDF civic association in Imbali was intimidated by aggressive threats from Inkatha.[35] The extent of growing Inkatha antagonism towards the UDF can be seen in Buthelezi's announcement in December 1985 that the UDF was a front for the ANC and that any UDF members in the KwaZulu civil service would be fired.

On Christmas Eve 1985, many UDF-aligned township dwellers around Pietermaritzburg turned off their electricity, and, in rural areas such as KwaShange, adults did not go to work and schoolchildren did not go to school in protest against the state of emergency. This was a clear sign that Inkatha did not have unanimous support in the townships and some rural areas.[36]

The 1980s were characterised by black schoolgoers identifying themselves as a site of struggle against apartheid and there were many school boycotts. Inkatha moved repressively against such school-based activism in the Pietermaritzburg region in 1980 and this alienated many young pupils from the movement. In 1983, school-based demonstrations and boycotts took place in Pietermaritzburg and Hammarsdale and were met with police repression.[37]

Students were also the victims of Inkatha vigilante groups, which were set up in the Midlands townships with the blessing of local sympathising councillors and the police, ostensibly to halt crime and gangsterism. In 1985, student leaders in the Sobantu and Imbali townships of Pietermaritzburg were assaulted and some were killed by vigilantes. There were retaliatory youth attacks on vigilantes.[38]

Conflict in itself does not result in fissure, nor does political tension inevitably lead to killing.[39] What transpired in the court indictment in November 1995 against Magnus Malan (minister of defence under President P.W. Botha and one of the architects of the state repression policy during the decade of apartheid) and others, and evidence led during the trial in 1996, show that what had long been assumed as a hidden hand behind the Natal conflict was indeed true.[40] As reported in the *Mail & Guardian*:

> According to the indictment, Buthelezi approached the South African military in 1985 for help with information, protection

> and military capacity. He needed it because the supporters of the ANC planned to neutralise him (though this threat seems to have been discovered by the security services and may well have been largely disinformation). General Tienie Groenewald, chief director of military intelligence, allegedly gave Buthelezi's shopping list at a meeting on 25 November 1985 to General Malan and it was eventually agreed that the SADF [South African Defence Force] would provide him with a contra-mobilisation capability, an offensive capability and an intelligence capability.[41]

Some 200 Inkatha soldiers were secretly trained in the Caprivi Strip. One of their first actions was the murder of four trade unionists in Mpophomeni.[42] Another, a month later, was the KwaMakutha massacre, when thirteen women and children at a prayer meeting in a UDF official's house were murdered by a kombi load of AK-47-wielding Caprivi 'graduates' who, allegedly, had demanded a chance to practise their new skills.[43]

Alongside increasing Inkatha's military capacity was the development of an even more secret network of bases, from which the security police would go out to abduct and then torture, cross-examine and put to death or co-opt ANC underground operatives.[44] It was only in March 1997 that Truth and Reconciliation Commission investigators, on the basis of evidence from amnesty applicants, began to unearth the bodies of executed victims on farms rented by the police near Pietermaritzburg, Camperdown, Verulam and a number of other sites. The Vlakplaas base of Eugene de Kock (former South African Police colonel, torturer and assassin, active under the apartheid government) in the Transvaal was not unusual, but part of a wider security infrastructure for the elimination of the government's political enemies. The founder of Vlakplaas was Brigadier Jac Buchner, who arrived in Pietermaritzburg to head the security police in 1987. In 1989, he was appointed commissioner of the KwaZulu Police and moved to Ulundi until his departure in late 1992.[45]

From March to August 1987, the death toll began to rise in the Pietermaritzburg region.[46] There was a hardening of the confrontation between the Inkatha vigilantes and the UDF youth organisations, particularly in KwaShange, Imbali and Mpumalanga.

Vigilantes invaded schools and armed groups were often bussed into areas in recruitment drives. On 5 and 6 May 1987, 90 per cent of Pietermaritzburg workers responded to the call from COSATU and the UDF for a stay-away in protest against the whites-only elections. This seemed to be a defeat for Inkatha and Buthelezi, who had urged his supporters to campaign against a stay-away. Inkatha blamed the success of the stay-away on the Transport and General Workers' Union, as striking bus drivers effectively made it impossible for many workers to get to work even if they had wanted to.[47]

Other factors amplified the manifestations of this national conflict in KwaShange. In September 1987, there were devastating floods that destroyed hundreds of houses in KwaShange, Vulindlela and greater Edendale. The relationship of these floods to the violence that followed is a matter of considerable conjecture. It was popularly believed that people in the Msunduzi River valley were so frustrated by the damage caused by the floods that when Inkatha launched a coercive recruiting drive, it was the last straw and they fought back. Another suggestion is that corruption in the distribution of flood relief aid led to anger directed at Inkatha and KwaZulu structures and, in turn, led to resistance to recruitment.

By the end of October, Inkatha had lost control of much of Edendale, and the centre of conflict moved to Vulindlela, where UDF comrades were making gains. By the end of December, there was heavy fighting in Vulindlela and tribal leadership was in disarray.[48] There was large-scale detention of UDF youth (nearly 400 in December) and a growing number of reports about Inkatha leaders, who were alleged to have engaged in acts of violence with impunity from arrest and prosecution.[49] The only public attempts to halt their activities were the interdicts brought against them by the legal firm Cheadle, Thompson and Haysom, acting for COSATU.

At the end of 1987, many young UDF comrades felt a flush of victory at having beaten Inkatha. The next year was to disappoint them. It was impossible for them to take on both Inkatha and the state, locally personified in the figures of David Ntombela, a KwaZulu Legislative Assembly member from Vulindlela, and Jac Buchner.[50]

At the beginning of 1988, chiefs and *izinduna* in Vulindlela were no longer performing their official functions, and agricultural work was seriously affected. Some 79 people were killed in the area in January. The extent of the disruption and fear in the region can be seen in the fact that at one stage there were no children in the pediatric section of Edendale Hospital, as parents were too scared to leave their children there. Large numbers of refugees sought refuge in safer areas or were accommodated in domestic servants' quarters in white Pietermaritzburg.[51]

An Inkatha counter-attack, named 'Operation Doom' or 'Operation Clean Up', started in January 1988. The UDF were disabled by the massive detentions and savage police reaction to any gathering. Police provided what was, in effect, back-up to Inkatha forces, so that they could move and fight with impunity. With this support, Inkatha was able to restore much of its control in the Vulindlela area. There are reports of police handing over captured comrades to Inkatha or tribal authorities, who then killed them (as in the well-documented case of thirteen-year-old Makithiza Ndlovu, killed on 1 January 1988). Inkatha also seemed to be increasingly well armed. January ended with an Inkatha invasion of Ashdown, allegedly facilitated by the security forces, who allowed an enormous meeting of 15 000 Inkatha supporters to take place nearby, at which the crowd was allegedly incited to attack the UDF and COSATU.[52]

The police established bases in the Edendale and Vulindlela areas. They complained about the difficult terrain of these areas, especially at night, but they believed they could contain the unrest.[53] Heavy police reinforcements, including KwaZulu police and 150 kitskonstabels were deployed to the 'hot spots'. Many of them were Inkatha supporters with records of involvement in previous acts of violence.[54]

As the civil war worsened, the number of refugees moving into towns and other areas increased. Many women were domestic workers in Pietermaritzburg, and they moved with their children to stay with their employers. Schooling was disrupted by the resignation of many teachers. Mtholangqondo High School in KwaShange, for example, was heavily affected by this, because almost all teachers who taught there were from outside the area of KwaShange and 'were not prepared to risk their lives, because the area was boiling'.[55]

Scholars were refused entry into schools (or were too afraid to attend), after a card system was instituted at some Department of Education and Training schools. Many KwaZulu Department of Education and Culture schools refused to accept non-Inkatha pupils. There were reports of a large drop in enrolments in schools near Pietermaritzburg, and intermittent interruptions of schooling continued in the first half of 1988.

In February, the collusion between the police and Inkatha received official blessing when the minister of law and order, Adriaan Vlok, presenting a trophy to the Pietermaritzburg Town Hill Police Station, said: 'Police will face the future with moderates and fight against radical groups. Radicals, who are trying to destroy South Africa, will not be tolerated. We will fight them. We have put a foothold in that direction, and we will eventually win the Pietermaritzburg area.'[56]

By March 1988, Vlok's police had averted the danger of total UDF victory, with the kitskonstabels, massive detentions and the round-up of youths that took place. On 21 March in Ashdown, for example, 259 people were detained, and in Sobantu there were 218 detentions.

What all this meant was that Natal in the late 1980s was divided into 'no-go' areas, under control of one or other of the contending parties. Within greater Edendale, Inkatha had lost control of the urban townships around Pietermaritzburg (except for a few small pockets), but, with police support, they had regained control of the abutting tribal area of Vulindlela.

Although emergency rule was extremely repressive and large numbers of UDF members were detained, in June there were huge COSATU- and UDF-organised stay-aways in the region. The long, low-level civil wars started to impact on UDF refugee groups, mainly in schools and church halls in Edendale, and this allowed Inkatha 'warlords' time to rally their forces. The conflict spread to more rural tribal areas, with a politicisation of what may originally have been tribal factionalism.

In September 1988, there was an abortive attempt at peace mediation in the establishment of an Inkatha and COSATU Joint Complaints Adjudication Board, its jurisdiction limited to Pietermaritzburg and Vulindlela. The murder of Nicholas Kwilili Duma of Imbali, a witness to the Complaints Adjudication Board, led to COSATU's withdrawal from the board on 8 May 1989.

This COSATU withdrawal, according to Moses Ndlovu, had negative effects. It was like pouring petrol onto a small flame. It made the Vulindlela political violence worse. The situation was already bad but, after the withdrawal of COSATU, the violence escalated. Hope for peace disappeared and it was obvious what that meant for areas such as KwaShange, Nxamalala and other regions that were UDF-aligned.

Notes

1. See www.sahistory.org.za; personal communication with Mwelele Cele, manager of Killie Campbell Africana Library, 14 August 2008; S. Marks, *The Ambiguities of Dependence in South Africa: Class, Nationalism and the State in Twentieth-Century Natal* (Johannesburg: Ravan Press, 1986).
2. Interview with Nunu Mchunu, KwaShange, 12 March 2008.
3. B. Pogrund, *Robert Sobukwe: How Can Man Die Better* (Johannesburg: Jonathan Ball, 2006), p. 276.
4. M. Buthelezi, 'Commemoration of Robert Mangaliso Sobukwe', Graaff-Reinet Civic Centre, 28 February 1998.
5. Buthelezi, 'Commemoration of Robert Mangaliso Sobukwe'.
6. Interview with Nunu Mchunu, KwaShange, 12 March 2008.
7. This tension between Inkatha and the ANC in exile has been explored in a number of studies, notably A. Jeffery, *The Natal Story: Sixteen Years of Conflict* (Johannesburg: South African Institute of Race Relations, 1997); G. Maré and G. Hamilton, *An Appetite for Power: Buthelezi's Inkatha and the Politics of Loyal Resistance* (Johannesburg: Ravan Press, 1987); Mzala, *Gatsha Buthelezi: Chief with a Double Agenda* (London: Zed Books, 1988); C. McCaul, *Towards an Understanding of Inkatha Yesizwe* (Johannesburg: Development Studies Group, University of the Witwatersrand, 1983); J. Aitchison, 'The Origins of the Midlands War' and 'KwaZulu-Natal: The Pre-election Wars of the 1990s', in *The Role of Political Violence in South Africa's Democratisation*, edited by R. Greenstein (Johannesburg: Community Agency for Social Enquiry, 2003).
8. See G. Maré, *Ethnicity and Politics in South Africa* (London: Zed Books, 1993); Maré and Hamilton, *An Appetite for Power*; Mzala, *Gatsha Buthelezi*; Jeffery, *The Natal Story*.
9. J.C. Eby and F. Morton, *The Collapse of Apartheid and the Dawn of Democracy in South Africa, 1993* (Chapel Hill, NC: University of North Carolina Press, 2003), p. 52.
10. Aitchison, 'The Origins of the Midlands War'.
11. Aitchison, 'The Origins of the Midlands War', p. 49.
12. Interview with Nunu Mchunu, KwaShange, 14 March 2008.
13. Interview with Nunu Mchunu, KwaShange, 14 March 2008.
14. Interview with Nunu Mchunu, KwaShange, 14 March 2008.
15. Interview with Nunu Mchunu, KwaShange, 14 March 2008.
16. Interview with Nunu Mchunu, KwaShange, 15 March 2008. See also Aitchison, 'The Origins of the Midlands War'; Aitchison, 'KwaZulu-Natal'; Jeffery, *The Natal Story*.
17. See interview, Walter Felgate and R.W. Johnson, *Focus*, January 1998: 20.

18. Aitchison, 'The Origins of the Midlands War'; Aitchison, 'KwaZulu-Natal'; P. Denis and P. Dlamini, 'Multi Layers of Memory: The History of Mpophomeni Told and Retold', *Alternation* 22(2), 2015: 73–99.
19. Interview with Moses Ndlovu, KwaShange, 11 August 2003; Aitchison, 'The Origins of the Midlands War'.
20. Interview with Moses Ndlovu, KwaShange, 11 August 2003.
21. Interview with Nunu Mchunu, KwaShange, 15 March 2008; interview with Chris Hlengwa, KwaShange, 14 March 2008; interview with Moses Ndlovu, KwaShange, 11 August 2003.
22. Interview with Nunu Mchunu, KwaShange, 14 March 2008.
23. Interview with Nunu Mchunu, KwaShange, 14 March 2008. See also Maré and Hamilton, *An Appetite for Power*.
24. Thabo Mbeki, 'Isikhumbuzo senkosi Bhambatha', Greytown (Ngome), 12 June 2006.
25. See also documentary on Jacob Zuma, *From Rural Inkandla to Union Buildings*, SABC 2, 10 May 2009.
26. Aitchison, 'The Origins of the Midlands War'; Aitchison, 'KwaZulu-Natal'.
27. Interview with Moses Ndlovu, KwaShange, 11 August 2003.
28. Interview with Nunu Mchunu, KwaShange, 14 March 2008.
29. Aitchison, 'The Origins of the Midlands War'. See also Maré and Hamilton, *An Appetite for Power*; Mzala, *Gatsha Buthelezi*.
30. Aitchison, 'The Origins of the Midlands War'; interview with Moses Ndlovu, KwaShange, 11 August 2003; interview with Nunu Mchunu, KwaShange, 12 March 2008.
31. P. Zulu, 'Durban Hostels and Political Violence: Case Studies in KwaMashu and Umlazi', *Transformation* 21, 1993: 1–23.
32. D. Booth and M. Biyela, 'Exploring the Spatial Dimension of Black Resistance and Political Violence in South Africa: The Case of Durban', *Urban Geography* 9(6), 1988: 629–53; D. Hindson, M. Byerley and M. Morris, 'From Violence to Reconstruction: The Making, Disintegration and Remaking of an Apartheid City', *Antipode* 26(4), 1994: 323–50.
33. D. Bonnin, 'Claiming Spaces, Changing Places: Political Violence and Women's Protests in KwaZulu-Natal', *Journal of Southern African Studies* 26(2), 2002: 301–16; D. Bonnin, 'Legacies of Political Violence: An Examination of Political Conflict in Mpumalanga Township, KwaZulu-Natal, South Africa', *Transformation* 62, 2006: 59–83.
34. Aitchison, 'The Origins of the Midlands War'; Aitchison, 'KwaZulu-Natal'. See also Bonnin, 'Claiming Spaces, Changing Places'.
35. Interview with Moses Ndlovu, KwaShange, 11 August 2003.
36. Interview with Chris Hlengwa, KwaShange, 14 March 2008; interview with Moses Ndlovu, KwaShange, 11 August 2003; interview with Nunu Mchunu, KwaShange, 12 March 2008. See also Aitchison, 'The Origins of the Midlands War'; Aitchison, 'KwaZulu-Natal'.
37. Aitchison, 'The Origins of the Midlands War'; Aitchison, 'KwaZulu-Natal'. See also Bonnin, 'Claiming Spaces, Changing Places'.
38. Interview with Chris Hlengwa, KwaShange, 15 March 2008; interview with Moses Ndlovu, KwaShange, 2003. See also Aitchison, 'The Origins of the Midlands War'; Aitchison, 'KwaZulu-Natal'.

39. Aitchison, 'The Origins of the Midlands War'; Aitchison, 'KwaZulu-Natal'. See also Bonnin, 'Claiming Spaces, Changing Places'.
40. Z. Magubane, 'Attitudes towards Feminism among Women in the ANC, 1950–1990: A Theoretical Re-interpretation', in South African Democracy Education Trust, *The Road to Democracy in South Africa, Volume 4, 1980–1990* (Pretoria: Unisa Press, 2010). See also Aitchison, 'KwaZulu-Natal'.
41. 'Buthelezi Onearly [*sic*] Arrested', *Mail & Guardian*, 8 December 1995, https://mg.co.za/article/1995-12-08-buthelezi-onearly-arrested.
42. Interview with Nunu Mchunu, KwaShange, 12 March 2009; interview with Moses Ndlovu, KwaShange, 11 August 2003.
43. Aitchison, 'The Origins of the Midlands War'; Aitchison, 'KwaZulu-Natal'; Booth and Biyela, 'Exploring the Spatial Dimensions of Black Resistance'; Hindson, Byerley and Morris, 'From Violence to Reconstruction'.
44. Malan's evidence quoted in Aitchison, 'The Origins of the Midlands War'; Aitchison, 'KwaZulu-Natal'.
45. See John Aitchison's, testimony at the Truth and Reconciliation Commission hearings, http://www.justice.gov.za/trc/hrvtrans/hrvpmb/pmb7_2.htm.
46. Interviews in KwaShange with unnamed informants.
47. Interview with Nunu Mchunu, KwaShange, 12 March 2008; interview with Moses Ndlovu, KwaShange, 11 August 2003.
48. Aitchison, 'The Origins of the Midlands War'; Aitchison, 'KwaZulu-Natal'.
49. Interview with Moses Ndlovu, KwaShange, 11 August 2003. See also Aitchison, 'The Origins of the Midlands War'; Aitchison, 'KwaZulu-Natal'.
50. Aitchison, 'The Origins of the Midlands War'; Aitchison, 'KwaZulu-Natal'; interview with Moses Ndlovu, KwaShange, 11 August 2003; interview with Nunu Mchunu, KwaShange, 12 March 2008.
51. Aitchison, 'The Origins of the Midlands War'; Aitchison, 'KwaZulu-Natal'.
52. Aitchison, 'The Origins of the Midlands War'; Aitchison, 'KwaZulu-Natal'.
53. Interview with Chris Hlengwa, KwaShange, 14 March 2008.
54. Aitchison, 'The Origins of the Midlands War'; Aitchison, 'KwaZulu-Natal'; interview with Chris Hlengwa, KwaShange, 14 March 2008.
55. Interview with Sbongile Madi, teacher at Mtholangqondo High School at the time of the violence, KwaShange, 2008.
56. Aitchison, 'The Origins of the Midlands War', p. 61.

7

Signs of Coming Bloodshed

THE STRUGGLE FOR liberation in South Africa, which started in earnest in the 1960s and carried on into the early 1990s, and political violence from the 1980s to 1996 in the Natal Midlands, left many South African societies, especially women and children, deeply psychologically wounded. This chapter explores the role of women, their place in the violence and in the production of knowledge concerning the events. Women in KwaShange are now at the heart of acts of remembrance because political wars have moved out of the battlefield and into every corner of civilian life. That is why women, as well as men, now construct the story and disseminate it. Women join men in forming a new class of historical actors, who are now termed 'witnesses', people who were there, people who saw the war at close range, people whose memories are part of the historical record. Their testimony documents the crimes they saw, but their stories and their telling of them in public are historical events in their own right. This chapter focuses upon how women in KwaShange remember and how they share their memories of *udlame* (political violence).

Zulu traditions, beliefs and practices form a network of customs that are passed orally from generation to generation and are often accepted without question.[1] For the most part, Zulu people have strong religious beliefs, traditions and customs, especially in the area of dreams, prophecies and visions. Many Zulu people believe that dreams and visions are an important part of human life that communicate messages to living people from uNkulunkulu or uMvelingqangi (God) and the ancestors.[2]

Belief in dreams and visions, however, is not exclusively Zulu, but is found in all cultures. In 1925, psychoanalyst Carl Jung, who had toured north-east Africa, recalled a conversation he had about dreams with an African traditional healer: 'I remember a medicine-man in Africa, who said to me almost with tears in his eyes: "We have no dreams anymore since the British are in the country."' When Jung attempted to find out why the British colonial presence had caused Africans to stop dreaming, the traditional healer replied, 'The District Commissioner knows everything . . . God now speaks in dreams to the British and not to the medicine-man . . . because it is the British who have the power.' From this conversation, Jung deduced that, for Africans, 'Dream activity has emigrated.'[3] According to Jung's biographer, Frank McLynn, the diviner's point was that Africans were unable to dream under colonial conditions because the European colonial administrator did all the dreaming for them, since 'power speaks to power'.[4] This dream loss was reflected in broader social, economic and political realities within which indigenous people lived during the colonial period.

Dreams and visions are indicators of what the dreamer – and probably his/her society – have reason to fear. For instance, during the colonial period, dreams revealed a changing world in which indigenous people would undergo dispossession and displacement, as well as a disruption of their traditional lifestyles.[5]

An example from nineteenth-century Xhosa life is Nongqawuse's vision, which inspired and preceded the disastrous cattle killing of 1856/1857. As a young girl, she claimed to have received a message from the ancestors that almost led the Xhosa people to commit suicide. She saw the faces of her ancestors appearing in a pool. They told her that they would drive all the white settlers out of the country. A huge wind would come up and blow all the settlers into the sea. But first, as an act of faith to prove their belief in the world of the spirits, the Xhosa would have to kill all their cattle and destroy all their crops. Xhosa religion taught that the ancestors appreciated the sacrifice of cattle because that was a man's most valued possession. Those who refused would be turned into frogs, mice and ants and would be blown into the sea by a mighty whirlwind.[6]

Close to our own times, prophecies, dreams and visions have continued to provoke debates. Renowned Zulu diviner and prophet Credo Mutwa, in an exclusive interview in *Drum* magazine, stated:

> Nontetho, a 1930s prophetess . . . was locked up in a Pretoria mental hospital where she eventually died, a sad, lonely old woman. She was not mad. This is the same woman who foresaw a great black leader who would rule over us for a short period. She called the leader Mandla. Could she have referred to Mandela who, after 27 years in prison, led the nation for only five?[7]

Then there was Thokozile Magwaza, who predicted violence in Richmond, Shobashobane and many other KwaZulu-Natal trouble spots, long before it became front page news. *Drum* magazine recorded that Magwaza had warned King Cyprian, the then Zulu monarch (Goodwill Zwelithini's father and predecessor), about looming violence among his subjects 'but she was ridiculed from one side of Zululand to the other'.[8]

Mutwa added: 'When the sun marries the moon [an eclipse], it usually precedes some disaster or other.' During one such period, he warned the apartheid architect, H.F. Verwoerd, that he saw a bayonet hanging over his head. Verwoerd dismissed the vision as nonsense, saying only blacks died by knives. Shortly afterwards he was fatally stabbed in parliament.[9]

In 1999, Thabo Mbeki was in power, but Mutwa predicted he would not see out his term in office. His prophecy was fulfilled in June 2008, when Mbeki was asked to step down by the ruling African National Congress (ANC). Mutwa also predicted the energy crisis and power cuts that swept through southern Africa.[10]

Dreams and visions have often served as warnings, guides and sometimes indications of a condition or state of anxiety of the mind. They have often been in the form of great mysteries to interpret, but they are also regarded as treasures, especially when taken up into religious texts such as the Bible. Pharaoh's prophetic dream of the seven years of plenty, followed by seven years of famine is an excellent example of a dream that is both prophetic and reflects the anxieties of a ruler.[11] In Zulu culture, dreams and visions have often served another purpose: they have been seen as a link to the mysterious space that separates man from uNkulunkulu.[12]

Dreams and visions are very much part of most Zulu people's lives and religions. They have historically been instrumental in the naming of a child and have given direction to communities as to who should be a chief or headman, for example. The latter are of particular note among members of the Shembe church, where dreams and visions are seen as communications with the spiritual realm, and there is a direct link between dreams and the elders of the church considering the next leader, as in the appointment of Vela Shembe (some members of the church dreamt that he had to become the church leader).

Dreams and visions in KwaShange affected and influenced the political history of the area. They reflected the deeper fears and hopes of the times in which the people of Vulindlela lived, before and during dispossession, displacement and trauma. The dreams discussed here are those of women who were relatively powerless, but aware of the signs of coming conflict and seeking influence in their group. These dreams were a clear reflection of the extent of the psychological effects this violence had on the KwaShange populace. The dreams were not symptoms of any primitive mentality. They were situated within the violent disruptions of an apartheid zone and during the time of an armed struggle.

Dreams and visions in KwaShange

Memories of political violence in KwaShange abound in stories about prophetic dreams and visions that people, mainly women, experienced during the period of violence.

The sharing and telling of the dreams and visions of residents of Vulindlela help outsiders to understand the atmosphere of fear and dread that prevailed and confirms the abnormal times that the residents were living in. They are evidence of the most salient signs of anxiety and the psychological effects this violence had on ordinary people.

This chapter presents five dreams experienced by women from 1985 to 1990 and recorded between 2008 and 2010. The dreamers and narrators of these dreams claim that they had these dreams and visions before the violence started and during the violence. These dreams were told and recorded long after the events of violence in KwaShange, making the possibility of a reconstruction of memories real.

Differences – even antagonisms – existed before open conflict broke out in 1987. It is likely that a half-conscious awareness of these produced some of the dreams that I record below.

MaDlomo

> I saw [in a vision] Vulindlela covered in flames of fire. A number of young and old men lying on the streets, some bodies were eaten by dogs. There were white men accompanied by multitudes of black men in traditional attire carrying shot guns and petrol bombs, who were killing men and burning houses. Women and children were all pushed to the Msunduzi River; they were drowning and I heard them screaming very loudly, asking for help, but there was no one to help them.[13]

This is a summary of a dream told by MaDlomo, a KwaShange survivor of political violence. It is typical of many dreams that were narrated by women interviewees. MaDlomo had this dream in 1985. She believes that this was a revelation of what was about to happen in Vulindlela.

MaDlomo describes herself as a devout Christian and her revelations, in fact, display remarkable similarities to those related in the Old Testament, for example, in the narrative that describes how Moses received the Ten Commandments from God on Mount Sinai. Although MaDlomo strongly supported all attempts at KwaShange youth mobilisation, she was not directly or actively involved in any political activities. But she did have political influence in the sense that leaders, including Moses Ndlovu and Nunu Mchunu, consulted her on a regular basis.[14] In particular, she was consulted in connection with the interpretation of dreams and her prayers were often requested for important decisions and meetings.

MaZuma Khanyile

MaZuma Khanyile was 68 years old when I interviewed her in 2009. She was born in Vryheid. She was the second wife of the late Vusumuzi Khanyile, who was killed in 1987 in Pietermaritzburg, when Inkatha and the United Democratic Front (UDF) fought each other. She recalled:

> In March 1985 I heard a voice talking to me, saying I must wake up, go outside and pray. I was not dreaming but I was awake. It was a voice that came from nowhere. I did so, I

> went outside and prayed . . . after about 30 minutes, I opened my eyes and I looked up in the sky. The moon was red. It was strange. I was terrified. I did not go back to sleep but I went to an old lady [MaKhumalo], my neighbour; I knocked and requested her to wake up and see the moon that looked strange. MaKhumalo was a member of the Apostolic Faith Mission. She was a well-respected old lady in the community. She looked at the moon and she began to prophesy, saying that what she saw in the moon meant that there was going to be a spilling of blood. There was going to be a war but she was not able to tell where and who would be fighting. From then we began to have women's prayer meetings in the area, every Thursday. After uManyano gatherings from our respective denominations, we would meet and pray against the evil we saw in a form of a vision.[15]

In February 1991, MaZuma Khanyile saw a vision:

> It was on a Sunday morning, I was feeding my two-year-old baby; I was feeding him soft porridge. Before I finished feeding my baby, in the very bowl I saw blood. The bowl was full of blood. I became so scared and I left it there . . . I stood up and went to call my other two kids who were outside playing children's games. I told them to come back home and I went out to tell one community leader that I suspected that we were going to be attacked that day. I do not know where that came from, but I had a strong feeling that what I saw in the bowl was meant to warn us that there was going to be an attack. I took my children and we went into hiding. The same day, in the afternoon, indeed there was an attack in the area. Luckily, some people took my call seriously and prepared themselves for the attack I had seen in a vision. On that day about seventeen of the attackers were killed in KwaShange.[16]

MaNdlovu Zondi

MaNdlovu Zondi was 65 years old in 2009. She was born in Nkandla. Her eldest son was killed in 1988 by the police as he was one of the UDF leaders in the area. Her daughter died in the same year, in the bus that was stoned in Mvundlweni (an Inkatha area opposite KwaShange). She told me:

> In June 1985, I had a strange dream. I saw the whole area of KwaShange covered with water. All houses were covered with water and people were drowning. I was outside this huge dam . . . as I was standing watching people drowning. Suddenly a voice that came from nowhere said to me, why are you standing? Run . . . I ran to the bank of this huge dam full of dirty water . . . I was running very fast . . . When I reached Zwartkop Mountain, I saw that the whole area of Inadi was full of water. It was on a Sunday night when I had this dream. The following Sunday I went to church and just before the service started I spoke to one elderly woman. I told her about this terrible dream I had had. She advised me to share the dream with church members . . . the same old lady had a gift of prophecy; she began to interpret the dream. She said the pool of water I saw was tears – she said something horrifying was going to happen in the area – women and children were going to be in such a pain. There was going to be a lot of death.[17]

MaNdlela Ngubane

In 1985, a 54-year-old woman, MaNdlela Ngubane, lost her son, Zenzele, who was eighteen years old. He was killed one night in KwaShange but to this day no one knows who killed him.

> It was in 1986; I cannot remember the day this thing started, but it was just after nine at night when my husband and I went to sleep. When I entered into my bedroom, I saw bioscope playing on the wall in my bedroom. It was a big screen; I saw violence that I had never seen in my life. The bioscope showed me the area of KwaShange. I saw people that I know fighting against each other. I saw big weapons I had never seen before. I saw houses burning . . . this bioscope continued for about ten minutes – after that I fainted, I became unconscious, I was told. When I woke up . . . it was almost midnight and some neighbours were in my bedroom, praying. Nobody else

> saw what I saw . . . my husband did not see the bioscope. The same night, I saw writing on the wall. Words were written in a language that I did not understand.
>
> This thing continued for about a month. I remember one day I was out of my house, doing some washing for my children. I heard a voice that said to me I must go my bedroom. I was terrified, but I went. When I entered, the bioscope was playing again – the same thing that I had seen was playing again. This played for about ten to fifteen minutes and it was followed by some words written on the wall. The words were written in a very strange language.
>
> It happened for the third time: this time I had gone to town. Before I finished what I was doing in town, the voice came to me: it said I must go to my bedroom. I was terrified; instead of going home, I looked for a public phone and I phoned my aunt in Mpophomeni. When I told her about this, she told me that I am mad. I must go to a diviner.[18]

One day, MaNdlela went to fetch some firewood from a forest not far from her house. It was during this day that she received her first revelation, on 9 August 1985, on the Ntabaskopho Mountain. She had already collected enough firewood and was ready to tie it together and depart for her home when she suddenly heard a voice calling her name. Her name was called three times; and then the voice told her that she should leave the firewood and rush home. The voice never identified itself but she recognised it as her late son's voice. MaNdlela doubted the voice, as she was well aware that her son was dead, but, once again, it instructed her to go quickly. In addition to this instruction, the voice also told her that when she arrived home she must go straight to her bedroom. When she arrived home, MaNdlela told her husband (who was outside the house tightening the fence) what had happened. Her husband, who obviously thought that she was talking nonsense, ignored her. She decided to proceed to her bedroom as per instruction and there, on the wall was a 'big screen' playing a sort of 'action movie'. She saw violence she 'had never seen before'. This was taking place in Vulindlela and she saw some KwaShange people. Woman and children were crying, trying to escape. When she told her husband what she had seen he ridiculed her. The following day she went to do some washing in a nearby river called the Inembe. The same voice came to her and instructed her to go to her bedroom. She did so and the same thing happened. Almost a month later, she was in Pietermaritzburg at about 10h00, when the same voice came to her and told her to go back home and go straight to her bedroom. She saw a hand, writing on a wall in a language foreign to her, not English or Afrikaans, because she could recognise those two. The movie started again, showing a house in flames of fire. It dawned on her that this was a prophetic vision. She thought that the world was coming to an end. She began going to church but she was still hesitant to discuss it with church leaders because her children and husband ridiculed her and thought that she was going crazy.[19]

These accounts reveal the gender divisions in KwaShange during the times of violence. The testimonies of these women – and the absence of men's accounts of dreams – seem to imply that dreams and visions were experienced only by women, not men. One man claimed:

> It is only women who had dreams and had time to see visions because they slept and they had time to relax . . . we men were always alert, on guard . . . there was no time to relax for us to see visions, let alone sleeping for us to dream. But these miracles [dreams and visions] helped us to know what Inkatha was planning. Our ancestors and uNkulunkulu were on our side; they kept us updated about what was about to happen.[20]

Women, in this society, saw visions and had dreams, whereas rituals and *muthi* were for males only. Dreams and visions in KwaShange are reported to have mobilised, alerted and revived people, and they played a unique role in the discourse about political violence.

These dreams and visions also reveal the abnormality of the time: times were 'muddled'. The Zulu term for 'muddled' (*dungeka*, *ukudunga*) is a metaphor derived from stirring up mud in water. Although it could be applied to a state of mind, signifying confusion, it could also be applied to the disturbance of a household by an *idungandlu* (literally, a house muddler), or the disturbance of a village by an *idungamuzi* (village muddler).[21] All of these meanings, certainly, were at play in the dreams of KwaShange women, who experienced their bodies, their homes, their families and their sense of community as 'stirred up' and under attack by forces threatening to kill them.

Although it has been claimed that violence broke out in this area only in 1987, there were undoubtedly symptoms that it was imminent in the years before 1987, and the three dreams presented here are evidence of this. When the ANC took the decision to resort to an 'armed struggle' against the apartheid regime in the 1960s, they began to plant bombs throughout the country.[22] The 1987 floods that destroyed communities in the Midlands exacerbated the political violence between the UDF and Inkatha in the area. This political strife and catastrophic weather had psychological effects on Natal and Zululand residents. It was a period of great uncertainty about the future, and, to add to this, when violence had already erupted, families turned against each other. This conflict was unprecedented in rural areas such as KwaShange.

These dreams and visions show the context of the violence experienced by non-combatants: appropriation of cattle, control of territory and the practice of torture. The recounting of dreams and visions allows people to understand and extract meaning from their experiences and to relate this meaning to their everyday lives. Two 'dreamers' envisage television screens on which violence is played out – evidence that their visions relate closely to the conditions of the modern world as they know them. In this way, dreams and visions provide a framework for understanding themselves and the world, offering a means for finding solutions, from thwarted desires to the highest spiritual aspirations, encompassing practical problems and the inconsistencies of daily life. The use of dreams and visions as instruments to mobilise political support was not merely a phenomenon of the period of political violence. During the colonial and apartheid eras, dreams and visions played a role in the struggle against oppression and in ethnic revival attempts. The same can be said in respect of recent dreams connected with political violence.

Therefore, it could be reasoned that dreams and precognitive visions of the violence indicate evidence of trauma and memory among survivors. They also indicate, firstly, the fact of a cultural continuity, in that the historical evidence shows these responses to be native to peoples of Nguni origin – in their preparations for war and modes and perception of war. Secondly, psycho-social reactions (both precognitively and in memory) towards such abnormal or 'muddled' times lead to the question – are such dreams and precognitive visions a method adopted by memories of survivors to attempt to explain such anomalies and traumatic incidents or is there is an element of foretelling involved? Importantly, although there is no scientific empirical evidence for this, Zulu culture allows for such possibilities in its belief system.

The dreams and visions of KwaShange's violence support both views. Meleko Shelembe's quote above gives insight into the function of precognitive visions – dreams and visions giving warning, with the explanation of it being an act of God and ancestors on the side of the community being warned. It is also true that such 'ominous signs' are the construct of memory to explain what the survivors have experienced.

This lends further credence to its having at least some role to play in healing, handling and dealing with trauma. If one accepts that a survivor needs to continue with 'ordinary daily life' and continue to cope, then it must also be accepted that they would need a satisfactory explanation for such a horrendous disruption of the course of that normal life. One can see the need for survivors to return to normal daily life and how the responsibility for the re-establishment of daily life would fall on women, who tend to the children's needs.

Notes

1. D. Chidester, 'Dreaming in the Contact Zone: Zulu Dreams, Visions, and Religion in Nineteenth-Century South Africa', *Journal of the American Academy of Religion* 76(1), 2008: 27–53.
2. Chidester, 'Dreaming in the Contact Zone'.
3. Jung quoted in Chidester, 'Dreaming in the Contact Zone': 28.
4. F. McLynn, *Carl Gustav Jung: A Biography* (New York: St Martin's Press, 1997), p. 282. See also B.W. Blake, *Jung in Africa* (New York: Continuum, 2005); Chidester, 'Dreaming in the Contact Zone'.
5. Chidester, 'Dreaming in the Contact Zone'.
6. J. Peires, *The Dead Will Arise: Nongqawuse and the Great Cattle-Killing Movement of 1856–57* (Johannesburg: Ravan Press, 1989). See also T. Makhura, 'Missionary and African Perspectives on the Politics of Witchcraft among the Xhosa and Zulu Communities in the 19th Century Cape and Natal/Zululand', paper prepared for the Wits Institute for Social and Economic Research, Johannesburg, 15 September 2003.
7. *Drum*, 1 July 1999.

8. *Drum*, 1 July 1999.
9. *Drum*, 1 July 1999.
10. *Drum*, 1 July 1999.
11. See King James Version, Genesis 41.
12. Interview with MaNdlela Ngubane, KwaShange, 14 March 2009.
13. Interview with MaDlomo, KwaShange, 17 April 2009.
14. Interview with MaDlomo, KwaShange, 17 April 2009.
15. Interview with MaZuma Khanyile, KwaShange, 17 April 2009.
16. Interview with MaZuma Khanyile, KwaShange, 17 March 2009. See also Chapter 8.
17. Interview with MaNdlovu Zondi, KwaShange, 15 March 2009.
18. Interview with MaNdlela Ngubane, KwaShange, 15 March 2009.
19. Interview with MaNdlela Ngubane, KwaShange, 15 March 2009.
20. Interview with Meleko Shelembe, KwaShange, 14 Septermber 2008.
21. C.M. Doke and B.W. Vilakazi. *Zulu-English Dictionary* (Johannesburg: Wits University Press, 1958).
22. Interview with Moses Ndlovu, KwaShange, August 2003.

8

Ritual Murder and *Muthi*

EIGHTEEN-YEAR-OLD Loyiso Njokweni disappeared on Christmas day in 2010 from his sister's house. He was originally from the village of Inanda, a semi-urban area outside Durban, but he was visiting his sister at the time.[1]

His headless body was discovered on 17 January 2011 and his head was found two weeks later, in a witch-doctor's freezer. The police arrested an *isangoma* and the man he had instructed to murder the boy. The *isangoma* intended to use the head, or parts of it, for *muthi*.[2]

In the surrounding areas, people were anxious to know if missing body parts of their dead relatives would also be found in this house. They were hoping to reclaim the bodies for a respectful burial and to obtain closure. Thulani Zulu explained: 'Today I have bad luck because my father was buried without his "manhood" [genitals].'[3] Another interviewee said: 'I am hoping that they will find my son's skull, left hand and arm. His children are troublesome in the community, and they use drugs. The youngest daughter has HIV; I think it is because of this problem.'[4]

Newspapers reported that almost 1 000 people marched to the house of this witch-doctor and burned down the structure when they did not find any of their relatives' body parts.[5] This was reminiscent of the ritual murders for *muthi* that were prevalent in Vulindlela in the 1980s and 1990s. The community believes that *izangoma* (diviners) and *izinyanga* (traditional healers) sold human body parts to Chief Shayabantu Zondi and David Ntombela, who were believed to be using strong *muthi*.

Traditional healers use various items that have symbolic meanings for obtaining power: for example, nail clippings, hair cuttings,[6] and faeces to make powerful *muthi*.[7] This *muthi* is then ritualised to enhance its efficacy by invoking the blessing of the ancestors. It is then considered ready for consumption, to be smoked, or scattered in or around the desired location, or burned to release the healing properties. Some kinds of *muthi* are not only used to cure disease, but can be applied to ward off evil spirits and bring good luck, mainly in business.

Many Zulu people believe that to manufacture strong medicine, body parts obtained from animals (including human beings) must be harvested when the subjects are still alive.[8] The part used for the *muthi* will retain the spirit of the animal or human, which will enhance its potency. The more difficult the problem, the more extreme the intervention and the higher up the 'food chain' the *isangoma* will go to obtain the part that will help to get the desired result.

Sometimes *izangoma* use animals for *muthi*. Moving from the use of animals to human beings, the traditional healer crosses the line from legal to illegal and indicates that he or she believes that it is necessary to solve the patient's problem.

Belief in witchcraft and ritual murder were prevalent during the political violence of the 1980s in the Midlands. The accused in the story referred to above was also implicated in ritual killings of United Democratic Front (UDF) supporters during this period.

Traditional healers and *muthi*

Muthi and associated rituals have played an important role in the lives of Zulu people for many centuries. According to Karen Flint:

> Healers provided medical, ecological, social, political and military assistance to the nation. Each king and chief in the kingdom relied on his or her own healer or healers to help obtain political power. Furthermore, the judicial system relied on healers to determine guilt for petty crimes and witchcraft as well as resolving the occasional dispute over political succession.[9]

Controversy around the use of *muthi* and the role of traditional healers in South Africa during the pre-colonial period is well documented.[10] Wars were fought not only with weapons but also with the use of *muthi*. 'Strengthening of warriors'[11] and 'doctoring of wars'[12] were regarded as more important than any weaponry. Some Zulu fiction, popular dramas and oral histories mention the prominence of traditional healers and war-doctors. Each clan and village had healers who were experts in *muthi* and rituals associated with battles.[13]

For example, the role played by the use of *muthi* has been recorded in the history of the rise of King Shaka and the establishment of the Zulu kingdom.[14] This *muthi* and the expertise displayed by Shaka's healers and diviners is said to have contributed hugely to the rise to power of the Zulus and their dominance over other prominent clans.

Even though Shaka used *muthi*, he opposed the witchcraft of others. According to Jeff Guy, the action of the sea had a strange fascination for Shaka.[15] Any person suspected of being a witch 'was required to throw his stick into the sea . . . and [the stick] of a witch never returned [with the advancing and receding waters]. The owner of the stick that never returned was in consequence killed on the spot on the grounds that he was a witch.'[16]

During the colonial period, white people, and especially the missionaries, were critical of rituals, *muthi* and the witchcraft associated with it.[17] Guy, referring to a number of court cases that took place in northern Natal where people were accused of preparing for war, reasons that colonial officials (and the missionaries) misunderstood African ritual practices and reduced all rituals of healing and strengthening to war-doctoring. Because the missionaries believed that *muthi* was immoral, they influenced the colonial officials, who rewrote some of the African customary law to have it aligned more closely with Judaeo-Christian ways. 'Smelling out' by *izangoma* was made illegal because those identified in this way were often put to death. The colonial officials tried their best to label any use of *muthi* as witchcraft. The prohibition of *muthi* and magical rituals would escalate into suppression and attack and trials, as was seen in the Bhambatha rebellion of 1906 and subsequent courts martial and trials.[18]

There are records of human body parts being used for *muthi* in the twentieth century. Warriors were strengthened or doctored to overcome their enemies. It was considered essential that liquid used for the sprinkling should contain material particles (*insila*) connected with the person of the chief whose people were about to be attacked.

Secret messengers would be sent out beforehand to obtain substances as powerful as some of the chief's hair, parings of his nails, his spittle scraped from the ground or something as innocuous as scrapings from the floors of his huts or any utensils he may have used.

Muthi was used during the Bhambatha uprising.[19] Guy dedicates a whole chapter to court cases against people who he argues were falsely accused of having performed ritual killings and used human body parts for *muthi*.[20] He felt that in most cases these accusations were not true and that colonial officials and Zulu headmen who had a grudge, or were rivals for the power of the accused, falsely blamed them for the deaths and mutilation of human bodies for *muthi*. During the Bhambatha uprising in 1906, a force of Natal Police, under Lieutenant Colonel G. Mansel, marched from Greytown along the Keate's Drift road and set up camp at Burrups. They passed through the Mpanza valley to Keate's Drift and returned that evening along the same road. Bhambatha's men were ready for them. They had been doctored for war by the war-doctor Malaza, whose medicine was designed to make them impervious to the white man's bullets.[21] Chakijana had posted them in three groups: one above a prominent rock near the road, one below it and one in a drainage ditch.[22] According to the South African Military History Society:

> At around 7 pm the police group approached along the road, unable to manoeuvre effectively as it was fenced on both sides. The advance guard, under Inspector O. Dimmock, bore the brunt of the attack. Four of his men were wounded and four (Sgt Brown, L. Sgt Harrison and Troopers Aston and Greenwood) were killed. Three bodies were retrieved (Sgt Brown's body was found later, severely mutilated) and the wounded men were placed in the carriage . . . Although two or three of Bhambatha's men were wounded, it was claimed that Malaza's medicine had saved them from death. Dinuzulu's men witnessed this and they were no doubt impressed.[23]

Muthi killing: Stories of the 1980s and 1990s

In the upheavals of the 1980s and 1990s, Natal and Zululand witnessed ritual killings and *muthi* use that involved mutilating bodies and cannibalism, not only to strengthen warriors but also to weaken their opposition. UDF supporters labelled Inkatha supporters as witches and vice versa. The UDF and Inkatha accused each other of using *muthi*.

In the past, the reaction to a witch was violent, especially among the Nguni, Tsonga and Sotho people, where death was the usual penalty, but mutilating bodies was not common. Among the Nguni, the homestead of a witch was razed by fire.[24] In Vulindlela, the consensus is that the 'old tradition' of punishment was acceptable for 'witches' although mutilation and the removal of bodily parts were perceived by some people as something that was invented by the youth as a political tool to destroy their enemies.[25] The youth were not, however, the only participants in these acts. There were many elders who were passive participants or directly involved.[26] Such acts provoked widespread horror and incomprehension.

In 1985, Anglican Archbishop Desmond Tutu spoke out against necklacing, which was being practised during the countrywide political unrest:

> If you do this kind of thing [human body mutilation for *muthi* ritual and necklacing], I will find it difficult to speak for the cause of liberation. If the violence continues, I will pack my bags, collect my family and leave this beautiful country that I love so passionately and so deeply . . . I say to you that I condemn in the strongest possible terms what happens [in black communities].[27]

The minister of foreign affairs, Pik Botha, stated that he 'would not allow the future of South Africa to be decided by perpetrators who commit these kinds of acts [body mutilation and necklacing]'.[28]

In 1985, *The Sowetan* reported that such deeds were 'becoming almost fashionable among blacks . . . this is the beginning of a terrible phase that spells doom to the black nation . . . this kind of savagery is completely out of step with the sophisticated thinking and behaviour of the twentieth century'.[29] *The Star* warned, 'The children should know from their history books that this type of thing was common in the Dark Ages and cannot be countenanced in 1985.'[30] The perpetrators of these activities were reported by *The Star* as justifying these killings, saying, 'For how long will you tell us to show mercy to these "system" people when they kill us once we are in their hands? Why don't you allow us to deal with these dogs in the same way they treat us?'[31] The perpetrators said that they were angered by attackers; in other words, these acts were caused by anger '. . . and it is not possible to do this to the victim if you are not angry enough'.[32] Other perpetrators said it was done 'in order to show others how "criminals" and "witches" are dealt with'.[33]

Some scholars who have explored political violence in the Midlands have considered it an inappropriate subject to ponder.[34] The increased incidence of *muthi* murder in times of political stress has only been documented in a few historical studies.[35] My own view is that the opposing forces saw the use of *muthi*, and magical means in general, as essential parts of their conflict. The result of ignoring these matters has meant that the reasons why warriors were mutilated and body parts mixed with *muthi* and eaten has been largely unexplored, the clichés left unquestioned. Even members of communities who were sympathetic to the use of *muthi*, and who were directly affected by the violence, will now refuse to discuss the practice and how it was used by war-doctors and warriors in the 1980s and 1990s. Although I am a former member of the Vulindlela community and a witness to much of the violence, I had the utmost difficulty in persuading former combatants to discuss these matters. Eventually, through the influence of a local *induna*, they agreed to be frank with me, but insisted on remaining anonymous. Exactly what happened is known only by people who witnessed and partook in the rituals, and those who disclosed specific details warned me not to write about them.

Other evidence of the use of magical practices is contained in Truth and Reconciliation Commission reports, police and coroners' reports and the Congress of South African Writers video footage.

Human body mutilation continued even after the violence subsided.[36] Some authors have suggested that South Africa is still witnessing what is described as an 'epidemic' of occult-related violent crime.[37] It is believed that more than 300 people have been murdered for their body parts in the last decade in this country, although some accounts put the figure far higher, with one investigation reporting that there were 250 *muthi* killings in the Limpopo Province alone in a single year.[38] The actual frequency of *muthi* murder is difficult to gauge because in a country with a high murder rate, estimated at about

43 murders per 100 000 people, it is likely that not every *muthi*-related murder is recorded as such.[39] Though predominantly a phenomenon of the country's more rural provinces, police records indicate that several *muthi*-related killings take place each year in urban Soweto.[40] In 2000, a commission of inquiry into witchcraft was set up by the government after a spate of deaths in Soweto, in which young boys aged between one and six had been kidnapped and murdered.

The South African Police Service, in an article posted on its website, linked ritual murder to the centuries-old belief that human blood and body parts are essential to the preparation of *muthi*.[41] Nonkonyana Mwelo, chairperson of the Eastern Cape branch of the Congress of Traditional Leaders of South Africa, however, claimed that he 'does not believe' human organs are being used by witch-doctors for *muthi*, and he does not see any use for body parts as *muthi* and cannot understand why bodies are being mutilated in this way other than as a result of ordinary criminality.[42] In contrast, the chairperson of the South African Council of Churches, Reverend Thivhilaheli Nedohe, stated: 'This kind of murder only shocks people who want to be shocked. If we have to go back into history, we will see that these deeds have been happening, and will persist, as long as the perpetrators continue to believe in it.'[43]

Traditional healers and the use of *muthi*: KwaShange testimonies

My own recollections

The abduction and death of Loyiso Njokweni described at the beginning of this chapter happened in Mafakatini in Vulindlela. In February 1990, about seventeen people were killed in the area and some of their bodies were mutilated for *muthi*. Of the incident, I recall:

> I found that I was obliged to hide when an attack took place. After an hour or so I came out of hiding. Walking home, I came across my neighbour, Sipho Ndlovu, and he told me: 'We have finished them' [meaning that they, as ANC supporters, had killed Inkatha vigilantes]. I did not believe him but as I walked further I was 'welcomed' by a 'stream' of blood and three mutilated human bodies, one of which had an arm, head and the abdomen cut open, and the insides were out. The other

> two bodies were butchered as well, but I was too nauseated to get closer to see what body parts had been removed. In retrospect, I have been informed by some of the informants who participated in this act, that 'manhood', i.e., genitals, had been removed for *muthi* purposes. This is the scene I have carried in my mind since then, one of three memories which are more prominent than any of the other horror images I recall from the wreckage of the KwaShange violence. This event was well covered by the media; where on 10 February 1991 an ANC 'ambush' took place in KwaShange and seventeen Inkatha members were killed.[44] The following day the police went around trying to find people who had committed the act. They asked particularly women and youngsters like me at that time. However, when they asked me what I had seen, I mentioned that I saw three dead bodies, but I had to 'close my eyes' as it was too horrible to bear.[45]

The memory of this scene was triggered by a response I received from informants in KwaShange, when I asked about the effects of the violence in KwaShange almost twenty years after the violence. MaZamisa Shange gave an insightful reply. She said:

> Do not even ask. Today we are a fragmented, cursed and sick community and we will never again be the community that we once were before this violence started. We talk all the time when we have community meetings about a number of people who were buried without some of their body parts. A number of people were killed and their bodies were mutilated and even today nothing has been done to correct that and I am telling you nothing will heal our community until those body parts are discovered. Today we have insane people [in our community] because of this revolting act . . . young people who partook . . . *thula mntaka Zamisa kungaze kuthiwe uthe* [oh! let me shut up otherwise I will be accused of divulging community issues].[46]

An elderly woman, MaNdlela Nduli, said:

> Your Jacob Zuma [assuming that I am Jacob Zuma's ANC supporter] has abandoned our community. Our children killed people during the violence. They used strong *muthi* . . . and all these other [evil] things they did. But when Mandela and Jacob Zuma got what they wanted [freedom and positions of power], they are now too busy building schools, roads and toilets. They forget the basics [rituals that need to be done after a war]. You know, those people who participated in these *muthi* rituals are now addicted to killing and harassing. Now that there are no Inkatha people to harass, they harass us, the community members themselves.[47]

An elderly man, Mancinza Zondi, added:

> Like in any other conflict, the use of *muthi* was prevalent in the civil war of the 1980s and 1990s. In fact, I can say that *muthi* was more important than any other weapon that was used. We were fighting against people who were known for using very strong *muthi*. I can tell you today that [this is] the reason why we [KwaShange] were strong and most feared by our neighbouring areas. It was not because we had big guns. No, no, no . . . but we used very strong *muthi* to strengthen ourselves and our families. There is no one in the area that did not use *muthi*. The few that refused [to use *muthi*] were all killed. I am just saying this because I want you to know what a big role *muthi* played in the war of the 1980s and 1990s.[48]

He went on to say:

> It is sad that even today we have some of our people who died and were buried without some of their body parts. We have people who were kidnapped by Inkatha people who declared them dead, but even today we do not know where they were buried. We had a baby that was stolen when she was only three months old, even today we do not know what happened to that baby; her grandparents were consumed by fire in a burning house. As a result, we have things that happened in our community of which the consequences will still persist

> until we find closure to the matter. Until then we will still have the stigma we are having today. Could you [myself as researcher] find where those body parts are? Could you talk to the communities we fought with and arrange for us to have a proper cleansing ritual?[49]

Community members stress the significance of cleansing rituals for the survivors. What happened had profound psychological effects. The people would have preferred ritual cleansing to infrastructure development. Government would have done better if it had ensured cleansing of communities by doing cultural rituals to wash away all the misfortunes incurred by youths or child warriors and older men who had killed people and used their body parts.

From the 1980s to the 1990s, at the time of the unrest, the use of *muthi*, witchcraft and magic was so prevalent and regarded as so dangerous by Zulu communities that there were dramas on Radio Zulu aimed at conscientising people. In KwaShange, Phillip Thabethe was given the alias 'Makhekhe', after one of the characters of the drama, because he was alleged to have been seen performing magic and killing his opponents to gain power as an Inkatha warlord.[50]

Generally, people who lived in areas affected by the violence were very susceptible to fear of the mysterious or unknown. They had become used to 'normal' war, where Inkatha and UDF were fighting, but they were defeated by the supernatural, where 'strange things happened'. They believed in the effects of rituals and 'medicines'. *Izinyanga* (war-doctors) were aware of the immensely powerful psychological effect of rituals and medicines on the warriors doctored for war. This belief in invincibility through 'supernatural' means and protection, coupled with their discipline and tactics, usually worked well for the KwaShange ANC warriors. However, occasionally the use of *muthi* had disastrous results – for example, when they charged opponents who had firearms, in the belief that their doctored shields were impenetrable to bullets.

When talking to me, some interviewees indicated that certain leaders used *muthi* that had a lot of magic. They believe that the kind of *muthi* used was acquired outside South Africa. Some people in KwaShange believed that Inkatha leaders got their *muthi* from Mozambique. For instance, Innocent Dlamini was one of the most feared leaders of Inkatha in the area because of his cruelty. He killed many people in the KwaShange area, even before the political violence between Inkatha and the UDF started in 1986. Many people who were known to have resisted taking Inkatha membership, and who were opposed to the idea of making every community person a member of Inkatha, feared him.

Discussing his fate, Vikizitha Mbanjwa said:

> It was on a Friday, September 1987; I had just come into the area on the 5 pm bus. I saw Brahman [Amon Kubheka] across the uMsunduzi River. He was herding his cattle. I was so terrified because I had never expected to see him there. I felt dizzy . . . in less than a minute he was right in front of me. His cattle were where he had been on the other side of the river. This is where he stabbed me [showing his big scar]; luckily a group of young men, my neighbours who were just passing by, noticed and they came to assist me – I managed to escape.[51]

A group of five interviewees described a similar occurrence:

> It was on a Saturday morning before 6 am in 1987 – after Chief Shayabantu [Zondi] had attacked and killed people in KwaShange – we saw his car, a Ford Cortina, going through KwaShange to *Induna* Guvaza Khanyile's homestead. We ambushed the chief, having all kinds of ammunition you can think of. Our intention was to kill him. We hid under the bridge. We saw his car come from a distance: he was driving very fast but when he was just about to pass the bridge, we all fell asleep. When we woke up, the car had already passed.[52]

Thulebona Zuma said:

> In 1990, after the Seven Days' War, when many people were still in refugee camps in Edendale, because we had a lot of time doing nothing at home [as young men] we were hurting that David Ntombela and his people are having a nice time [at Elandskop] while our people were struggling in refugee camps. We decided to attack him, in revenge for what he

> and his people had done. We left here on Friday night, we had invited some uMkhonto weSizwe soldiers to come and assist us to 'finish' with Ntombela. We went there . . . when we were just about to arrive at Ntombela's homestead, strong mist came from nowhere . . . we got mystified, we couldn't see [Ntombela's homestead] anymore but instead we saw a big dam where David Ntombela's homestead was. We began quarrelling among ourselves and we almost killed each other on our way back.[53]

Muthi murder is only one component of this belief system, which underpins other magical phenomena, such as the appearance of a *tokoloshe* and mythical dinosaur-like creatures, with the power to magically transform a human being into an apple, or a homestead into a dam and gun bullets into grapes.[54]

The mutilation controversy

On 10 February 1991, Inkatha attacked the ANC-aligned community of KwaShange. MaMthimkhulu Khanyile was awakened in her house at Mpumuza, near Sweetwaters in the Midlands, by a distraught Manzini Zungu, who had just escaped the attack at KwaShange. MaMthimkhulu and other neighbours who had relatives in KwaShange immediately gathered together and set out to the scene of the disaster.[55] Her description of what she saw there provides a vivid insight into the aftermath of the KwaShange ambush:

> As we approached the area a fearful and horrible sight presented itself, and the stillness of the spot was awful; there were our men lying all about the place, some naked and some only half clad. On the opposite side of the road I need not attempt to describe to you what I saw; all the bodies were full of spear wounds and nearly all of them were disembowelled . . . I did not see not even one body that was not mutilated.[56]

The accounts of MaMthimkhulu and other survivors of the KwaShange 'ambush' mirror the sense of shock that KwaShange survivors of the incident felt upon their return to their homes, after hiding in river banks and valleys: 'We saw the dead bodies of men strewed about on every side, and horribly mutilated.' MaZamisa observed: 'Our children mutilated them and pierced them with spears all over their bodies.' Thina Madlala, a KwaShange resident, noted that 'every man who was killed or wounded was ripped up, and his bowels torn out'.[57] To suffer a sudden, unexpected and astonishing catastrophe was bad enough, but the treatment of the dead understandably angered those who witnessed it. 'It was enough to make your blood boil,'[58] commented one (anonymous) man. 'To see men cut open, the worst ever was done in the violence in the Midlands,' said a retired policeman who was called just after the ambush. Vulindlela Inkatha supporters offer bizarre explanations, which hint at witchcraft practices and even cannibalism.

There is a good deal of current information about the treatment of the dead from local traditional healers' sources – about the practices themselves, and with specific reference to this clash between Inkatha and the ANC. The warriors of both Inkatha and the ANC repeatedly stabbed, disembowelled and mutilated the bodies of the rival party's men killed in action. They were in pursuit of three distinct post-combat rituals, all of which reflected the extent to which death in combat was regarded as an important part of interaction with the spirit world.[59]

A feature common to the descriptions of all the informants was that the dead of both sides often bore multiple stab wounds. In the fierce frenzy of action, it is likely that many enemies were stabbed more than once before they fell because despite the Zulu warrior's famed expertise with their stabbing weapons, it was probably impossible to dispatch an enemy with a single clean thrust, especially if he was parrying with his own weapons. Given the large wounds made by the blades of the stabbing spears and the bullets, the act of inflicting death itself was likely to be messy.[60] Bodies were also stabbed again after death in a practice known as *ukuhlabana* or *ukuhlomula*.[61] Ian Knight says this was less to do with mercy to a fallen enemy (delivering the final and fatal blow) than it was a desire on the part of warriors to mark their role in the kill.[62]

Members of the ANC and Inkatha all came from communal and traditionalist mindsets, which were reinforced by complex pre-battle rituals, intended to bind the army together as a whole.[63] In action, therefore, those men who had been involved in the fighting, but had not actually killed an enemy, were entitled to some part of the 'glory' attached to the victory. In particular, the old practice of *ukuhlabana* had evolved in the hunt; after cornering and dispatching a particularly dangerous animal, the act of participation was recognised when the men each came up and stabbed the dead beast.[64] While the man who had actually killed it was allowed his particular share of the glory, *ukuhlabana*, or stabbing the corpse after it was dead, reflected the participation of the other members of the hunt.[65]

The same rule applied in warfare, particularly when fighting an enemy who had stood his ground bravely and had therefore been a dangerous opponent. Mancinza Zondi, an ANC warrior who fought against Inkatha during the KwaShange ambush, explained:

> Indeed we stabbed our opponents, even those who had already been stabbed and were lying down. This is called *abahlabana*; then again those *abahlabana* became more numerous by reason of the fact that we had been fighting such formidable opponents. This custom was observed here [KwaShange] because it was recognised that fighting against such fearsome enemies and killing some of them was of the same high grade as lion-hunting, because Inkatha had SAP [South African Police] support, and they were known to be using strong *muthi* supplied by their war-doctors.[66]

With regard to the second ritual, namely the custom of disembowelling a fallen enemy, termed *ukuqaqa,* this was directly related to the traditional Zulu view of the spiritual realm and its relationship with the world of the living. Prior to embarking on a campaign, the warriors were prepared for war in a complex set of rituals that set them aside from civilian life,[67] and protected them against the harmful effects of *isinyama* (or literally 'darkness') – the harmful spiritual consequences that flowed from shedding human blood. They could not return to ordinary society until they had undergone parallel cleansing ceremonies at the end of the campaign, for fear of contaminating their families with *isinyama.*[68] As part of the cleansing rituals, certain practices had to be observed with regard to the bodies of men who had been killed in battle. Specifically, it was necessary for a warrior to remove part of the clothing of a man he had killed and to wear it until he had undergone the necessary cleansing ceremonies. This practice was known as *ukuzila* – abstention from everyday life while in a dangerous state of spiritual pollution.[69] Men who had killed in battle, but who had not yet been cleansed, were known as *izinxeleha*. Those who had particularly distinguished themselves by their tally in battle were said to be wet with yesterday's blood. As part of these observances, it was also necessary to slit open the stomach of the enemy.[70] In the hot sun, any corpse begins to decompose quickly, and the gases given off by the early stages of decay cause the stomach to swell. In Zulu belief, this was the soul of the dead warrior, trying to escape to the afterlife. The man who killed him was obliged to open the stomach in order to allow the spirit to escape. If he did not, he would be haunted by the ghost of his victim, who would inflict various horrors upon him, including causing his own stomach to swell, until eventually the killer went mad. To allow the spirit free passage, a cut was made vertically down the stomach, from the sternum to the groin.[71]

Ngubane, the present-day traditional healer of KwaShange, suggested that, as part of the ritual, it was necessary for the killer to run the blade of his spear along his own tongue, touching the blood. The purpose of this remains obscure, but probably has to do with the killer gaining supernatural ascendancy over his enemy by ritually 'eating' his spirit. It is perhaps no coincidence that the warrior's cry of exultation is '*ngadla*' (I have eaten).

The fact that both practices were followed in Vulindlela and elsewhere in Natal and KwaZulu is verified by the accounts of traditional healers. Mzila, an *inyanga* and descendant of Bhambatha Zondi's war-doctors said:

> It is the custom for one man killing another to take off the deceased's things and put them on, even the penis cover. He mourns with them by so doing . . . If he has killed two or more, he will take articles from each and put them on. He will not put on his own things until the doctor has treated him and given him medicines . . . to cleanse him from contagion or war killing. We took the ANC things at Vulisaka; they were all stripped. This was done to mourn them.[72]

It is not clear whether the disembowelling was always carried out in the immediate aftermath of the victim's death, or later, once the full fury of the fighting had passed. Certainly, at least some bodies were disembowelled immediately after death.

Details and rules of the normal practices of 'doctoring'

Interviewees from both the ANC and IFP disclosed that they never went to war without being specially strengthened by war-doctors in their respective communities. This process took a few days and began as soon as all the warriors had arrived at the secret gathering place.[73] The purpose was to 'bring together the hearts of the people'. Rituals were performed entailing sprinkling troops with liquids with magical properties, the bare-handed killing of a bull and the disposal of the carcass in prescribed ways, and the cleansing of the individual warriors by inducing communal vomiting through the use of emetics and ablutions.

In battle, it was often preferred that the victim remain alive during disembowelment. When body parts, including internal organs, were removed while the victim was still alive, it was believed that the power of the resultant medicine would be enhanced. Harvested body parts are usually mixed with other medicinal plant matter or cooked. The product is sometimes eaten, but may also be carried by the person who aims to benefit from its power. The use of human body matter in the production of traditional medicine does not always involve killing; for instance, a living person's nail clippings or hair cuttings may secretly be collected, or already dead bodies may be exhumed and used for *muthi* purposes.

The normal practices of 'doctoring' consist of three aspects: the 'doctoring' and protection of the individuals in a war zone, the 'doctoring' or strengthening of an army or *impi* and the cleansing ceremonies after a battle.

No warrior would go to war unless he had first taken some *muthi* for protection. He would go to the place where *muthi* was kept, usually in a war-doctor's homestead, to fortify himself. Warriors also had to abstain from sexual intercourse. Anybody who was injured or had a wound was not allowed to take part in certain rituals or use certain kinds of *muthi*. This was one of the main reasons why women were not allowed to be near the area where *muthi* rituals were being practised, let alone take part in them. Women are said to have a 'natural wound' – they are born with it [the vagina] – and this disqualifies them from participating. They are also believed to be 'weak'; it is believed that they cannot keep secrets to themselves. When cornered by rivals, they could easily tell the enemy what *muthi* the warriors used. Discussing the kind of *muthi* used with 'outsiders' would be dangerous, because, if rivals knew, they could apply the same *muthi* or find *muthi* specifically to counter this *muthi*.

Prominent war-doctors of Vulindlela

Some war-doctors took advantage of the times, and, regardless of where they were located, they opportunistically assisted groups that promised to pay more. Sometimes an *inyanga* situated in an Inkatha area secretly gave *muthi* to ANC warriors, and vice versa.

Inkatha had a number of war-doctors they trusted. These included Jamile in Durban, and Mchunu, who lived in the neighbouring KwaMpande area. They also consulted with Mbanjwa in Richmond, in the ePhatheni area. Khangela Zondi in Mvundlweni was a brutal war-doctor. My informants claimed that every day in Mvundlweni, Inkatha people used to jump through huge flames of fire during daylight, so they would be seen in order to intimidate the people of KwaShange.[74]

Other war-doctors in KwaShange were Gabuza, who was also an expert on lightning and rain-doctoring, and Mchunu, who was the most feared war-doctor in Vulindlela. His son, Senzo, was a supporter of the UDF. In 1987, when Inkatha attacked UDF supporters in Vulindlela, Senzo, like many other UDF youth supporters, sought refuge in Edendale. After almost a year, he went home to visit his parents and Inkatha attacked and killed him. This angered Mchunu the war-doctor and he secretly approached the UDF in KwaShange, intent on avenging his son. He told the KwaShange people what kind of *muthi* Inkatha was using at that particular time and he gave them (the ANC in KwaShange) the same *muthi*, which disempowered Inkatha warriors and made the KwaShange ANC warriors the strongest and most feared.

Body parts used for *muthi*

One anonymous informant, who participated in a ritual murder, said:

> We did it [ritual murder]. It had to be done; otherwise we were not going to win. We were going to be finished [by the

> enemies] . . . we captured one of them; we were instructed [by the war-doctor] that we should not injure the person because *muthi* does not work if the person is already dead. We took him to a stream. We cut his genitals, left eye, left hand and when he was dead we cut open his abdomen and removed the liver and heart.[75]

Mthandeni Dlamini described the killing of his son in 1989 in KwaShange:

> My son (fifteen years old) – Thulani's severed head, arms, legs and genitals were found in a forest, neatly packed separately, in black plastic rubbish bags. It was obviously *muthi* murder. We suspect that Inkatha killed him with the purpose of using his body parts for *muthi* purposes. This was common here.[76]

A person whose body parts were selected to be used for *muthi* was not supposed to have any scar on his body and he was not supposed to be injured. The body parts had to be removed while the person was still alive, so that those who took the body parts would be more powerful. When the person cried while they cut the body parts, the sounds would 'be heard' by the community he belonged to and that would make them lose the battle. They preferred to obtain body parts from the man who was leading the warriors but, because of the nature of violence, they usually did not know who the leader was, so they ended up mercilessly cutting anybody's body parts.[77]

The rival group the deceased man belonged to would be disempowered by the *muthi* mixed with his penis and testes. When the testes were mixed with *muthi*, the rival *impi* would all drink the *muthi* and call the name of the enemy camp and say negative things about them, to weaken them. Each person would be expected to roar like a lion and proclaim '*ngahlabana*' (fight). Everyone who had taken part in this ritual would be expected to stab an enemy, even if he was already lying down injured or dead.[78]

The left hand had to be removed and was used to stir *muthi* and sprinkle warriors with *muthi*. They used the skull to sit on. Someone prominent in the community had to sit on the skull while the battle was in progress, otherwise they would be defeated by the enemy.

They also removed the eyes of the enemies because they believed the eyes could be mixed with *muthi*, called *nkungwini*, which would make their enemies see mist or a dam or something else, but not see them. The eyes would be mixed with other *muthi*, which would confuse the attackers and they would end up fighting themselves. Inkatha was known to be strong on this *muthi*. David Ntombela had been attacked several times, but his assailants, the UDF supporters, could not win because of the *muthi*. He drove confidently and alone in Edendale, without bodyguards.[79] Inkatha was known to have a powerful medicine, *babengadubuleki* (a charm against gun bullets). Even if you tried to stab such people with a spear, it would not work.[80]

The liver and heart were mixed with a certain unnamed substance and the combatants had to drink this mixture. This was aimed at making them brave and vicious when faced by the enemy.

Taboo and unwritten cultural ethics

Despite the diversity of existing traditions, stories and memories, the topic of *muthi* and magic is still taboo in Zulu society. The dramas played on Radio Zulu mentioned earlier attempted to break this taboo. They enabled the exploration of issues of power and violence in a way that was both public and intensely private. The airing of a topic as feared, as secret and yet as pervasive as witchcraft was opened up for debate, even though there was often official silence. As an insider to Zulu culture, I am aware that by trying to understand the details of the subject, I am breaking an unwritten 'law', an issue of cultural ethics.

All the people I spoke to, especially those who participated in violent activities, were reluctant to talk about their use of *muthi*. People were most reluctant to talk about cases of actual anthropophagy on the part of warriors even though I did my best to reassure interviewees, saying *Lokhu kuphakathi kwami nawe* (This is between you and me). Informants would say, *Ungayithikuxu* (Do not tell anyone), *Ufunelani ukwazi, uzokwenzani uma usuwazi* (Why do you want to know, what are you going to do with this?). Others would say *Ngizokutshela kodwa uma usungithutha ngiyothi angazani, angikutshelanga* (I am going to tell you, but when you discuss this with other people, I will deny it and say I do not know, I never discussed this thing with you) or *Akukhulunywa ngo muthi* (You do not tell anyone about *muthi* you used).

I have therefore protected the anonymity of my informants on this matter. The primary reason for these informants' fears may be the sensitivity of the subject because war *muthi* involves human body parts. People are scared to talk about it because further questions may be asked, such as, did you personally take part in the ritual? If the victim had to be alive during the process, does this not constitute murder? The South African Police have dossiers and the reports of pathologists who had to stitch up victims before burial but these records are not accessible, even to researchers.[81] If someone is arrested and there is evidence against him, he goes on trial, but it is believed that he can use *muthi* to escape the consequences. In KwaShange, community members believe this is why David Ntombela and many Inkatha leaders, known to have committed violent crimes, were not sentenced.

The warriors who participated in these rituals and the families of people whose body parts were removed are still psychologically affected. They believe that even today, after the war, they carry the stigma associated with these rituals and that it affects them every day. After the battle, or when the violence came to an end, it was important to conduct cleansing ceremonies, but only a few families were able to do this.

Notes

1. *The Witness*, 31 January 2011; see also *Daily Sun*, 31 January 2011.
2. *Daily Sun*, 31 January 2011. *Muthi* refers to medicine that not only heals or destroys the physical body but also helps people and leaders to usurp (political) power from rivals and kin. In the context of war, *muthi* helps to fight and defeat rivals or enemies. My interviewees generally cited any success by a rival group during attacks as evidence of the use of *muthi*. Acquisition of proper *muthi*, and the powerful doctors (*izinyanga*) who administered it, were considered essential to Vulindlela during the violence.
3. Interview with Thulani Zulu, KwaShange, 29 January 2011.
4. Interview with MaNzimande Ngubeni, KwaShange, 29 January 2011.
5. *Daily Sun*, 31 January 2011; *The Witness*, 31 January 2011; *Echo* 31 January 2011.
6. L. Vincent, 'New Magic for New Times: Muthi Murder in Democratic South Africa', *Tribes and Tribals* 2, 2008: 43–53.
7. Interview with Senzesenkosi Mkhize, Richmond, 13 June 2010.

8. Interview with Senzosenkosi Mkhize, an *inyanga*, Richmond, 13 June 2010.
9. K. Flint, *Healing Traditions: African Medicine, Cultural Exchange, and Competition in South Africa, 1820–1948* (Ohio: Ohio University Press, 2008), p. 67.
10. See Flint, *Healing Traditions*; A.T. Bryant, *Zulu Medicine and Medicine-Men* (Cape Town: C. Struik, 1966); J. Brownlee, 'Account of Amakosa, or Southern Caffers', in *Travels and Adventures in Southern Africa, Vol. 1*, edited by G. Thompson (London: Henry Colburn, 1827).
11. In Zulu this is called *ukuqiniswa kwamabutho*.
12. In Zulu this is called *ukunyangwa noma ukuqiniswa kwempi*.
13. Flint, *Healing Traditions*. See also Bryant, *Zulu Medicine and Medicine-Men*.
14. Webb and Wright in Flint, *Healing Traditions*.
15. J. Guy, *The Destruction of the Zulu Kingdom: The Civil War in Zululand, 1879–1884* (Pietermaritzburg: University of Natal Press, 1994).
16. M.M. Fuze, *The Black People and Whence They Came: A Zulu View*, translated by H.C. Lugg and edited by A.T. Cope (Pietermaritzburg: University of Natal Press and Durban: Killie Campbell Africana Library, 1979), pp. 62–3.
17. See, for example, P. Chabal and J.P. Daloz, *Africa Works: Disorder as Political Instrument* (Oxford: James Currey, 1999); P. Delius, 'Witches and Missionaries in the Nineteenth Century "Transvaal"', *Journal of Southern African Studies* 27(3), 2001: 429–31; L. Vail (ed.), *The Creation of Tribalism in Southern Africa* (Oxford: James Currey, 1989).
18. J. Guy, *The Maphumulo Uprising: War, Law and Ritual in the Zulu Rebellion* (Pietermaritzburg: University of KwaZulu-Natal Press, 2005). See also B. Carton, *Blood from Your Children: The Colonial Origins of Generational Conflict in South Africa* (Pietermaritzburg: University of Natal Press, 2000).
19. T. Magwaza, Y. Seleti and M.P. Sithole (eds), *Freedom Sown in Blood: Memories of the Impi Yamakhanda: An Indigenous Knowledge Systems Perspective* (Polokwane: Ditlou Publishers, 2006). See also J. Guy, *Remembering the Rebellion: The Zulu Uprising of 1906* (Pietermaritzburg: University of KwaZulu-Natal Press, 2006).
20. Guy, *The Maphumulo Uprising*.
21. South African Military History Society, 'Newsletter No. 328', KwaZulu-Natal Branch, October 2002, http://samilitaryhistory.org/2/d02octne.html. See also Guy, *The Maphumulo Uprising*.
22. South African Military History Society, 'Newsletter No. 328'. See also P.S. Thompson, *Bambatha at Mpanza: The Making of a Rebel* (Pietermaritzburg: P.S. Thompson, 2004).
23. South African Military History Society, 'Newsletter No. 328'.
24. D. Hammond-Tooke (ed.), *The Bantu-Speaking People of Southern Africa* (London: Routledge & Kegan Paul, 1947).
25. Interview with Nunu Mchunu and Chris Hlengwa, KwaShange, 24 March 2009; interview with Mhlekwa Ndawonde and MaZamisa Shange, KwaShange, 11 April 2010.
26. Interview with Nunu Mchunu and Chris Hlengwa, KwaShange, 24 March 2009.

27. Quoted in J. Ball, 'The Ritual of the Necklace', Research Report for the Centre for the Study of Violence and Reconciliation, March 1994.
28. Quoted in Ball, 'The Ritual of the Necklace'.
29. Quoted in Ball, 'The Ritual of the Necklace'.
30. Quoted in Ball, 'The Ritual of the Necklace'.
31. Quoted in Ball, 'The Ritual of the Necklace'.
32. Quoted in Ball, 'The Ritual of the Necklace'.
33. Quoted in Ball, 'The Ritual of the Necklace'.
34. Ball, 'The Ritual of the Necklace'.
35. See, for example, J. Comaroff and J. Comaroff, 'Occult Economies and the Violence of Abstraction: Notes from the South African Postcolony', *American Ethnologist* 26(2), 1998: 279–303; J. Comaroff and J. Comaroff, 'Alien Nation: Zombies, Immigrants and Millennial Capitalism', *South Atlantic Quarterly* 101(4), 2002: 779–804; J. Comaroff and J. Comaroff, 'Policing Culture, Cultural Policing: Law and Social Order in Postcolonial South Africa', *Law and Social Inquiry* 29(3), 2004: 513–45.
36. M. Wa Afrika, 'Patient's Penis Skinned in *Muthi* Murder', *Mail & Guardian*, 29 May 1998. See also J. van Niekerk, 'Failing or Future: Responding to the Sexual Abuse of Children', *SA Crime Quarterly* 3, 2003: 11–16.
37. Comaroff and Comaroff, 'Occult Economies and the Violence of Abstraction'.
38. Vincent, 'New Magic for New Times'.
39. Vincent, 'New Magic for New Times'.
40. A. Nicodemus, 'Soccer Fan Brutally Killed for Muthi', *Mail & Guardian,* 11 June 1999.
41. http://www.saps.org.za/7-crimeprev/7-sangoma2.htm; http://www.factnet.org/cults/Sangoma/index.html. See also Comaroff and Comaroff, 'Policing Culture, Cultural Policing'.
42. 'Two Held for Cape "*Muthi*" Killing', *Cape Argus*, 8 August 2006.
43. Vincent, 'New Magic for New Times': 45.
44. *Sunday Tribune*, 17 February 1991; *Sunday Star*, 17 February 1991. See also M. Mchunu, 'Culture Change, Zulu Masculinity and Intergenerational Conflict in the Context of Civil War in Pietermaritzburg (1987–1991)', in *From Boys to Men: Social Constructions of Masculinity in Contemporary Society*, edited by T. Shefer, K. Ratele, A. Strebel, N. Shabalala and R. Buikema (Cape Town: UCT Press, 2007).
45. My testimony during Father Lapsley's Healing of Memories Workshop, Pietermaritzburg, 2005.
46. Interview with MaZamisa Shange, KwaShange, 14 March 2010.
47. Interview with MaNdlela Nduli, KwaShange, 14 March 2010.
48. Interview with Mancinza Zondi, KwaShange, 14 March 2010.
49. Interview with Mancinza Zondi, KwaShange, 14 March 2010.
50. See L. Gunner, 'Wrestling with the Present, Beckoning to the Past: Contemporary Zulu Radio Drama', *Journal of Southern African Studies* 26(2), 2000: 223–37.
51. Interview with Vikizitha Mbanjwa, KwaShange, 12 October 2010.
52. Interview with a group of anonymous men, KwaShange, 12 October 2010.
53. Interview with Thulebona Zuma, KwaShange, 12 October 2010.

54. Interview with Nunu Mchunu, KwaShange, 14 March 2009; interview with Chris Hlengwa, KwaShange, 14 March 2009; interview with a group of ten Inkatha members, Mpumuza, 17 February 2010; interview with MaZamisa Shange, KwaShange, 11 June 2010. See also Comaroff and Comaroff, 'Alien Nation'; Comaroff and Comaroff, 'Policing Culture, Cultural Policing'.
55. Interview with MaMthimkhulu Khanyile and Manzini Zung, KwaMpumuza, 13 October, 2010.
56. Interview with MaMthimkhulu Khanyile, KwaMpumuza, 13 October 2010.
57. Interview with Thina Madlala, KwaShange, 11 April 2009.
58. The Zulu expression '*ukushiselwa igazi*' is equivalent to 'make your blood run cold' in English.
59. Interview with Nunu Mchunu, KwaShange, 19 March 2009; interview with Chris Hlengwa, KwaShange, 19 March 2009. See also I. Knight, *Brave Men's Blood: The Epic of the Zulu War, 1879* (Barnsley: Pen & Sword, 2006).
60. Interview with Mancinza Zondi, KwaShange, 19 March 2010; Knight, *Brave Men's Blood* states the same about the Anglo-Zulu War of 1879.
61. Interview with Mancinza Zondi, KwaShange, 19 March 2010; interview with Nunu Mchunu, KwaShange 20 October 2010.
62. Knight, *Brave Men's Blood.*
63. For Inkatha see A.T. Bryant, *The Zulu People as They Were before the White Man Came* (Pietermaritzburg: Shuter and Shooter, 1949); H.L. Samuelson, *Zululand: Its Traditions, Legends, Customs and Folk-lore* (Pinetown: Mariannhill Mission Press, 1930); R.C.A. Samuelson, *Long, Long Ago* (Durban: Knox, 1929). See also Guy, *The Maphumulo Uprising.*
64. Interview with Nunu Mchunu and Mancinza Zondi, KwaShange, 20 October 2010; interview with Nelson Zondi, Engome, 2004.
65. Interview with Nunu Mchunu and Mancinza Zondi, KwaShange, 20 October 2010.
66. Interview with Mancinza Zondi, KwaShange, 20 October 2010.
67. Interview with Nunu Mchunu and Mancinza Zondi, KwaShange, 20 October 2010; Knight, *Brave Men's Blood*; Guy, *The Maphumulo Uprising.*
68. Knight, *Brave Men's Blood*; Guy, *The Maphumulo Uprising.*
69. Knight, *Brave Men's Blood*; Guy, *The Maphumulo Uprising.* This was also confirmed by Nunu Mchunu and Mancinza Zondi.
70. Knight, *Brave Men's Blood*; Guy, *The Maphumulo Uprising.*
71. Interview with Ngubane (traditional healer), KwaShange, 21 October 2010. See also Knight, *Brave Men's Blood*; Guy, *The Maphumulo Uprising.*
72. Interview with Mzila, Engome, 24 September 2004.
73. During political violence warriors met in secret places, where nobody knew where they were except other warriors; this was mainly because when police came they usually asked children where older people were. In most cases, children would disclose the hidden information without suspecting anything. This was the main reason why warriors had to hide. The rituals were normally performed at night, in some cases at the house of the *inyanga,* or in the field, hill, river or valley, depending on the kind of *muthi* they used.
74. Interview with group of twelve men, KwaShange 14 May 2010.
75. Interview with anonymous informant, KwaShange, 19 April 2008.
76. Interview with Mthandeni Dlamini, KwaShange, 15 November 2009.

77. Interview with Ngubane (traditional healer), KwaShange, 14 May 2010; interview with Mdunge (traditional healer), KwaMpande, 15 May 2010; interview with Ndlala (traditional healer), northern Zululand, 15 June 2010.
78. Interview with Ngubane (traditional healer), KwaShange, 14 May 2010; interview with Mdunge (traditional healer), KwaMpande, 15 May 2010; interview with Ndlala (traditional healer), northern Zululand, 15 June 2010.
79. Interview with Fanozi Ndlovu, Edendale, 17 May 2010; interview with a group of twelve men, KwaShange, 14 May 2010; interview with Moses Ndlovu, KwaShange, 18 August 2003.
80. Interview with Fanozi Ndlovu, Edendale, 17 May 2010.
81. 'Police Tell of Muthi Murder', *Daily Dispatch*, 30 October 2001, Vincent, 'New Magic for New Times'; see also Comaroff and Comaroff, 'Policing Culture, Cultural Policing'. In 2008, I was denied access to records of *muthi* murders and suspected cannibalism by the police authorities in Pietermaritzburg.

9

The Aftermath and Ritual Cleansing

DURING THE CONFLICT in Vulindlela, which lasted more than ten years, many young males were drawn into armed conflict as active combatants. The political violence left many people, young men in particular, 'damaged in their spirits'.[1]

After the gradual subsiding of the violence, in the climate of exhaustion within the KwaShange community and the general will to leave behind what was increasingly seen as destructive madness, there was a great need for reconciliation between opponents and reintegration of the community.

Background

During the political violence, male children as young as fourteen were trained to fight and defend their families. They participated in killings and in rituals associated with war. These men, then adolescents, who earned respect for their heroism in the 1980s, are now regarded as villains and are ostracised by their communities. Linda Williams suggests that a society under stress, in violent conflict, will have higher rates of depression, anxiety, panic and violence. If, as is often the case in war-torn societies, the conflict has continued, or has broken out sporadically for years, violent behaviour may eventually become *accepted* and may be common to large portions of the population, and thus may be considered a cultural phenomenon.[2] Maria Schuld notes that post-conflict societies sometimes experience levels of violence comparable to those in time of civil war.[3] Adam Curle notes that in societies torn by civil conflict alienation tends to escalate into post-traumatic stress syndrome. Violence generally continues to exist within the social fabric of societies coming out of conflict for decades or even centuries after the war.[4]

Biomedical psychotherapeutic notions of mental distress and trauma constitute 'Western' social and cultural constructs, which may often be ineffective in contexts where cultural beliefs and world views are different.[5] The biomedical approach to war trauma should thus be regarded as only one of several ways of dealing with post-war healing, since there are other ways of understanding health and healing in post-conflict situations, which are culturally prescribed and favoured by the victims and communities themselves.

Trauma is a worldwide phenomenon, but little research has been done on how it presents itself in different cultures.[6] Remedies for trauma are often culturally specific and imported remedies may be ineffective in South African communities damaged by violence.

There is a need to understand trauma from a non-clinical perspective, which is informed by an African cultural belief system. In Vulindlela, trauma is conceptualised as *ukuhlukumezeka*. This implies a disruption between the supernatural and natural domains of life. This disruption appears in anthropological literature as stigma or contagion, which is believed to make people vulnerable to traumatic events, such as political violence, poverty, unemployment and HIV/AIDS. Such traumas are understood to rupture social relations. For many KwaShange Zulu people, trauma, rather than being an individual condition, is seen as a general consequence of a disruption in the balance between the supernatural and natural/social worlds.[7] The discourse of trauma is central to social functioning and it is possible to understand mental health as a socio-cultural construct.[8] In terms of this view, to ensure efficacy, an approach to healing should include therapeutic strategies that draw on the appropriate world views.

Historically, trauma interventions within the Zulu context took into account local understanding, as well as the indigenous capacity for dealing with 'social scars'.[9] Although research has been conducted in the area of trauma among victims of violent crime in South Africa,[10] little attention has been paid to the way in which individuals construct and theorise their traumatic experiences and the impact that these explanations have on the healing process. This chapter will investigate the traditional understanding in KwaShange of the traumatic violence of the past and how this impacts on the individual's socio-cultural view of reality.

The methods of ritual cleansing after battles that are employed in traditional Zulu society are not unique but are mirrored elsewhere in traditional societies in Africa, Asia and Australia.[11] The debate in South Africa, however, is whether these methods of dealing with trauma can be relied upon or whether contemporary Western-style trauma counselling should be preferred to traditional Zulu ways of dealing with post-traumatic stress disorder (PTSD). A large proportion of the country's population is rural and still wedded to traditional culture. Even when they reside and work in urban areas, the same appears to be true. Traditional counselling methods have major advantages in comparison to other types in that the individuals being treated have confidence in the processes, which are informal and less intimidating, allowing patients to be more at ease and less uncomfortable and alienated.

Battle fatigue

Dominant Western psychotherapeutic models are often seen as universal and applicable everywhere. However, this assumption has been challenged as Western psychology is also a culturally constructed system. Modern psychology locates the causes of psycho-social distress within the individual and devises responses that are primarily based on individual therapy.[12] Recovery is achieved through helping the individual 'come to terms' with the traumatic experience and healing takes place in private sessions aimed at 'talking out' and externalising one's feelings. War-related PTSD was recognised in the 1980s in the United States and was based on research carried out with veterans of the Vietnam War.

The situation may be different in other socio-cultural contexts. Jo Boyden and Sara Gibbs have shown that in Cambodia, individual therapy conducted by modern psychotherapists can be ineffective because it does not account for the part that ancestral spirits and other spiritual forces play in the causation and healing processes.[13] By focusing exclusively on the individual, family and community efforts to provide support and care are undermined. Studies on healing war trauma in Mozambique have shown that recalling the traumatic experience through verbal externalisation as a means of healing is not always effective.[14] In many instances, people would rather not talk about the past and prefer to start afresh after certain ritual procedures, which do not necessarily involve verbal expression, have been performed.

In KwaShange and in other areas affected by political violence in the Natal Midlands, the vast majority of young men who were born during the political violence are between 23 and 26 years of age at the time of writing. There is also a sizeable group of those who were 'heroes' in the Vulindlela conflict. For these young men, trauma is not 'post', but rather 'current', and part of their everyday life.[15] Most of the population of KwaShange is still living with the ongoing aftermath of violent and traumatic circumstances. There is a need to adapt biomedical models to the day-to-day situation experienced by these people.

Understanding war trauma

In Zulu culture, there are particular ways of understanding war trauma. People believe that war-related psychological trauma is directly linked to the anger of the spirits of those killed during the war. These spirits are called *imimoya emibi* (spirits of those who did not have a proper burial, which would place them in their proper positions in the world of the ancestors). Such people are believed to be unsettled and bitter, likely to cause harm to their killers or to passers-by.[16] In Vulindlela, this is a common understanding. Many people interviewed mentioned that the spirits of people killed during the violence – especially those that died in February 1991 – had to be appeased, to ensure peace.

Ritual pollution, known as *insila*, is an important aspect of post-war healing in Zulu cultural understanding. Pollution may arise from being in contact with death and bloodshed. Individuals who have been in a war, who killed or saw people being killed, are called *banequnga* (polluted by the wrongdoings of the war). They are seen as the vehicles through which the spirits of the dead might enter and afflict the community. These spirits may afflict not only the individual who committed the offences but also an entire family or group. After the war, when combatants and refugees return home, they are believed to be potential contaminators of the social body. The spirits of the dead can disrupt life in their families and villages. The cleansing process is seen as a fundamental condition for collective protection against pollution and for the social reintegration of war-affected people into society.[17] In KwaShange, this did not happen immediately after the war. People who participated in the February 1991 KwaShange 'ambush' were regarded as especially polluted. Some community members attributed disasters that followed to a lack of cleansing, but others believe that Inkatha buried their dead with strong *muthi* in their graves so that the person who killed them would be cursed.

The traditional concept of warriorhood

I use the archaic word 'warrior' because in traditional Zulu thinking there are a number of complex ideas surrounding the word – particularly concerning the reasons why males conform to traditional military roles. Some men in KwaShange claim that they did not take part in political violence because they wanted to destroy or kill; they claim they sought to observe traditional warrior values 'to protect their community from the unruly behaviour exhibited by Inkatha'.[18] Warriors were driven by a conviction that if they had to kill, they needed transcendent reasons to do so.[19] Throughout history, the only reason for fighting that has survived moral scrutiny is the fear of a direct attack with a real, immediate threat to one's people. Almost all cultures, past and present, have had warriors and have also had stories and rituals to help them recover from combat and guide them through life. The presence of warriors is so universal that many psychologists understand 'warrior' to be one of our foundational psycho-spiritual archetypes.[20]

In traditional cultures or communities such as KwaShange, men and boys who participated in violent activities were defined as warriors. This was not the same as being a professional soldier. Warriors were not members of a huge, anonymous military institution used for the violent execution of political ends. Rather, a warrior was one of the foundational roles that kept a community whole and strong. Warriors were fundamentally protectors, not destroyers.[21]

Warriors, however, were not so highly valued or nurtured in KwaShange after the violence, and they were often not accorded social status. A veteran, especially one who in the process of defending the community lost his opportunity to go to school, participated in strengthening rituals, or smoked dagga (cannabis), appears to many, and sometimes to himself, as a failure in terms of normal civilian identity.

Impacts of violence and case studies of the cleansing of former warriors

Father Benedict Mbhele is a leader of the Roman Catholic Church in Vulindlela and a trained psychologist. He interacted with some former warriors in KwaShange. He told me that culpability, worthlessness, ostracisation from the community and life itself was the legacy that the 1980s to 1990s political violence left to young warriors in KwaShange.[22]

Nobuhle Zungu, a social worker who specialises in trauma counselling at the University of KwaZulu-Natal, comes from KwaShange. Her family was deeply affected by violence. Zungu came into contact with some of the former warriors immediately after the violence came to an end. She says:

> Dealing with young men who were traumatised (using 'Western' psychotherapeutic techniques) because of the 1980s violence was an impossible mission – it just did not work. Because I come from a family that deals with similar kinds of issues in a cultural way, I advised families of my patients to consider using cultural therapeutic means – these rituals are what my family did to all of us at home. As a trauma counsellor, I still go back to cultural means of dealing with my own past issues.[23]

Rather than feeling that their participation in defending their community had restored their families' honour, these former warriors spent years ravaged by nightmares, homelessness, drug and alcohol abuse and sitting with guns at 'the ready',[24] first, because they are wanted by relatives and friends of people they killed or second, because of crimes they committed in the area.[25]

Oscar Khanyile's story: An example of the impact of violence

Oscar Khanyile was sixteen years old in 1987 when he participated in 'defending the KwaShange community from Inkatha'. He feels that, as a former warrior, he does not fit into the new South Africa. The only place he belongs to is 'prison or six feet underground'.[26]

I asked him why he was active while still so young, as he could have opted not to participate. 'I wanted to finally be accepted as one of the community's respectable guys,' Khanyile answered. 'Participating in a fight against ill-doings of Inkatha cronies in a righteous cause would expunge my family's past (they were seen as newcomers, insignificant in KwaShange) and earn a place in the community.' He did not know that by becoming a young warrior he would return with *isinyama nokuhlukumezeka* (PTSD) and feel less than ever like 'one of the respectable guys'.[27] He went on: 'Participating in a war or violence on a battlefield fosters stigma at home. When we participated in wars related to the struggle, we inevitably brought its *isinyama* stigma and horror back to our homes. We could not help it.'[28]

Khanyile claims he has been trying to find the will to end it all. He never married but has five children with three different women. He neglects his children and cannot keep a job. He could not come back to his family homestead because he had never been cleansed.[29]

War echoes down the generations. We all carry the wounds of war, known or hidden. Khanyile was wounded by his father's participation in the conflict and his own. He has been ostracised by the community and now his children, in turn, are wounded by his history.[30] When a warrior suffers from PTSD, his entire family and community are inevitably affected. Many former warriors have symptoms of PTSD, which include sleep disturbances, substance abuse, depression and problems with intimacy, employment and authority. The same trauma was mentioned by interviewees in other areas affected by this violence, for example, Shobashobane, Zingolweni and Richmond, where political violence survivors and former warriors suffer similarly.

Traditional ways of ritual cleansing and reconciliation.

Ukukhumelana umlotha is a Zulu proverb that describes ritual cleansing and reconciliation of people who have fought or have been enemies. Traditionally, the two parties would be guided by an elderly woman. After formal discussions and reaching an agreement, the old woman would take them to a ploughed field and the parties would eat ash and wash each other's hands.[31] This process is called *ukuthelelana amanzi*;[32] some people call it *ukuhlambulukelana* or *ihlambo* (to wash each other's hands).[33] Zenze Mkhize and four elderly women interviewed in KwaShange understand *ukuthelelana amanzi* or *ukukhumelana umlotha* as a process, not an event.

War poisons the spirit and warriors return contaminated. This is why, among the Zulu and in other traditional cultures, returning warriors are usually put through significant rituals of purification before reuniting with their families and communities.[34] In traditional cultures, it was believed that unpurified warriors could be dangerous. Even in modern societies, the absence of rituals to reintegrate a warrior into a peaceful community helps to explain why suicide, homicide and other destructive acts occur among former warriors.

Warriors could be freed from the nightmares resulting from the human blood on their hands.[35] As in the case of individual cleansing, communities would, under the supervision of an acknowledged healer (*inyanga*), undergo treatment, including *izintelezi* (a medicinal mixture for expelling and keeping certain evil spirits at bay), *imibhemiso* (a medicinal mixture for inhalation), *imbiza* (a medicinal mixture for internal cleansing by vomiting and otherwise expelling unhealthy substances) and *amakhubalo* (herbal remedies recommended for healing, recovery or prevention of ailments and evil spirits).

The blood and other parts of a beast (preferably *imbuzi emhlophe* – a white goat), which has been selected, dedicated and slaughtered under the eyes of the officiating *inyanga*, form part of the *ihlambo* (a medicinal mixture for the cleansing and purifying ritual), celebrated around the fireplace in the main hut until shortly before sunrise.[36] Other animals, preferably *izinkomo* (cattle), are slaughtered and *utshwala* (beer) is brewed for the feast on the following day, at which every neighbour, stranger or well-wisher from afar is welcome.

In traditional cultures, warrior-cleansing was often guided by diviners and traditional healers, and a particular traditional healer presided over 'warrior medicine'.[37] A diviner was responsible for overseeing the spiritual lives and well-being of the society's warriors and communicating with ancestors on behalf of the warriors and communities concerned. Slaughtering an animal was considered to be the most important of all the activities.[38]

The actual ceremonies arranged by individual families in KwaShange resemble the rituals described but they are not identical to it. Sipho Nxele, a former warrior, exhumed bodies of enemies from graves to get their body parts and then reburied them. He felt as though he had 'dirtied and damaged his soul'.[39]

KwaZulu-Natal government's intervention

In 1994, the KwaZulu-Natal government realised that even though some families had performed cleansing rituals, anger and resentment among communities still existed. The government established peace committees within communities, but the efforts of the peace committees to mediate a peace process always ended after a short period and fights erupted.

The Premier's Office of KwaZulu-Natal, in partnership with other government departments, such as Safety and Liaison and Arts and Culture, requested the organisation Sinani to help them organise cleansing ceremonies in a culturally acceptable way.[40] The aim of these ceremonies was 'to calm down the spirits of the dead and build up a climate of peace'. The two parties, Inkatha and the African National Congress (ANC), met to try to finally break the deadlock of war and make peace possible.[41] Provincial cleansing ceremonies, for the most part effective, were carried out. In Richmond, five representatives from each of the four political parties worked together and managed to stop political violence in the area. In Umbumbulu, about 40 traditional leaders and councillors worked actively together to bring peace among the nine villages in this area. In Estcourt, peace-making strategies were initiated by religious leaders, who managed to draw in the political leadership of the area. The peace in Estcourt is fragile and the leaders are working hard to ensure that it deepens.[42]

On 7 November 2010, the KwaZulu-Natal government, working with some people in Vulindlela, organised a community ritual cleansing and reconciliation ceremony. This was aimed at bringing about peace and reconciliation to families, neighbours and residents in the areas where there had been fighting in the 1980s and 1990s due to their political alignment. This ceremony received wide public attention because of the nature of the violence in Vulindlela, but it did not go unchallenged by Inkatha.

Also in November 2010, the national government's campaign to cleanse the communities that were at war in the 1980s and 1990s moved to Vulindlela. State President Jacob Zuma, KwaZulu-Natal Premier Zweli Mkhize, the Zulu monarch Goodwill Zwelithini, and Chief Sondelani Zondi from Vulindlela were present. In their speeches, they emphasised their deep commitment to *ukubuyisana* (reconciliation) in very convincing terms. The national, provincial and local leadership of Inkatha had said it was not going to participate in the cleansing ritual and reconciliation ceremony.

The Zulu monarch, in his address, affirmed the good intentions expressed by the hosting communities. He admonished young and old, reprimanded grumblers and troublemakers and encouraged the reconciling communities to continue steadfastly in their efforts. Representatives of mainstream religious communities, such as Christianity, Islam and Hinduism, as well as *inkolo yendabuko* (ancestral religion) and *abakwaShembe* (an indigenous faith society, the Nazarene Baptists) opened with prayers.

As I was standing watching the process of cleansing and listening to the speeches about reconciliation, I began to question whether this was a fitting way of carrying out this ritual. I left the stadium and went to KwaShange to ask survivors' opinions. I conducted interviews with members of the community who were directly touched by the violence.

Muzikayifani Khumalo, a KwaShange violence survivor, said:

> I did not know about it. I only heard this morning on the radio that Jacob Zuma is coming and the king [Goodwill Zwelithini] . . . No, no! Even if I heard, I am the last person who would have set my foot there. What reconciliation? What reconciliation? What cleansing? Who is cleansing whom? [He is crying.] Look at my condition right now – you see [referring to his mud house].[43] Is he [David Ntombela] prepared to return my cattle? Is he going to return our cattle? How can you speak of reconciliation . . . Macingwane, if people who looted our homes and our property are known and they live [a] good life and we are still struggling because of their doings?[44]

Makhosonke Mshengu replied:

> I knew about this meeting, last week there was a loud speaker when our headman encouraged community members to attend. He said he got the instruction from *komkhulu* [the chief]. I did not go. I want to be honest with you – I did not attend. How do you say sorry to a person who lost his relative

> because of you? I think what happened – happened and there is nothing we can do now. My brother was killed in front of his wife and children and since then things never got back to normal . . . I do not think that going there would have made any difference. I was drinking at home . . . life goes on.[45]

Zodwa Ntsusha said:

> I can only reconcile if Inkatha supporters tell me who killed my father and, more importantly, if they were to tell the truth about where his body parts are hidden or buried. I would like those to be exhumed and be buried properly. My mother spent every cent she had consulting with diviners and traditional healers trying to see if they can help us to find closure, but it did not happen – she passed away in 2003 and left us with stigma. I finished Standard 10 [Grade 12] but I do not have money to further my studies. My elder brothers are alcoholics. The eldest brother is not well, he often gets terrible headaches – he has a gun bullet that cannot be removed from his head because of Inkatha. I cannot find employment – I have a stigma because no proper ritual was done after my father's death.[46]

Some survivors disapproved of the cleansing ritual and reconciliation ceremony and it was not a success for everyone. Instead of healing survivors, some felt that they were re-wounded. Firstly, some people did not know about the gathering. Secondly, concerned communities were not given time to prepare. Reconciliation is not an event; it is a process. Communities that were at loggerheads claimed that they felt aggrieved because they still do not know the truth about what happened. National, provincial and local leaders of Inkatha and the ANC, whose speeches incited people to violence, never apologised to the victims. The Inkatha leadership even refused to go before the Truth and Reconciliation Commission. This was an indication that they were not prepared to tell the truth and/or reconcile with their former enemies. I concur with the statement made by Albert Mncwango of Inkatha that 'not enough ground work has been done to prepare the people in the area [for the gathering]. The IFP and the ANC still have a lot of issues to talk about.'[47]

I believe that truth-telling is a precondition for reconciliation. It creates opportunities for people to see the past in terms of shared suffering and collective responsibility. In the case of Vulindlela, both Inkatha and ANC supporters suffered, and they have a collective responsibility to bring about peace in the area for the sake of future generations. More important, still, is the recognition that victims and offenders are members of the same community and simply have to get on with each other.

The leadership of both parties in the conflict should help the community of Vulindlela to reach agreement; partnership appears more sensible than sustained conflict. Common interests may be found in roles and identities that cross former lines of division, such as religion, gender and generation or region. Empathy, however, does not lead to a fully harmonious community. Conflicts and controversy are part of all human communities. Moreover, empathy does not exclude the continuation of feelings of anger and resentment, nor does it require that the victims be ready to forgive and forget. Pardoning the offenders will, of course, broaden the basis for empathy, but for some victims it may be too distant, or too sudden, a goal. To pursue it relentlessly may result in an abrupt end to the entire reconciliation process. At this stage, it may be unjust to ask victims to forgive if perpetrators do not express regret and remorse, as has been the case in Vulindlela.

Notes

1. Words of an elderly woman in KwaShange, who preferred to remain anonymous.
2. L.M. Williams, 'Adult Memories of Childhood Abuse: Preliminary Findings from a Longitudinal Study', *APSAC Advisor* 5(3), 1992: 19–22.
3. M. Schuld, 'The Prevalence of Violence in Post-Conflict Societies: A Case Study of KwaZulu-Natal, South Africa', *Journal of Peacebuilding and Development* 8(1), 2013: 60–73.
4. A. Curle, *Another Way: Positive Response to Contemporary Violence* (Charlbury: Jon Carpenter Publishing, 1995).
5. There is a degree of remarkable similarity in beliefs and healing practices after a war, across Africa. See A. Honwana, 'Sealing the Past, Facing the Future: Trauma Healing in Mozambique', in *The Mozambique Peace Process in Perspective*, edited by J. Armon, D. Hendrickson and A. Vines (London: Conciliation Resources, 1998).
6. Honwana, 'Sealing the Past, Facing the Future'.

7. See S. Ndlovu, 'Trauma, Identity and Culture among Rural isiZulu Speakers', unpublished paper presented at Critical Method Nine, Durban, 2004.
8. L.A. Barnett, 'Critique, Culture and the Cough: Examining Conceptualisations of Healing', unpublished paper presented at Critical Method Nine, Durban, 2004.
9. Honwana, 'Sealing the Past, Facing the Future'.
10. V. John, 'Natal's War: Monitoring Internal Refugees and Assessing Their Distress', unpublished report, Centre for Adult Education, University of Natal, Pietermaritzburg, 1990. See also P. Denis, R. Ntsimane and T. Cannell, *Indians versus Russians: An Oral History of Political Violence in Nxamalala (1987–1993)* (Pietermaritzburg: Cluster Publishers, 2010).
11. Honwana, 'Sealing the Past, Facing the Future'.
12. J. Boyden and S. Gibbs, *Children and War: Responses to Psychological Distress in Cambodia* (Oxford: INTRAC, 1997).
13. Boyden and Gibbs, *Children and War*.
14. Honwana, 'Sealing the Past, Facing the Future'. See also A. Vines, *Renamo: Terrorism in Mozambique* (York: Centre for Southern African Studies, University of York, 1991).
15. C. Nordstrom, *A Different Kind of War Story* (Philadelphia: University of Pennsylvania Press, 1997). Carolyn Nordstrom researched war and violence in Mozambique. She emphasises the point that violence in Mozambique continued well beyond military attacks, land mines and direct war situations and she touches on the backlash of poverty, hunger and displacement.
16. Honwana, 'Sealing the Past, Facing the Future.'
17. Honwana, 'Sealing the Past, Facing the Future'.
18. Interview with Moses Ndlovu, Chris Hlengwa and Mancinza Zondi, KwaShange, 2003 and 2009.
19. E. Tick, 'Heal the Warrior, Heal the Country', *Yes! Magazine*, 20 May 2008, http://www.yesmagazine.org/issues/a-just-foreign-policy/heal-the-warrior-heal-the-country.
20. Tick, 'Heal the Warrior, Heal the Country'. See also A. Honwana, 'Negotiating Post-War Identities: Child Soldiers in Mozambique and Angola', in *Contested Terrains and Constructed Categories: Contemporary Africa in Focus*, edited by G. Bond and N. Gibson (New York: Westview Press, 1999).
21. Interview with Mancinza Zondi, KwaShange, 12 June 2010.
22. Interview with Father Benedict Mbhele, leader of the local branch of the Roman Catholic Church. Similar cases were noted by Tick, 'Heal the Warrior, Heal the Country'.
23. Personal communication with Nobuhle Zungu, University of KwaZulu-Natal, Pietermaritzburg, 2009.
24. Tick, 'Heal the Warrior, Heal the Country'.
25. Personal communication with ex-combatants in KwaShange.
26. Interview with Oscar Khanyile, KwaShange, 14 March 2010.
27. Similar responses were noted by Tick, 'Heal the Warrior, Heal the Country'.
28. Interview with Oscar Khanyile, KwaShange, 14 March 2010.
29. Interview with Oscar Khanyile, KwaShange, 14 March 2010.
30. Tick, 'Heal the Warrior, Heal the Country'; interview with Oscar Khanyile and his uncle Sdumo Khanyile, KwaShange, 12 June 2010.

31. Interview with Zenze Mkhize (traditional healer), KwaVulindlela, November 2010.
32. Interview with Zenze Mkhize (traditional healer), KwaVulindlela, November 2010. See also A-I. Berglund, *Zulu Thought-Patterns and Symbolism* (London: Hurst and Company, 1976).
33. B. Khumalo-Seegelken, 'Cleansing and Reconciling in Southern Africa Today', http://www.benkhumalo-seegelken.de/dokumente/UkuBuyisana_2011.doc.
34. Interview with Ngobese (traditional healer), Impendle, 14 August 2010.
35. Interview with Zenze Mkhize (traditional healer), KwaVulindlela, November 2010. See also Khumalo-Seegelken, 'Cleansing and Reconciling in Southern Africa Today'.
36. Khumalo-Seegelken, 'Cleansing and Reconciling in Southern Africa Today'.
37. Interview with Ngobese (traditional healer), Impendle, 14 August 2010.
38. Interview with Ngobese (traditional healer), Impendle, 14 August 2010.
39. Interview with Sipho Nxele, KwaShange, 14 March 2010.
40. Sinani facilitates intensive residential workshops that make use of small group support to offer a space for people to reflect on their lives. The workshops cover a sharing of an overview of one's life, discussing particularly painful past experiences, dealing with anger, dealing with loss, personal reconciliation, making decisions and goal-setting for the future (see https:// www.survivors.org.za).
41. https://www.survivors.org.za.
42. https://www.survivors.org.za.
43. Khumalo's house was burnt in March 1990 during the Seven Days' War. He never recovered from this. His son, who was a teacher, was killed in one of the KwaShange attacks in 1988, allegedly by Inkatha supporters because he refused to join Inkatha youth meetings.
44. Interview with Muzikayifani Khumalo, KwaShange, 10 November 2010.
45. Interview with Makhosonke Mshengu, KwaShange, 10 November 2010.
46. Zodwa Ntsusha is 26 years old. She was born in 1986 during the violence. Her father was killed when she was only five years old; interview with Zodwa Ntsusha, KwaShange, 10 November 2010.
47. Albert Mncwango, IFP national spokesperson, *The Witness*, 11 November 2010.

10

Remembering the Violence

WHEN MEMORY IS viewed with reference to past events, the way in which memory represents these events can deviate from reality in many ways. An event or character stored in memory can be, and often is, altered by time and influenced by perception. This book focuses on the history of political violence and how it is remembered by survivors: it relies heavily on oral sources and memories of the turmoil. How the interviewees remember violence has been affected by national, provincial and local discussions about 'forgiving and forgetting' the atrocities of the 1980s and 1990s, which are still topical in Vulindlela and the province of KwaZulu-Natal. Issues of national or community memory have been privileged so much that they undermine individual survivor's memories.

Memory has a role in the construction of history. Even the way a person is questioned about an event can alter the memory being retrieved. Also, memory is only concerned with what has been remembered, not what has been omitted. Thus, there can be variance between what has been recounted and what actually occurred. Memory is not merely a passive representation of events that occurred.

Memory of trauma is even further removed from actual experience, since 'what occurs is not integrated into experience or directly remembered, and the event must be reconstructed from its effects and traces'.[1] All memories undergo similar transformation. Just as personal memory is filtered through other experiences, 'official' or sanctioned state memories also alter, based on changes in political regimes.

The ambiguities of collective approaches to memory

Memorial projects or commissions, such as the Truth and Reconciliation Commission (TRC) urge people to reconcile and forgive each other for their wrongdoings. People may not necessarily forget the past because their government has told them to. Memories persist, even if they are not in line with the popular expectations of leaders or government officials.[2] Surely the erection of memorials is prescribed remembering – how then can the victims forgive and forget? Yet, it is supposed to be for healing.

After the first democratic elections in South Africa, there were a number of initiatives intended to reconstruct memories of violence to aid the healing process.[3] The government introduced projects such as the TRC, commissions of inquiry and commemoration projects, which are usually employed to revisit and recompose memories.[4] This notion of having one national memory has been criticised. Jaspal Singh and Rajendra Chetty state that this idea of a collective approach to memory is problematic because memory, like truth, is subjective and dependent on the experiences of individuals. 'There can never be one whole [memory], that the idea of collective history and memory is fraught with complications, and that . . . the production of any history narrativising the past always contains an element of fiction,' they claim.[5]

Brandon Hamber and Richard Wilson label the collective approach to memory initiatives, such as the TRC, as 'a hostage to their own memory' and therefore as obstructions to the process of selective forgetting advocated by reconciling national political leaders. They challenge the call by the then state president, F.W. de Klerk, for South Africans to simply 'let bygones be bygones'.[6] Elsewhere, Hamber argues that 'it is critical that victims are not expected to forgive the perpetrators, or forget about the past because some form of reparations (or comprehensive report on the nature and extent of past violations) has been made'.[7]

Kgereshi Mokwena agrees that a collective approach to memory initiatives, such as the TRC, tacitly implies that pursuit of national unity is a unitary and coherent process, which it is not, in fact, and that the national process of dealing with the past and individual processes of dealing with the past are largely concurrent and equivalent. A national process of uncovering and remembering the past is said to allow the country to develop a common and shared memory, and, in so doing, it creates the sense of unity and reconciliation for its people.[8] Mokwena argues:

> The collective approach refers to an initiative, for instance by an entity such as a government, to reconstruct and represent memory through the use of a Truth Commission, commissions of inquiry and projects such as public memorials and monuments. Such a move is believed to be helping the nation to develop a common and shared memory which is pivotal to the enhancement of unity and perhaps reconciliation, as in the case of South Africa. In some cases, the collective process would seek to re-enact one memory for the entire nation and individuals within it, in spite of their different experiences.[9]

Hamber and Wilson state that the collective national approach to memory reconstruction ascribes a collective identity to a nation, an identity of a traumatised people,[10] and this makes it dubious. National processes, such as the TRC, fail to recognise that each of the traumatised individuals live in a world of his or her unique circumstances. This results in the national process failing to take account of the individual's personalised trauma, especially if the process was a high-profile initiative, handling well-known cases involving high-profile political activists.[11]

A similar dilemma was noted in smaller communities, where people who had committed atrocities in their past were expected to join hands with the victims and work with the state to promote peace and harmony in the country, forgive each other and forget all the wrongs done against them.

This coerced forgetting was rejected in some local communities. In 2009, I was requested by the community to organise a committee that would express their views about their unhappiness at the KwaZulu-Natal government's announcement of the erection of a Heroes Arch in Slangspruit.

When I raised questions on behalf of my community as to why victims of the war in rural Vulindlela were ignored with regard to these memorials, I was told to raise it on the right platform. There had been reports in 2012 about a large monument to be built in 2019 in Imbali to commemorate the victims of political violence. People in other areas surrounding Pietermaritzburg, equally affected by the violence, were left wondering why they were excluded. One example of how a collective approach to memory can go wrong is the Peace Monument erected in Imbali in 1998 in honour of those who died during the violence. The choice of the location of the monument confounded people from neighbouring areas. Families of the victims and the people of Vulindlela were disappointed and frustrated by this act of government. Many residents of KwaShange expressed their discomfort about the African National Congress (ANC) government selecting where political violence was to be remembered. Many people said that Edendale was given more attention for everything, including services: '*Asisezukuyivotela i-ANC thina, sikhathele*' (We are not going to vote for the ANC, we are sick and tired [of being treated this way]).[12]

Sabine Marshall reasons that 'the government invests in monuments to achieve specific objectives . . . In South Africa, the government tends to assume a particular strong and somewhat paternalistic role, where government officials see themselves as public representatives who must develop strategies and make decisions on behalf of and in the interest of "the people" who elected them.'[13]

Nonjabulo Khumalo, a political activist in KwaShange, who was part of the group I interviewed, expressed her unhappiness: '*i-ANC esayilwela, sayilwela sisebancane. Uhulumeni osimele sonke thina esalwela umzabalazo kodwa iqhakambisa abantu baseyiDeni abahlukumezeka. Thina? . . . Thina?*' [she was in tears] (The ANC we fought for, we fought for from our very young age, our own government has singled out Edendale victims of violence [as if they were the only ones] . . . What about us? What about us? [from neighbouring KwaShange]).[14]

This is a shared view among many KwaShange victims of violence. Since emotional healing requires space for individuals to reflect and heal at their own pace, collective processes, such as the TRC, seem to take away that individual space by emphasising a collective approach. This may submerge individual memories under the collective's uniform memory.

Thus, single programmes initiated on a national scale may not, in practical terms, be in a position to deal with the trauma experienced by every individual throughout the country and especially not with the trauma of people in small communities, where the sense of 'nation' is weak. Even the much publicised TRC could not attain that kind of influence.

Organisations such as Sinani and the Khulumani Support Group thus took upon themselves the responsibility of filling in the obvious gaps and providing psychological support to victims and survivors of violence at the individual level.[15] The TRC Evaluation Report, compiled by Khulumani and the Centre for the Study of Violence and Reconciliation, states that the TRC's national programme for healing was far above the individual survivor's needs level and could not deal with their trauma and healing.[16] The victims' memorial in Imbali was the ruling party's initiative and represented the party's views and agenda as opposed to the full history and the healing needs of the victims of the violence. Most victimised families in Vulindlela thus boycotted it. In KwaShange, interviewees said that they were not consulted on how to commemorate or where the commemorative structures were to be built, nor was there consultation on the name of the memorial.

A similar debate occurred regarding the reconciliation and cleansing ceremony in November 2010 in Vulindlela, which was intended to commemorate the victims of the violence and reconcile communities that were at loggerheads.[17] According to interviewees in Vulindlela, the memorial ceremony was conducted by local, provincial and national politicians, without the local peoples' knowledge.[18] Many complained that the memorial and reconciliation ceremony aggravated their trauma, since hearing about the memorial revived terrible memories. Some said that they went to the extent of organising to disrupt the ceremony because it would re-traumatise them and perpetuate the haunting experiences and memories, instead of helping them in their personal healing. Yet, the memorial was supposed to be 'the community's' way of commemorating those who died from 1987 to 1996. It does not seem as though individual survivors were regarded as members of 'the community', since many of the directly affected survivors were excluded.

The politics of the Midlands violence was extremely complex and memorials should have reflected this if they claimed to aim at the healing of memory. It was, however, seen by most of the community as a partisan process biased towards the ANC; this in spite of some of these very victims having been supporters of the ANC. Supporters who found they now live in the 'wrong' zone to be remembered cannot depend on the government for their trauma to be recognised or assuaged. Many interviewees believed the violence would rekindle. Thus, it is best to recall none of it, rather than recall a one-sided picture of such terrible experiences.

Counter-collective memories and individual memories

In KwaShange, people were reluctant to participate in national and provincial initiatives to create community memorials. They did not participate in the TRC; they opposed the memorial in Imbali; and they opposed the memorial, cleansing and reconciliation ritual organised by the national and provincial governments in 2010 in Vulindlela.

One of the reasons is that in 1991, when KwaShange ANC combatants killed seventeen Inkatha combatants, Harry Gwala, the ANC leader in the Midlands in the 1990s, promised that the ANC government would erect a memorial stone in KwaShange to honour those 'heroes' that fought in the battles [and killed Inkatha combatants] but no one in the ANC-led government has implemented Gwala's vision.

Another reason seems to be anger at giving equal recognition to Inkatha since Inkatha leaders were considered 'traitors':

> Inkatha betrayed black people and the struggle in general. How could we submit names of our people to the Imbali memorial where in the same memorial stone there is a list of names of Inkatha members; who are we fooling here? Whose story should be told?[19]

The attitude displayed by some KwaShange residents counteracts the government's large-scale plan. Daniel Bouchard reasons that counter-memory can exist in opposition to the official (hi)story:

> Individuals who do not subscribe to the dominant memory, who refuse to forget or remember what it prescribes, become part of society's counter-hegemonic groupings. Their memories exist in private spaces and individual minds. Their memories are subaltern and exist as a potentially threatening undercurrent to the social order. Their ability to survive depends on what

claims to political resources and state power the group is able to muster. Yet, even in totalitarian societies, the state does not completely control individual or social memory. Agents of civil society can play an active role in strategies of remembrance; sometimes in collaboration with the state, sometimes against it.[20]

Examples from interviews in Vulindlela

Earlier events can be reconstructed in the process of remembering, as they are retrospectively instilled with new meaning. This was evident in my interviews. The interviewees largely remembered events in the past by connecting these with current systems of meaning. These reconstructed memories on occasion strengthened resentment between individuals in Vulindlela communities. One interviewee, asked to share his memories of violence, said:

> The reason why we have all these problems today in our communities is because the ANC allowed young people to control us – there is endless and uncontrollable crime in our community. Women were raped during the period of violence, women are still raped today. Schools were boycotted and broken into by the very same *amaqabane* [comrades]; we have similar problems even today. People were killed and their bodies mutilated then, have you heard [on the news], even today these things are happening? Who do you blame? The youths that did not get opportunities to go to school during the violence period are responsible for all problems we are faced with and the ANC is responsible. Bheki Cele says people should return their illegal guns to the police. They [ANC] gave these guns to the ANC supporters to kill us. They are testing their own medicine.[21]

One woman in KwaShange had an interest in being a ward councillor. She said:

> You see, the reason why our infrastructure development is delayed in KwaShange is because Inkatha won the elections in the province in 1994. They deliberately created a system that made it difficult for us [supporters of the ANC] to get

> development in our areas. We fought for this democracy. Many people in KwaShange lost their lives. Even today [2009], our area is not developed because, even though the ANC is in control of KwaZulu-Natal, many officials are still IFP [Inkatha Freedom Party] and they deliberately bypass ANC-supporting communities. I want to be a councillor so as to 'settle the score'. Firstly, for all our people that Inkatha killed during the time of violence [in the 1980s and 1990s]. Secondly, to develop ANC-supporting areas in Vulindlela, as they have been ignored since 1994.[22]

According to another woman interviewee in an IFP area:

> Now that there is no more fighting in our area, we need to seriously consider appointing women in the leadership of our communities. Women suffered a great deal; they were the ones who made sure that children are taken care of while men were fighting. The tension that existed between us [IFP] and ANC is the reason why we are not progressing as women in rural areas. I think we should put aside our differences as women and fight for our rights. Women are reliable. They are not corrupt as men are. I think one thing that the violence taught is that we should not allow men to do as they wish with our lives. The reason why violence got out of hand was because men were dominating – and look where that brought us, to this endless circle of pain, suffering and lack.[23]

These testimonies show that memories of violence are reconstructed. The earlier events are given new meanings as they are interpreted through the needs of the present day. Giving the past new meaning concludes that everybody is affected by political actions or systems in this country.

Memories in KwaShange are often referred to as proof or evidence of what really happened. In the aftermath of violence, people draw on memories when justifying their actions today. One man shared his memory of violence and used it to justify why his son had to be appointed as the ward councillor in KwaShange:

> I suffered a lot for this community. I was found guilty of a crime I did not commit – but a state gun that was signed out under my name was used to kill Inkatha youth – the killing was justified because if the youth were not killed, many people would be dead by now. The Inkatha youth was planning to attack and kill many people here . . . Now I am not able to support my family because I cannot be employed . . . My son should at least be given opportunities by the ANC-led government to be a councillor. This will help my family to 'put food on the table'.[24]

The debate in KwaShange as to who should become the ward councillor, and why, is built partly on constructed memories of previous times – the violence of the 1980s. The use of memories as proof of previous suffering and the reasons for benefiting in the current dispensation is common in KwaShange. Interviews show that people use memories of violence in their strategies to gain political authority and benefit from the current government of the ANC.

Tacit carriers of community memory are often found in the form of ruins of homesteads, shops and buildings, which belonged to people who were either killed or displaced during the violence. Families, even those who have relocated, will keep these places untouched, as reminders, as sacred ground and for the graves of their forefathers. It can be argued that these sites also tell the 'silent' story of the violence. The survivors use these as proof when they claim compensation from the provincial government and to show that their suffering really happened.

Interviewees remembered details of their experiences in these ruins. For example, Thembe Dlomo remembered that his son had been wearing his grey raincoat because it had been raining. He also recalled that his son had been standing and leaning on the wall when the bullet hit him, and he was able to point to the section of the house that was standing. Many were overcome with emotions that they had suppressed.

Zulu philosophy claims, '*Umenzi uyakhohlwa kodwa umenziwa akakhohlwa* (The doer of bad deed forgets, but the sufferer does not). This Zulu expression is normally used when there has been a quarrel.

My interviews with KwaShange people who were ANC supporters and with IFP supporters from neighbouring areas proved this proverb to be correct. Many interviewees from KwaShange remembered only bad things that were done to them by Inkatha combatants. Gonyela Ndlovu was a United Democratic Front (UDF) child combatant in 1988 in KwaShange; in the same year he and another seven young UDF combatants were apprehended by police in Mvundlweni while they were carrying out an attack. They killed three men at the bus stop who were waiting for transport to Pietermaritzburg. In an interview, Gonyela Ndlovu said:

> Inkatha combatants were merciless; they often attacked unexpectedly and killed people. I cannot even count how many times we were attacked. They usually came at awkward times, early in the morning, 03h00, when everybody is fast asleep, and they burnt houses. Many people [in KwaShange] were killed in these attacks.[25]

Ndlovu's memory is selective. He seemed to have forgotten about the many atrocities and human rights violations he committed. All that he remembers, when asked about his experiences of violence, are atrocities committed by Inkatha combatants towards him and the KwaShange people. This testimony is representative of many such stories in KwaShange, where people speak as if they had not attacked Inkatha supporters, despite evidence to the contrary.

In Mpumuza, an IFP neighbouring area, Christopher Manzini (in a wheelchair), who was injured in KwaShange in the February 1991 massacre, said:

> *Ngingaxola kodwa ngeke ngikhohle* [I will forgive but I will not forget] what was done to us in KwaShange. Today I am in a wheelchair because of their brutality. I am grateful, however, because I am still alive because many of my neighbours did not survive. They died. They were killed and mutilated in KwaShange. Others disappeared; even today we do not know where their remains are.[26]

Many interviewees, particularly those who committed human rights violations, minimised their actions during the violence. This is a form of denial. They did not deny that human rights violations occurred, but they questioned the emotional responses or experiences of victims. They made statements such as '*banehaba*' (they are exaggerating) or '*banozwela kakhulu*' (they are too sensitive):

> This was common during those days; there was a war. Did they expect us to fold our arms when they attacked us? Did they not kill our people; did they not destroy our property? Did they not loot? For me it was not a big deal. These things should not be blown out of proportion. All I know is that we defended ourselves from people who attacked us. We eliminated *ophumasilwe* [warlords] and I do not regret we got rid of them because otherwise this area would be something else if they did not die . . . so I am saying it is not a big deal.[27]

Many survivors of this turmoil have compartmentalised their memories. Because their stories are no longer regarded as heroic, as they used to be during the times of violence, they chose what they would discuss. Painful and traumatic memories – especially the terrible things they did to their enemies – were not shared.

In some instances, they denied that certain gross human rights violations were committed. Many refused to revive these suppressed traumatic memories. Common immediate responses were to remain silent or to show anger, particularly when asked about atrocities and body mutilations. Then they either changed the subject or discontinued the interview if I was persistent. Three people threatened me, which was obviously a defence mechanism. Eventually some did open up – after developing trust that I was genuinely prepared to listen and was not judgemental. The interviews took place privately.

At the beginning of the interviews in 2008, there were high levels of resistance, mainly from men. Men who were young combatants at the time of the violence refused to share their memories. This group of people had committed atrocious acts in the name of the community and showed symptoms of post-traumatic stress disorder. They tended to be alcoholics or use drugs, such as dagga. Most of them are unemployed and some have been in and out of prison. They were regarded as heroes at the time but after the violence had come to an end, they were seen by the same community as villains.

> I was not there. I never did anything wrong. I do not remember anything. I think if you want to know what happened, you should talk to your brothers and stop bothering the whole community. Why do you want to bring back things that we have forgotten about? Do you think it was nice? Do you think we enjoyed it?[28]

In September 2008, I phoned Nosihle Mkhathini and made an appointment to interview her. She promised that she would be ready. The following week I drove from Durban to meet with her in KwaShange, as per our arrangement. She did not come to welcome us (my research assistant and myself), but instead her older brother asked:

> Tell me, what are you going to gain with all this? . . . Do you realise that you are hurting people? Nosihle lost her three-month-old baby. Inkatha people attacked her boyfriend's family where she was at the time; they shot and killed everyone in the house, took the baby and burnt the house. She does not talk about this . . . because she does not want to talk about it. I would advise you to stop it. She will not talk to you about it.[29]

These examples attest to the fact that people have not dealt with their past experiences. Sipho Sokhela's reaction, for instance, shows that his memories of the violence are unbearable. He does not want to remember it. In order to avoid talking about it, he becomes defensive and he tells 'white lies'. He started by saying, 'I was not there', 'I did not do anything', 'I do not remember anything'. Nosihle Mkhathini's silent response is a defence mechanism against the fact that she lost her baby.

I continued working with members of the community, especially those who had a problem with sharing their memories, but I noted that many interviewees in the beginning were talking in generic terms – they avoided discussing personal experiences. To be on the safe side, many interviewees used words such as '*sezwa kuthiwa*' (we heard that this and that happened). It took much negotiation between me and the individuals concerned as well as the intervention of community leadership. It was only when I shared my own experiences of this violence with community members in a meeting that many began to trust me. Others even mentioned afterwards that they thought that I was interested in getting stories for newspapers or radio, because in 2004 I was working for SABC radio news and I was a regular commentator in *The Witness* newspaper in early 2009. As a result, many thought it was a journalistic project. It was only after I had assured them that I would not publish this in any newspaper or broadcast it on the radio that they agreed to talk to me. I referred to the safe, private place where we would do the interview. I had to promise that I would not bring a camera or tape recorder, as I had done before. I promised that I would come alone, without my research assistant. I also promised them anonymity. Even after this, it took them many months to agree to share their experiences. It was only in 2010 that I managed to break through and get some people to share – especially those who had been young combatants. An anonymous source said:

> Inkatha combatants were strong; they had ammunition and the sort of weaponry that we did not have. They came here at night with [Magnus] Malan and they were trained in Caprivi – so you see – they had a lot of support from the Boers. To cause them pain, we had to be brutal to those that we managed to capture. We always ran to hide when we saw them [Inkatha] attacking, but when they started killing women and children who could not defend themselves – we used to come and defend our women and children. That is when we really started mutilating their bodies. You must know that we need to be strong. It was the only way we could protect ourselves from their bullets.[30]

This is a typical example of a memory reconstructed. Firstly, at the time it was not known that it was Magnus Malan who worked with the state police in Vulindlela to kill people; it was only during the TRC hearings that Malan spoke out and asked for forgiveness. The memories of this interviewee are mixed with information he must have learnt from newspapers or heard on the radio in discussions after the violence. During the interview he spoke as if he saw Magnus Malan. Secondly, he spoke about Inkatha combatants as trained in the Caprivi. These details were not known at the time of the violence. They only surfaced after the violence, during the TRC's hearings.

When I interviewed those who were young combatants during the violence, especially when asked about their involvement in *muthi* rituals and human body mutilations, many denied that it happened. Others admitted that 'we heard about it but we do not know details because we never partook of those rituals'. When I persisted, on some occasions I was harshly treated and requested to stop, because 'it had nothing to do with you'. Some questioned me, 'Where are we going with this discussion?' and 'What are your intentions?' Others even asked, 'Why are you asking these questions?' Many of them refused ever to talk to me again about their experiences of political violence. Some, when asked, claimed that they had forgotten. They did not remember anything that happened because 'it was a long time ago'.

Memory triggers

Human beings have memory triggers that set off very strong recollections of past experiences. In KwaShange, interviewees spoke of a number of things that brought back memories of the violence of the 1980s. Many spoke of memory triggers such as sound, a particular scent, or something a person sees, that flashes him or her back into the past. These triggers caused them to relive past events so intensely that nothing else existed but the moment they were reliving. Many indicated that they had the same feelings as when the memory was born. Sgede remembers:

> I had been smoking dagga and drinking beer and joined [Inkatha] group that attacked and burnt Ziqubu's family [in 1987]. I assaulted Zakhe Ziqubu [owner of the home that was attacked], kicked and stabbed [a two-year-old baby] in the face, insulted Ziqubu's wife about being a UDF informer and of being a witch. I also got injured in the incident when UDF supporters came to defend the family. I must have also heard about the incident from my friends Tana and Latu Zuma, who were there when the attack was carried out. And I'm sure I

> brooded about the incident for days when I was in Edendale Hospital and then Plessislaer Police Station in Edendale.[31]

Sgede claims to have no memory of being part of the Inkatha group that attacked the Ziqubu family that night, or of anything he did or said. He also does not remember many other violent crimes he committed in the 1980s to 1990s. Sgede continued, 'But even if I cannot remember that night, I have never forgotten that it occurred.' Several things serve as memory triggers for him. One memory trigger is the Ziqubu homestead, which is still there and the same house was rebuilt. Following his friends' advice, Sgede has not set foot in there for more than 24 years. He fled to Elandskop that September (1987) but returned home many times to visit. 'And I could not walk past that homestead without remembering the incident [attack] I could not remember.'

Another memory trigger for Sgede is a scar on the face of Nelly Ziqubu (who was wounded when she was two years old). As she grows older, the scar grows bigger. Nelly Ziqubu's testimony about the incident contains a similar phenomenon. She cannot remember the actual incident, but because of the scar on her face and the information she received from her parents about how she was injured and by whom, she can talk about the incident as though she remembered it.

Another memory trigger for Sgede is Edendale Hospital and the Plessislaer Police Station, which is opposite the hospital. These two institutions are situated on the main Edendale Road and are visible when travelling by bus or other transport from KwaShange to Pietermaritzburg.

Two other memory triggers involve the name 'Ziqubu'. The homestead is close to the main road in KwaShange and the name of the bus stop close to the homestead is 'KwaZiqubu'. Every time the name is mentioned, Sgede remembers the night when he attacked the Ziqubu homestead. Ziqubu subsequently died because of the injuries he received during the attack. 'When I pass the grave, I think of that night of attack,' Sgede says.

Some people reported that they contracted terminal illnesses. A few have bullets, which cannot be removed, in their bodies. Many take medication, which itself is a constant reminder to them of what they went through.

Where do they remember?

Most of my interviews were conducted in KwaShange. The landscape, mountains, hills and rivers bring back memories of the violence. When asked about the violence, they point at things as their memory triggers. For instance, Moses Ndlovu walked with me to the Msunduzi River where his daughter was shot and killed during the Seven Days' War.

When do they remember?

Some memories are suppressed; some people said they had forgotten what happened. After some time, they started opening up when they developed trust in me. I did not record them, but they allowed me to take some notes.

Dreams and reconstructed memories

The concept of flashback (while the facts of the dream might not be accurate, the feelings are) implies the literal reinstatement of the sensory context of the traumatic event. Yet, the notion of a timeless, inflexible, photographic reproduction flies in the face of what we know about the dynamics of the brain.[32] In other words, the feeling of sensory reinstatement can be very powerful, but this metacognitive (knowing about knowing) sense of literal replaying is illusory. The same holds for traumatic nightmares. Although survivors reported that their nightmares are replays of the traumatic experiences, this cannot literally be true. To be sure, dreams tied closely to the traumatic events can be reconstructed and 're-experienced' during sleep, but such re-experiences are not reproductions.

Flashbacks can happen in a number of ways. While most people think of flashbacks as visual, they can tie into any of the senses. For example, one woman mentioned that she often gets a memory or flashback when she smells braai (barbecue) meat. Since 1987, she has never again eaten braai meat or wanted to be around where there is braai meat cooking. This ties into a memory in which she saw a person burning to death during one of the attacks in KwaShange. She was at close range and she could smell the burning body, which 'smelt like braai meat'.

Zenzile Hlomuka, for example, says that in 1987 she dreamt about a group of vigilantes attacking KwaShange, carrying traditional weapons and singing war songs.[33] Their commander was a short man with long hair, dark in complexion, and they were accompanied by a few white men. In the dream, the white men were carrying 'big machine guns' she had never seen before. In retelling her dream in 2009, Zenzile calls the commander of the *impis*, David Ntombela, and she identifies the white men that accompanied the combatants as state police led by Magnus Malan.

Zenzile admits that she only got to hear about David Ntombela in 1990. The same applies to Magnus Malan, who was not known in KwaShange in the 1980s. People got to know about him and his contribution to the KwaShange violence in 1996, when there were TRC hearings in Pietermaritzburg. This is a typical example of a reconstructed memory. Her narration is based on knowledge she acquired many years after she had dreamt. Her telling of the dream is influenced by what she heard in the TRC hearing, as well as what she read in the newspapers about state police.

Past-present relationships shape memory. Individual and collective or state memories are reconstructed. In KwaShange, individual memories are influenced by time, guilt and shame. The Midlands violence happened 15 to 25 years prior to the writing of this book. It is a relatively long period and much has been said in the media and the TRC, so interviewees reconstruct their memories based on what they have learnt or heard subsequently. Those who are alleged to have been violators of human rights are the ones who show signs of guilt and anger when asked to remember. How people consciously and unconsciously evaluate the external significance of their memories determines how they frame their memories and stories for disclosure or retain them as privately closed and inaccessible. Moreover, constructions of the private/public relationship are crucial in shaping what is remembered, how it is remembered, what is silenced or forgotten, what is expressed and how it is expressed and to whom.

Notes

1. D. LaCapra, *History and Memory after Auschwitz* (Ithaca: Cornell University Press, 1998), p. 21.
2. K.P. Mokwena, 'Commemorating Painful Experiences in a Divided Society, with Special Reference to the Thokoza Memorial: A Case Study' (MA thesis, University of the Witwatersrand, 2008).
3. Mokwena, 'Commemorating Painful Experiences in a Divided Society'.

4. B. Hamber, 'The Burdens of Truth: An Evaluation of the Psychological Support Services and Initiatives Undertaken by the South African TRC', *American Imago* 55(1), 1998: 9–28.
5. J. Singh and R. Chetty (eds), *Trauma, Resistance, Reconciliation in Post-1994 South African Writing* (New York: Peter Lang, 2010), p. 60.
6. Quoted in A.J. Vetlesen, *Evil and Human Agency: Understanding Collective Avoiding* (Cambridge: Cambridge University Press, 2005), p. 269.
7. B. Hamber, 'The Dilemmas of Reparations: In Search of a Process Driven Approach', in *Out of the Ashes: Reparation for Victims of Gross and Systematic Human Rights Violations*, edited by K. de Feyster, S. Parmentier, M. Bossuyt and P. Lemmens (Antwerp and Oxford: Intersentia, 2005), p. 148.
8. Mokwena, 'Commemorating Painful Experiences in a Divided Society'.
9. Mokwena, 'Commemorating Painful Experiences in a Divided Society', p. 17.
10. B. Hamber and R. Wilson, 'Symbolic Closure through Memory, Reparation and Revenge in Post-Conflict Societies', *Journal of Human Rights* 1(1), 2010: 35–54.
11. Hamber and Wilson, 'Symbolic Closure through Memory'.
12. Interview with a group of five women, KwaShange, 14 November 2010.
13. S. Marshall, *Landscape of Memory: Commemorative Monuments, Memorials and Public Statuary in Post-Apartheid South Africa* (Leiden: Brill, 2009), p. 338.
14. Interview with Nonjabulo Khumalo, KwaShange, 14 November 2010.
15. The Khulumani Support Group was formed in 1995 by survivors and families of victims of the political conflict of South Africa's apartheid past. It was set up in response to the pending TRC by victims who felt the commission should be used to speak out about the past to ensure that such violations never occurred again. See http://www.khulumani.net/khulumani/about-us/item/1-background.html.
16. Centre for the Study of Violence and Reconciliation and Khulumani Support Group, 'Submission to the Truth and Reconciliation Commission: Survivors' Perceptions of the Truth and Reconciliation Commission and Suggestions for the Final Report', 1988, https://www.csvr.org.za/publications/1705-submission-to-the-truth-and-reconciliation-commission-survivors-perceptions-of-the-truth-and-reconciliation-commission-and-suggestions-for-the-final-report.
17. I attended the ceremony as a community member and as a researcher.
18. Interview with Khethokwakhe Khuboni, KwaShange, 14 November 2010.
19. Interview with Mzoneli Mfeketho, KwaShange, 14 November 2010.
20. Quoted in G. Baines, 'The Politics of Public History in Post-Apartheid South Africa', https://www.academia.edu/926698/The_Politics_of_Public_History_In_Post-Apartheid_South_Africa.
21. Interview with Mhlephila Ndlovu, KwaShange, 14 March 2009.
22. Interview with Nozibele Mthombeni, KwaShange, 12 March 2009.
23. Interview with Thulile Mbongwa, KwaShange, 12 March 2009.
24. Interview with Ntandose Nhlumayo, KwaShange, 12 March 2009.
25. Interview with Gonyela Ndlovu, KwaShange, 14 April 2009.

26. Interview with Christopher Manzini, KwaMpumuza, 14 April 2009.
27. Interview with Ndonga Dlomo, KwaShange, 14 April 2009.
28. Interview with Sipho Sokhela, KwaShange, 11 May 2008.
29. Interview with Ndovela Mkhathini, KwaShange, 16 August 2009.
30. Interview with an anonymous source in KwaShange, 14 September 2010.
31. Interview with Sgede, KwaShange, 16 August 2009.
32. R. McNally, 'Debunking Myths about Trauma and Memory', *Canadian Journal of Psychiatry* 50(13), 2005: 113–17.
33. Interview with Zenzile Hlomuka, KwaShange, 15 March 2009.

Conclusion

THIS IS THE first scholarly work focused specifically on KwaShange. Its unique contribution to the literature on the Midlands violence lies in the insider experience, memories and interpretation, and the psychological effects on survivors many years after the violence ended. I have used my own memories to paint a picture of the psychological and emotional effects of this upheaval. I was, in effect, the instrument of information generation as I discovered that the insider-outsider dichotomy was too simplistic. I found myself on a constantly changing continuum between the two positions.

This book contains a historical background to KwaShange with the aim of determining the roots of violence in the 1980s and 1990s in order to offer insight into the disintegration of the community into civil war and its wider repercussions in the Vulindlela region. I also discuss the wider politics behind the conflicts of the period in Natal and Zululand, with a view to showing how provincial and national developments, particularly the emerging tension between Inkatha and the African National Congress at the national level of leadership, changed the climate in KwaShange and fuelled violence.

I have included biographies of four key ringleaders of the contending forces in KwaShange and presented the accounts of actual combatants. It is the inside story, told by one of its survivors.

The suffering experienced as a result of this violence, and its consequences, influenced the lives of the entire KwaShange population. This account of the political violence centres on the testimony of survivors, the details of what happened in local communities and the effects of the violence on the community members in the ensuing years. The social structure of the community was affected by it, and, by implication, successive generations were and are also affected as it has become part of some of the residents' identities.

The prevalence of the use of *muthi* and rituals associated with it is usually a subject avoided by most historians. War-doctors were at the core of political violence and *muthi* made from human body parts played a crucial role in the rise of communities and individuals to power. This book chronicles the psychological and social scars that *muthi* murders and the lack of cleansing services after the violence have left on the KwaShange community.

Previously neglected memories and prophetic dreams of women who were there, and who experienced war at close range, are now part of the historical record. Dreams and visions are part of most Zulu people's lives and beliefs. They are a culturally defined means of communication between the living and the ancestors or God, and they have a strong impact on communities' conceptions of reality.

This book describes how political violence is remembered by individuals, by the community and by the state, and how memories are influenced by time, guilt, shame and the accounts of others over many years.

I have investigated the ways in which an individual constructs and theorises his or her traumatic experiences, and the impact that these explanations have on the prognosis and the healing processes. Biomedical psychotherapeutic notions of mental stress, trauma and healing may be inappropriate and ineffective in contexts where cultural beliefs and world views are different, remedies for trauma often being culturally specific. The young people who were involved continue to bear emotional scars, and processes of healing the psychological wounds of war of these former child warriors needs to be carried out.

What is described did not take place in the public eye – it is more about the sacrifices, emotional torture, agony and psychological effects that almost every man, woman and child endured.

One of the great challenges the government faces today is to unify communities divided by political hatred or memories of losing their relatives. But, as this book shows, victims' and survivors' primary needs might be personal healing and not national reconciliation.

Select Bibliography

Primary sources

Killie Campbell Africana Library (KCAL), Black Sash Papers, Black Sash Records, Box 18: File – Miscellaneous, Affidavits 1988, 1989, 1990; File – Democratic Party, Information Sheets, 1989–1990 and Durban Network Funerals, 1989–1990; File – Democratic Party, Information Sheets, 1990–1991; Box 19: File – All Bulletin's Office Copy.

Pietermaritzburg Archives Repository (PAR), *State v. Hlengwa and others*, transcript of judgment by Justice N.S. Page, Natal Provincial Division of the Supreme Court, Pietermaritzburg, 11 April 1988.

Secondary sources

Adam, H. and K. Moodley. *The Opening of the Apartheid Mind: Options for the New South Africa*. Berkeley: University of California Press, 1993.

Agger, I. 'Psychosocial Assistance during Ethnopolitical Warfare in the Former Yugoslavia'. In *Ethnopolitical Warfare: Causes, Consequences and Possible Solutions*, edited by D. Chirot and M.E.P. Seligman. Washington, DC: American Psychological Association, 2001.

Aitchison, J. 'Numbering the Dead'. Unpublished mimeograph, 1988.

———. 'The Civil War in Natal'. In *People's Courts and Popular Politics: South African Review 5*, edited by G. Moss and I. Obery. Johannesburg: Ravan Press, 1989.

———. 'The Pietermaritzburg Conflict: Experience and Analysis'. Unpublished paper, Centre for Adult Education, University of Natal, Pietermaritzburg, 1989.

———. 'Interpreting Violence: The Struggle to Understand the Natal Conflict'. Unpublished mimeograph, 1990.

———. 'A Story of What Happened'. Unpublished mimeograph, 1990.

———. 'The Seven Days War: The Victims' Narrative'. Unpublished paper, Centre for Adult Education, University of Natal, Pietermaritzburg, 1991.

———. 'Numbering the Dead: The Course and Pattern of Political Violence in the Natal Midlands, 1987–1989'. Master's thesis, University of Natal, 1993.

———. 'KwaZulu-Natal: The Pre-election Wars of the 1990s'. In *The Role of Political Violence in South Africa's Democratisation*, edited by R. Greenstein. Johannesburg: Community Agency for Social Enquiry, 2003.

———. 'The Origins of the Midlands War'. In *The Role of Political Violence in South Africa's Democratisation*, edited by R. Greenstein. Johannesburg: Community Agency for Social Enquiry, 2003.

———. 'Numbering the Dead: Patterns in the Midlands Violence'. In J. Aitchison, W. Leeb and V. John, *Political Violence in the Natal Midlands: The Unrest Monitoring Project Papers, 1988–1994*. Pietermaritzburg: Centre for Adult Education, 2010.

Aitchison, J., W. Leeb and V. John. *Political Violence in the Natal Midlands: The Unrest Monitoring Project Papers, 1988–1994*. Pietermaritzburg: Centre for Adult Education, 2010.

Altbeker, A. *A Country at War with Itself: South Africa's Crisis of Crime*. Johannesburg: Jonathan Ball, 2007.

Amnesty International. 'South Africa: The Criminal Justice System and the Prosecution of Human Rights: The Role of the Prosecution Service'. *Amnesty International*, 1998. https://www.amnesty.org/en/documents/afr53/001/1998/en/.

Anderson, K. and D.C. Jack. 'Learning to Listen: Interview Techniques and Analysis'. In *The Oral History Reader*, edited by R. Perks and A. Thomson. London: Routledge, 1998.

Aurell, J. 'Autobiographical Texts and Historiographical Sources: Rereading Fernand Braudel and Annie Kriegel'. *Biography* 29(3), 2006: 425–45.

Baines, G. 'The Politics of Public History in Post-Apartheid South Africa'. https://www.academia.edu/926698/The_Politics_of_Public_History_In_Post-Apartheid_South_Africa.

Ball, J. 'The Ritual of the Necklace'. Research Report for the Centre for the Study of Violence and Reconciliation, March 1994.

Barnes, J.A. *Who Should Know What? Social Science, Privacy and Ethics*. Cambridge: Cambridge University Press, 1979.

Barnett, L.A. 'Critique, Culture and the Cough: Examining Conceptualisations of Healing'. Unpublished paper presented at Critical Method Nine, Durban, 2004.

Baskin, J. *Striking Back: A History of COSATU*. Johannesburg: Ravan Press, 1991.

Battersby, J. 'Edendale Journal; in Apartheid's Shadow, Zulu Wages War on Zulu'. *New York Times*, 9 November 1987.

Beinart, W. 'Political and Collective Violence in Southern African Historiography'. *Journal of Southern African Studies* 18(3), 1992: 455–86.

———. *Twentieth Century South Africa*. Cape Town: Oxford University Press, 1994.

Bekker, S. (ed.). *Capturing the Event: Conflict Trends in the Natal Region 1986–1992*. Durban: Indicator Project South Africa, 1992.

Bennett, M. and D. Quin (eds). *Political Conflict in South Africa: Data Trends 1984–1988*. Durban: Indicator Project South Africa, 1986.

Berglund, A-I. *Zulu Thought-Patterns and Symbolism*. London: Hurst and Company, 1976.

Bernard, H.R. *Research Methods in Anthropology: Qualitative and Quantitative Approaches*. Second edition. London: Altamira Press, 1995.

Bhengu, K. *Uphuya waseMshwathi* [Poor/Pauper Man from Shwathi]. Johannesburg: Educum, 1983.

Bird, J. *The Annals of Natal: 1495 to 1845*. Pietermaritzburg: P. Davis & Sons, 1888.

Blake, B.W. *Jung in Africa*. New York: Continuum, 2005.

Boister, N. and K. Ferguson-Brown (eds). *Human Rights Yearbook*. Cape Town: Oxford University Press, 1991.

Bonnin, D. '"I Am Poor, I Must Start All Over Again": The Impact of Political Violence on Household Economies: A Case-Study from KwaZulu-Natal'. *South African Review of Sociology* 32(2), 2001: 186–204.

———. 'Claiming Spaces, Changing Places: Political Violence and Women's Protests in KwaZulu-Natal'. *Journal of Southern African Studies* 26(2), 2002: 301–16.

———. 'Legacies of Political Violence: An Examination of Political Conflict in Mpumalanga Township, KwaZulu-Natal, South Africa'. *Transformation* 62, 2006: 59–83.

———. 'Space, Place and Identity: Political Violence in Mpumalanga Township, KwaZulu-Natal, 1987–1993'. PhD thesis, University of the Witwatersrand, 2007.

Booth, D. and M. Biyela. 'Exploring the Spatial Dimensions of Black Resistance and Political Violence in South Africa: The Case of Durban'. *Urban Geography* 9(6), 1988: 629–53.

Borland, K. '"That's Not What I Said": Interpretive Conflict in Oral Narrative Research'. In *Women's Words: The Feminist Practice of Oral History*, edited by S.B. Gluck and D. Patai. New York: Routledge, 1991.

Boyden, J. and S. Gibbs. *Children and War: Responses to Psychological Distress in Cambodia*. Oxford: INTRAC, 1997.

Bozzoli, B. *The Political Nature of a Ruling Class: Capital and Ideology in South Africa 1890–1933*. London: Routledge, 1981.

———. (ed.). *Class, Community and Conflict: South African Perspectives*. Johannesburg: Ravan Press, 1987.

Bozzoli, B. and M. Nkotsoe. *Women of Phokeng: Consciousness, Life Strategy, and Migrancy in South Africa, 1900–1983*. Woodbridge: Boydell & Brewer, 1991.

Brewer, J.D. (ed.). *Restructuring South Africa*. London: St Martin's Press, 1994.

Bromberger, N. and Y. Bhamjee. 'Unemployment in Pietermaritzburg with Special Reference to Sobantu'. Paper presented at the Association for Sociology in Southern Africa conference, University of the Western Cape, 1987.

Brookes E.H. and N. Hurwitz. *The Native Reserves of Natal*. Natal Regional Survey, Volume 7. Cape Town: Oxford University Press, 1957.

Brownlee, J. 'Account of Amakosa, or Southern Caffers'. In *Travels and Adventures in Southern Africa, Vol. 1*, edited by G. Thompson. London: Henry Colburn, 1827.

Bryant, A.T. *The Zulu People, as They Were before the White Man Came*. Pietermaritzburg: Shuter and Shooter, 1949.

———. *Olden Times in Zululand and Natal Containing Earlier Political History of the Eastern-Nguni Clans*. Cape Town: Struik, 1965.

———. *Zulu Medicine and Medicine-Men*. Cape Town: C. Struik, 1966.

Bulpin, T.V. *Natal and the Zulu Country*. Cape Town: Books of Africa, 1977.
Burns, J.F. 'Black versus Black in South Africa'. *New York Times*, 21 January 1988. http://www.nytimes.com/1988/01/21/world/black-vs-black-in-south-africa.
Buthelezi, M. 'Commemoration of Robert Mangaliso Sobukwe', Graaff-Reinet Civic Centre, 28 February 1998.
Campbell, C. 'Learning to Kill? Masculinity, the Family and Violence in Natal'. *Journal of Southern African Studies* 18(3), 1992: 614–28.
Carton, B. *Blood from Your Children: The Colonial Origins of Generational Conflict in South Africa*. Pietermaritzburg: University of Natal Press, 2000.
Carver, R. 'South Africa: After the Elections'. WRITENET for UNHCR, 1 May 1994. https://www.refworld.org/docid/3ae6a6c44.html.
———. 'KwaZulu-Natal: Continued Violence and Displacement'. WRITENET for UNHCR, 1 July 1996. https://www.refworld.org/docid/3ae6a6bc4.html.
Centre for the Study of Violence and Reconciliation and Khulumani Support Group. 'Submission to the Truth and Reconciliation Commission: Survivors' Perceptions of the Truth and Reconciliation Commission and Suggestions for the Final Report', 1988. https://www.csvr.org.za/publications/1705-submission-to-the-truth-and-reconciliation-commission-survivors-perceptions-of-the-truth-and-reconciliation-commission-and-suggestions-for-the-final-report.
Chabal, P. and J.P. Daloz. *Africa Works: Disorder as Political Instrument*. Oxford: James Currey, 1999.
Chidester, D. 'Dreaming in the Contact Zone: Zulu Dreams, Visions, and Religion in Nineteenth-Century South Africa'. *Journal of the American Academy of Religion* 76(1), 2008: 27–53.
Chirot D. and M.E.P. Seligman (eds). *Ethnopolitical Warfare: Causes, Consequences and Possible Solutions*. Washington, DC: American Psychological Association, 2001.
Clifford, J. 'Introduction: Partial Truths'. In *Writing Culture: The Poetics and Politics of Ethnography*, edited by J. Clifford and G.E. Marcus. Berkeley: University of California Press, 1986.
Cock, J. *Colonels and Cadres: War and Gender in South Africa*. Cape Town: Oxford University Press, 1991.
Coleman, P. 'Ageing and Life History: The Meaning of Reminiscence in Later Life'. In *Life and Work History Analyses: Qualitative and Quantitative Developments*, edited by S. Dex. London: Routledge, 1991.
Comaroff, J. and J. Comaroff. 'Occult Economies and the Violence of Abstraction: Notes from the South African Postcolony'. *American Ethnologist* 26(2), 1998: 279–303.
———. 'Alien Nation: Zombies, Immigrants and Millennial Capitalism'. *South Atlantic Quarterly* 101(4), 2002: 779–804.
———. 'Policing Culture, Cultural Policing: Law and Social Order in Postcolonial South Africa'. *Law and Social Inquiry* 29(3), 2004: 513–45.
Cosslett, T., C. Lury and P. Summerfield (eds). *Feminism and Autobiography: Texts, Theories, Methods*. London: Routledge, 2000.
Creswell, J.W. *Research Design: Qualitative and Quantitative Approach*. Thousand Oaks, CA: Sage, 1994.

Crotty, M. *The Foundations of Social Research: Meaning and Perspective in the Research Process*. Sydney: Allen & Unwin, 1998.

Curle, A. *Another Way: Positive Response to Contemporary Violence*. Charlbury: Jon Carpenter Publishing, 1995.

De Haan, M.J. *Mission on the Margin: A Case Study on Reformed Mission Prospects in eNkumane, KwaZulu-Natal*. Pietermaritzburg: Cluster Publications, 2010.

De Haas, M. 'Violence in Natal and Zululand: The 1980s'. In South African Democracy Education Trust, *The Road to Democracy in South Africa: Volume 6 (1990–1996): Part 1*. Pretoria: Unisa Press, 2013.

Delius, P. 'Witches and Missionaries in the Nineteenth Century "Transvaal"'. *Journal of Southern African Studies* 27(3), 2001: 429–31.

DeLyser, D. '"Do You Really Live Here?" Thoughts on Insider Research'. *Geographical Review* 91(1/2), 2001: 441–53.

Denis, P. *Never Too Small to Remember: Memory Work and Resilience in Times of AIDS*. Pietermaritzburg: Cluster Publications, 2005.

———. 'Indians versus Russians: An Oral History of the Political Violence in Nxamalala (1987–1992)'. *Journal of Natal and Zulu History* 24(1), 2006: 64–93.

Denis, P. and P. Dlamini. 'Multi Layers of Memory: The History of Mpophomeni Told and Retold'. *Alternation* 22(2), 2015: 73–99.

Denis, P. and G. Duncan. *The Native School That Caused All the Trouble: A History of the Federal Theology Seminary of Southern Africa*. Pietermaritzburg: Cluster Publications, 2011.

Denis, P. and R. Ntsimane (eds). *Oral History in a Wounded Country: Interactive Interviewing in South Africa*. Pietermaritzburg: University of KwaZulu-Natal Press, 2008.

Denis, P., R. Ntsimane and T. Cannell. *Indians versus Russians: An Oral History of Political Violence in Nxamalala (1987–1993)*. Pietermaritzburg: Cluster Publications, 2010.

Detainees Aid Committee. *Detention under Three Emergencies: A Report on the Natal Midlands, 1986–1989*. Pietermaritzburg: Detainees Aid Committee, 1989.

Dex, S. (ed.). *Life and Work History Analyses: Qualitative and Quantitative Developments*. London: Routledge, 1991.

Dlamuka, M. 'Connectedness and Disconnectedness in Thembeyakhe Harry Gwala's Biography, 1920–1995: Rethinking Political Militancy, Mass Mobilisation and Grassroots Struggles in South Africa'. PhD thesis, University of the Western Cape, 2018.

Doke, C.M. and B.W. Vilakazi. *Zulu-English Dictionary*. Johannesburg: Wits University Press, 1958.

Draper, J.A. (ed.). *Orality, Literacy and Colonialism in Southern Africa*. Atlanta: Society of Biblical Literature, 2003.

Duminy, A. and B. Guest (eds). *Natal and Zululand from the Earliest Times to 1910: A New History*. Pietermaritzburg: University of Natal Press, 1989.

Eby, J.C. and F. Morton. *The Collapse of Apartheid and the Dawn of Democracy in South Africa, 1993*. Chapel Hill, NC: University of North Carolina Press, 2003.

Ellis, S. 'The Historical Significance of South Africa's Third Force'. *Journal of Southern African Studies* 24(2), 1998: 261–99.

Epprecht, M. 'Health, Environment and Racialisation of Space in Pietermaritzburg/Edendale, 1880–1950: Revisiting the "Sanitation Syndrome"'. Paper presented at the History and African Studies Seminar, University of KwaZulu-Natal, 7 April 2010.

Etherington, K. *Becoming a Reflexive Researcher: Using Ourselves in Research.* London: Jessica Kingley Publishers, 2004.

Everatt, D. 'Analysing Political Violence on the Reef, 1990 to 1994'. In *The Role of Political Violence in South Africa's Democratisation*, edited by R. Greenstein. Johannesburg: Community Agency for Social Enquiry, 2003.

Field, S. *Lost Communities, Living Memories: Remembering Forced Removals in Cape Town.* Cape Town: David Philip, 2002.

Flint, K. *Healing Traditions: African Medicine, Cultural Exchange, and Competition in South Africa, 1820–1948.* Ohio: Ohio University Press, 2008.

Foster, K., M. McAllister and L. O'Brien. 'Coming to Autoethnography: A Mental Health Nurse's Experience'. *International Journal of Qualitative Methods* 4(4), 2005: 1–15.

Frankfort-Nachmias, C. and D. Nachmias. *Research Methods in the Social Sciences.* Fifth edition. London: Hodder Arnold, 1996.

Frenkl, V. *Man's Search for Meaning.* Boston: Beacon Press, 1959.

Freud, S. 'Thoughts for the Times on War and Death (1915)'. http://www.panarchy.org/freud/war.1915.html.

Frisch, M. *A Shared Authority: Essays on the Craft and Meaning of Oral and Public History.* Albany: State University of New York Press, 1990.

Fuze, M.M. *The Black People and Whence They Came: A Zulu View.* Translated by H.C. Lugg and edited by A.T. Cope. Pietermaritzburg: University of Natal Press and Durban: Killie Campbell Africana Library, 1979.

Gerrard, N. 'Some Painful Experiences of a White Feminist Therapist Doing Research with Women of Colour'. In *Racism in the Lives of Women: Testimony, Theory, and Guides to Antiracist Practice*, edited by J. Adleman and G. Enguidanos. New York: The Haworth Press, 1995.

Gobodo-Madikizela, P. *A Human Being Died That Night: A Story of Forgiveness.* Cape Town: David Philip, 2003.

Goldblatt, B. and S. Meintjes. 'Dealing with the Aftermath: Sexual Violence and the Truth and Reconciliation Commission'. *Agenda* 36, 1997: 7–17.

Greenstein, R. (ed.). *The Role of Political Violence in South Africa's Democratisation.* Johannesburg: Community Agency for Social Enquiry, 2003.

Grele, R.J. *Envelopes of Sound: The Art of Oral History.* Second edition. Chicago: Precedent Publishing, 1985.

Grunebaum-Ralph, H. 'Re-Placing Pasts, Forgetting Presents: Narrative, Place, and Memory in the Time of the Truth and Reconciliation Commission'. *Research in African Literatures* 32(3), 2001: 198–212.

Guelke, A. 'Interpretations of Political Violence during South Africa's Transition'. *Politikon* 27(2), 2000: 239–54.

Guest, B. and J. Sellers (eds). *Receded Tides of Empire: Aspects of the Economic and Social History of Natal and Zululand since 1910.* Pietermaritzburg: University of Natal Press, 1994.

Gunner, L. 'Wrestling with the Present, Beckoning to the Past: Contemporary Zulu Radio Drama'. *Journal of Southern African Studies* 26(2), 2000: 223–37.

Gutteridge, W. and J.E. Spence (eds). *Violence in Southern Africa*. London: Frank Cass, 1997.

Guy, J. *The Destruction of the Zulu Kingdom: The Civil War in Zululand, 1879–1884*. Pietermaritzburg: University of Natal Press, 1994.

———. *The View across the River: Harriette Colenso and the Zulu Struggle against Imperialism*. Cape Town: David Philip, 2002.

———. *The Maphumulo Uprising: War, Law and Ritual in the Zulu Rebellion*. Pietermaritzburg: University of KwaZulu-Natal Press, 2005.

———. *Remembering the Rebellion: The Zulu Uprising of 1906*. Pietermaritzburg: University of KwaZulu-Natal Press, 2006.

Gwala, N. 'Class Alliances in the Struggle against Inkatha'. *South African Labour Bulletin* 13(3), 1988: 85–90.

———. 'Political Violence and the Struggle for Control in Pietermaritzburg'. *Journal of Southern African Studies* 15(3), 1989: 506–24.

Haddad, B. 'African Women's Theologies of Survival: Intersecting Faith, Feminisms and Development'. PhD thesis, University of KwaZulu-Natal, 2000.

Halbwachs, M. *On Collective Memory*. Chicago: University of Chicago Press, 1992.

Hall, E.T. *Beyond Culture*. New York: Doubleday, 1976.

Hamber, B. 'The Burdens of Truth: An Evaluation of the Psychological Support Services and Initiatives Undertaken by the South African TRC'. *American Imago* 55(1), 1998: 9–28.

———. 'The Dilemmas of Reparations: In Search of a Process Driven Approach'. In *Out of the Ashes: Reparation for Victims of Gross and Systematic Human Rights Violations*, edited by K. de Feyster, S. Parmentier, M. Bossuyt and P. Lemmens. Antwerp: Intersentia, 2005.

———. 'The Impact of Trauma: A Psychosocial Approach'. Keynote address to A Shared Practice: Victims' Work in Action Conference, Limavady, Northern Ireland, 7–8 April 2004.

Hamber, B. and R. Wilson. 'Symbolic Closure through Memory, Reparation and Revenge in Post-Conflict Societies'. *Journal of Human Rights* 1(1), 2010: 35–54.

Hamilton, C. *The Mfecane Aftermath: Reconstructive Debates in Southern African History*. Johannesburg: Wits University Press and Pietermaritzburg: University of Natal Press, 1995.

———. *Terrific Majesty: The Powers of Shaka Zulu and the Limits of Historical Invention*. Cape Town: David Philip, 1998.

Hammond-Tooke, D. (ed.). *The Bantu-Speaking People of Southern Africa*. London: Routledge & Kegan Paul, 1947.

Hart, M. 'The Impact of Violence on Schooling'. Paper presented at the Centre for Adult Education Seminar on Violence, University of Natal, Pietermaritzburg, 1988.

Hart, M. and J. Gultig, 'The Effects of Violence on Black Schooling in Edendale and Vulindlela'. Paper presented at the Kenton conference, Cape Town, 1988.

Herd, N. *The Bent Pine: The Trial of Langalibalele*. Johannesburg: Ravan Press, 1976.

Hindson, D., M. Byerley and M. Morris. 'From Violence to Reconstruction: The Making, Disintegration and Remaking of an Apartheid City'. *Antipode* 26(4), 1994: 323–50.

Honwana, A. 'Sealing the Past, Facing the Future: Trauma Healing in Mozambique'. In *The Mozambique Peace Process in Perspective*, edited by J. Armon, D. Hendrickson and A. Vines. London: Conciliation Resources, 1998.

———. 'Negotiating Post-War Identities: Child Soldiers in Mozambique and Angola'. In *Contested Terrains and Constructed Categories: Contemporary Africa in Focus*, edited by G. Bond and N. Gibson. New York: Westview Press, 1999.

Horwath, D.R. and A.J. Norval (eds). *South Africa in Transition: New Theoretical Perspectives*. London: St Martin's Press, 1998.

Jeffery, A. 'Spotlight on Disinformation about Violence in South Africa'. *South African Institute of Race Relations Spotlight* 8(92), 1992: 1–57.

———. *The Natal Story: Sixteen Years of Conflict*. Johannesburg: South African Institute of Race Relations, 1997.

John, V. 'Natal's War: Monitoring Internal Refugees and Assessing Their Distress'. Unpublished report, Centre for Adult Education, University of Natal, Pietermaritzburg, 1990.

Johnston, A. 'Politics and Violence in KwaZulu-Natal'. In *Violence in Southern Africa*, edited by W. Gutteridge and J. Spence. London: Frank Cass, 1997.

Jones, B. 'Telling Family Stories: Interpretive Authority and Intersubjectivity in Life History Research'. *Journal of Contemporary History* 7, 2004: 2–11.

Kanuha, K. '"Being" Native versus "Going Native": Conducting Social Work Research as an Insider'. *Social Work* 45(5), 2000: 439–47.

Karon, T. 'An Interview with Harry Gwala', Dambuza, Pietermaritzburg, 8 January 1989. https://disa.ukzn.ac.za/int19890108043049.

Kelly, J. *To Swim with Crocodiles: Land, Violence, and Belonging in South Africa, 1800–1996*. East Lansing, MI: Michigan State University Press, 2018.

Kentridge, M. *An Unofficial War: Inside the Conflict in Pietermaritzburg*. Cape Town: David Philip, 1990.

Khumalo, F. *Touch My Blood: The Early Years*. Cape Town: Umuzi, 2006.

Khumalo-Seegelken, B. 'Cleansing and Reconciling in Southern Africa Today'. http://www.benkhumalo-seegelken.de/dokumente/UkuBuyisana_2011.doc.

Knight, I. *Brave Men's Blood: The Epic of the Zulu War, 1879*. Barnsley: Pen & Sword, 2006.

Koch, E. '"Nature Has the Power to Heal Old Wounds": War, Peace and Changing Patterns of Conservation in Southern Africa'. In *South Africa in Southern Africa: Reconfiguring the Region*, edited by D. Simon. Oxford: James Currey, Cape Town: David Philip and Athens, OH: Ohio University Press, 1998.

Koopman, A. and J. Deane, 'New Names for Old: Transformation in the Streets of Pietermaritzburg'. *Natalia* 35, 2005: 85–19.

Kosminsky, P. *Getting Back to Life When Grief Won't Heal*. New York: McGraw-Hill, 2007.

Krige, E.J. *The Social System of the Zulus*. London: Longmans, Green & Co., 1936.

Krog, A. *Country of My Skull*. Johannesburg: Random House, 2010.

Laband, J. and R. Haswell (eds). *Pietermaritzburg, 1838–1988: A New Portrait of an African City*. Pietermaritzburg: University of Natal Press, 1988.

LaCapra, D. *History and Memory after Auschwitz*. Ithaca: Cornell University Press, 1998.

Lambert, J. *Betrayed Trust: Africans and the State in Colonial Natal*. Pietermaritzburg: University of Natal Press, 1995.

Langhout, R.D. 'Where Am I? Locating Myself and Its Implications for Collaborative Research'. *American Journal of Community Psychology* 37(3/4), 2006: 267–74.

LeBaron, M. and B. Grundison. *Conflict and Culture: Research in Five Communities in British Columbia, Canada*. Victoria, BC: University of Victoria Institute for Dispute Resolution, 1993.

Lederach, J.P. *Preparing for Peace: Conflict Transformation across Cultures*. New York: Syracuse University Press, 1995.

Leeb, W. 'Daily Life, Daily Death in Pietermaritzburg'. In J. Aitchison, W. Leeb and V. John, *Political Violence in the Natal Midlands: The Unrest Monitoring Project Papers, 1988–1994*. Pietermaritzburg: Centre for Adult Education, University of Natal, 2010.

———. 'Misplaced, Displaced and Abandoned'. In J. Aitchison, W. Leeb and V. John, *Political Violence in the Natal Midlands: The Unrest Monitoring Project Papers, 1988–1994*. Pietermaritzburg: Centre for Adult Education, University of Natal, 2010.

Levine, L. (ed.). *Faith in Turmoil: The Seven Days War*. Pietermaritzburg: PACSA, 1999.

Lincoln, Y.S. and E.G. Guba. *Naturalistic Inquiry*. Thousand Oaks, CA: Sage, 1985.

Lloyd, R.B. 'Conflict Resolution or Transformation? An Analysis of the South African and Mozambican Political Settlements'. *International Negotiation* 6(3), 2001: 303–29.

Lynd, H. 'Secret Details of the Land Deal that Brought the IFP into the 94 Poll'. *Mail & Guardian*, 7 August 2019. https://mg.co.za/article/2019-08-07.

Magubane, Z. 'Attitudes towards Feminism among Women in the ANC, 1950–1990: A Theoretical Re-interpretation'. In South African Democracy Education Trust, *The Road to Democracy in South Africa, Volume 4, 1980–1990*. Pretoria: Unisa Press, 2010.

Magwaza, T., Y. Seleti and M.P. Sithole (eds). *Freedom Sown in Blood: Memories of the Impi Yamakhanda: An Indigenous Knowledge Systems Perspective*. Polokwane: Ditlou Publishers, 2006.

Makhura, T. 'Missionary and African Perspectives on the Politics of Witchcraft among the Xhosa and Zulu Communities in the 19th Century Cape and Natal/Zululand'. Paper prepared for the Wits Institute for Social and Economic Research, Johannesburg, 15 September 2003.

Malinowski, B. *Methods of Study of Culture Contact in Africa*. London: Oxford University Press, 1938.

Mandela, N. *Long Walk to Freedom: The Autobiography of Nelson Mandela*. London: Little, Brown and Company, 1994.
Manganyi, N. and A. du Toit (eds). *Political Violence and the Struggle in South Africa*. Johannesburg: Southern Book Publishers, 1990.
Marais, H. 'The Shattered Mould: Patterns of Violence in the Post-Apartheid Era'. In *The Role of Political Violence in South Africa's Democratisation*, edited by R. Greenstein. Johannesburg: Community Agency for Social Enquiry, 2003.
Maré, G. *Ethnicity and Politics in South Africa*. London: Zed Books, 1993.
Maré, G. and G. Hamilton. *An Appetite for Power: Buthelezi's Inkatha and the Politics of Loyal Resistance*. Johannesburg: Ravan Press, 1987.
Marks, S. 'The Myth of the Empty Land'. *History Today* 30(1), 1980: 8–12.
———. *The Ambiguities of Dependence in South Africa: Class, Nationalism and the State in Twentieth-Century Natal*. Johannesburg: Ravan Press, 1986.
Marshall, S. *Landscape of Memory: Commemorative Monuments, Memorials and Public Statuary in Post-Apartheid South Africa*. Leiden: Brill, 2009.
Mbiti, J.S. *African Religions and Philosophy*. London: Heinemann, 1969.
McCaul, C. *Towards an Understanding of Inkatha Yesizwe*. Johannesburg: Development Studies Group, University of the Witwatersrand, 1983.
McClendon, T.V. *Genders and Generations Apart: Labor Tenants and Customary Law in Segregation-Era South Africa, 1920s to 1940s*. Portsmouth: Heinemann, 2002.
Mchunu, M. 'Discipline, Respect and Ethnicity: A Study of the Changing Patterns of Fatherhood of Three Generations of Zulu Fathers and Sons in KwaShange, Inadi, Vulindela Area of Pietermaritzburg, KwaZulu-Natal, from the 1930s to the 1990s'. Master's thesis, University of KwaZulu-Natal, 2005.
———. 'Culture Change, Zulu Masculinity and Intergenerational Conflict in the Context of Civil War in Pietermaritzburg (1987–1991)'. In *From Boys to Men: Social Constructions of Masculinity in Contemporary Society*, edited by T. Shefer, K. Ratele, A. Strebel, N. Shabalala and R. Buikema. Cape Town: UCT Press, 2007.
McLynn, F. *Carl Gustav Jung: A Biography*. New York: St Martin's Press, 1997.
McNally, R. 'Debunking Myths about Trauma and Memory'. *Canadian Journal of Psychiatry* 50(13), 2005: 113–17.
Meer, F. (ed.). *Resistance in Townships*. Durban: Madiba Publishers, 1989.
Meintjes, S. 'Edendale 1850–1906: A Case Study of Rural Transformation and Class Formation in an African Mission in Natal'. PhD thesis, University of London, 1988.
Miles, M.B. and A.M. Huberman. *Qualitative Data Analysis: A Sourcebook of New Methods*. Thousand Oaks, CA: Sage, 1984.
Minnaar, A. *Conflict and Violence in Natal/KwaZulu: Historical Perspectives*. Pretoria: HSRC, 1990.
———. (ed.). *Patterns of Violence: Case Studies of Conflict in Natal*. Pretoria: HSRC, 1992.
———. 'The "Third Force": In Retrospect'. In *The Hidden Hand: Covert Operations in South Africa*, edited by C. Schutte, I. Liebenberg and A. Minnaar. Pretoria: HSRC, 1998.
Mkhize, S. *Uhlanga lwas'Embo: The History of the Embo People*. Durban: Just Done Production, 2007.

———. 'Spirals of Suffering: Political Violence in Richmond, KwaZulu-Natal, 1980 to 1999: An Autobiographical Narrative'. Paper presented at a conference at the Msunduzi Museum, 2009.

Mokwena, K.P. 'Commemorating Painful Experiences in a Divided Society, with Special Reference to the Thokoza Memorial: A Case Study'. MA thesis, University of the Witwatersrand, 2008.

Monaghan, J. and P. Just. *Social and Cultural Anthropology: A Very Short Introduction*. Oxford: Oxford University Press, 2000.

Morrell, R. (ed.). *Changing Men in Southern Africa*. Pietermaritzburg: University of Natal Press, 2001.

———. *From Boys to Gentlemen: Settler Masculinity in Colonial Natal, 1880–1920*. Pretoria: Unisa Press, 2001.

Morrell, R. and G. Hamilton (eds). *Political Economy and Identities in KwaZulu-Natal: Historical and Social Perspectives*. Durban: Indicator Press, 1996.

Morris, M. and D. Hindson. 'The Disintegration of Apartheid: From Violence to Reconstruction'. In *From 'Red Friday' to CODESA: South African Review 6*, edited by G. Moss and I. Obery. Johannesburg: Ravan Press, 1992.

———. 'South Africa: Political Violence, Reform and Reconstruction'. *Review of African Political Economy* 19(53), 1992: 43–59.

Motala, M. 'The Group Areas Act and the Effect of the Proclamations made in Pietermaritzburg Environs'. Paper presented at the Group Areas Conference, Pietermaritzburg, 28–29 January 1961.

Munthali, A.C. 'Change and Continuity: Perceptions about Childhood Diseases among the Tumbuka of Northern Malawi'. PhD thesis, Rhodes University, 2002.

Mzala. *Gatsha Buthelezi: Chief with a Double Agenda*. London: Zed Books, 1988.

Naidoo, K. 'The Politics of Youth Resistance in the 1980s: The Dilemmas of a Differentiated Durban'. *Journal of Southern African Studies* 18(1), 1991: 143–65.

Ndlovu, S. 'Trauma, Identity and Culture among Rural isiZulu Speakers'. Unpublished paper presented at Critical Method Nine, Durban, 2004.

Ngubane, H. *Body and Mind in Zulu Medicine: An Ethnography of Health and Disease in Nyuswa-Zulu Thought and Practice*. London: Academic Press, 1977.

Nicodemus, A. 'Soccer Fan Brutally Killed for Muthi'. *Mail & Guardian*, 11 June 1999.

Nora, P. 'General Introduction: Between Memory and History'. In *Realms of Memory: The Construction of the French Past, Volume 1: Conflicts and Divisions*, edited by P. Nora and L.D. Kritzman. New York: Columbia University Press, 1996.

———. (ed.). *Rethinking France: Les Lieux de Mémorie, Volume 1: The State*. Chicago: University of Chicago Press, 2001.

Nora, P. and L.D. Kritzman (eds). *Realms of Memory: The Construction of the French Past, Volume 1: Conflicts and Divisions*. New York: Columbia University Press, 1996.

Nordstrom, C. *A Different Kind of War Story*. Philadelphia: University of Pennsylvania Press, 1997.

Ntsimane, R. 'A Mirage Called Forgiveness: A Critique of the Truth and Reconciliation Commission'. In *Orality, Memory and the Past: Listening to the Voices of Black Clergy under Colonialism and Apartheid*, edited by P. Denis. Pietermaritzburg: Cluster Publications, 2000.

———. 'Trauma, Resilience and Reconciliation: Sinomlando's Psycho-Social Interventions in KwaZulu-Natal'. *Archives News* 1, 2007: 32–8.

Nuttall, S. and C. Coetzee (eds). *Negotiating the Past: The Making of Memory in South Africa*. Cape Town: Oxford University Press, 1998.

Nzimande. B. and S. Thusi. *Children of War: The Impact of Political Violence on Schooling in Natal*. Durban: Education Projects Unit, University of Natal, 1991.

Parle, J. *States of Mind: Searching for Mental Health in Natal and Zululand, 1868–1918*. Pietermaritzburg: University of KwaZulu-Natal Press, 2007.

Patton, M.Q. *Qualitative Research and Evaluation Methods*. Third edition. Thousand Oaks, CA: Sage, 2002.

Peires, J. *The Dead Will Arise: Nongqawuse and the Great Cattle-Killing Movement of 1856–57*. Johannesburg: Ravan Press, 1989.

Perks, R. and A. Thomson (eds). *The Oral History Reader*. London: Routledge, 1998.

Pigou, P. 'The State and Violence: What Has the Truth and Reconciliation Commission Found?' In *The Role of Political Violence in South Africa's Democratisation*, edited by R. Greenstein. Johannesburg: Community Agency for Social Enquiry, 2003.

Pogrund, B. *Robert Sobukwe: How Can Man Die Better*. Johannesburg: Jonathan Ball, 2006.

Popkin, J.D. *History, Historians, and Autobiography*. Chicago: University of Chicago Press, 2005.

Popular Memory Group. 'Popular Memory: Theory, Politics, Method'. In *The Oral History Reader*, edited by R. Perks and A. Thomson. London: Routledge, 1998.

Portelli, A. 'The Peculiarities of Oral History'. *History Workshop Journal* 12(1), 1981: 96–107.

———. *The Death of Luigi Trastulli and Other Stories: Form and Meaning in Oral History*. Albany: State University of New York Press, 1991.

———. *The Battle of Valle Giulia: Oral History and the Art of Dialogue*. Madison, WI: University of Wisconsin Press, 1997.

Radford J. and W. Leeb. 'An Investigation into the Effects of Job Loss on the Township of Mpophomeni'. Paper presented to the Industrial Court of Inquiry, Centre for Adult Education, Pietermaritzburg, 2010.

Said, E.W. 'Identity, Authority, and Freedom: The Potentate and the Traveler'. *Transition* 54, 1991: 4–18.

Samuel, R. and P. Thompson (eds). *The Myths We Live By*. London: Routledge, 1990.

Samuelson, H.L. *Zululand: Its Traditions, Legends, Customs and Folk-lore*. Pinetown: Mariannhill Mission Press, 1930.

Samuelson, R.C.A. *Long, Long Ago*. Durban: Knox, 1929.

Schuld, M. 'The Prevalence of Violence in Post-Conflict Societies: A Case Study of KwaZulu-Natal, South Africa'. *Journal of Peacebuilding and Development* 8(1), 2013: 60–73.

Schutte, C., I. Liebenberg and A. Minnaar (eds). *The Hidden Hand: Covert Operations in South Africa*. Pretoria: HSRC, 1998.

Shefer T., K. Ratele, A. Strebel, N. Shabalala and R. Buikema (eds). *From Boys to Men: Social Constructions of Masculinity in Contemporary Society*. Cape Town: UCT Press, 2007.

Shopes, L. 'Commentary: Sharing Authority'. *The Oral History Review* 30(1), 2003: 103–10.

Singh J. and R. Chetty (eds). *Trauma, Resistance, Reconciliation in Post-1994 South African Writing*. New York: Peter Lang, 2010.

Sitas, A. 'The Making of the "Comrades" Movement in Natal, 1985–91'. *Journal of Southern African Studies* 18(3), 1992: 629–41.

Sithole, J. 'Land Disputes, Social Identities and the State in the *Izimpi Zemibango* in the Umzinto District, 1930–1935'. *Journal of Natal and Zulu History* 27(1), 2009: 60–82.

———. 'The African National Congress in Natal, 1990–1995'. In South African Democracy Education Trust, *The Road to Democracy in South Africa: Volume 6 (1990–1996): Part 1*. Pretoria: Unisa Press, 2013.

Sithole, J. and S. Ndlovu. 'The Revival of the Labour Movement, 1970–1980'. In South African Democracy Education Trust, *The Road to Democracy in South Africa: Volume 2 (1970–1980)*. Pretoria: Unisa Press, 2006.

Smith, C. and F. Khumalo. 'Refugees and Disrupted Schooling in Natal'. In *Patterns of Violence: Case Studies of Conflict in Natal*, edited by A. Minnaar. Pretoria: HSRC, 1992.

Smith, T. 'Experiencing the Violence'. Paper presented at the Centre for Adult Education Seminar on Violence, University of Natal, Pietermaritzburg, 1988.

South African History Online (SAHO). 'The Nature and Character of Vigilantes in KwaZulu-Natal'. http://www.sahistory.org.za/archive/chapter-2-nature-and-character-vigilantes-kwazulu-natal.

South African Military History Society. 'Newsletter No. 328'. KwaZulu-Natal Branch, October 2002. http://samilitaryhistory.org/2/d02octne.html.

Southall, R. 'An Appetite for Power: Buthelezi's Inkatha and South Africa'. *African Affairs* 87(349), 1988: 635–6.

Spradley, J.P. *Participant Observation*. New York: Holt, Rinehart and Winston, 1980.

Stavrou, S. 'Underdevelopment: Natal's Formula for Conflict'. *Indicator SA* 7(3), 1990: 52–6.

Stavrou, S. and A. Crouch. 'Molweni: Violence on the Periphery'. *Indicator SA* 6(3), 1989: 46–50.

Sturken, M. *Tangled Memories: The Vietnam War, the AIDS Epidemic, and the Politics of Remembering*. Berkeley: University of California Press, 1997.

Taylor, R. 'The Myth of Ethnic Division: Township Conflict on the Reef'. *Race and Class* 33(2), 1991: 1–14.

Taylor, R. and M. Shaw. 'The Natal Conflict'. In *Restructuring South Africa*, edited by J.D. Brewer. London: St Martin's Press, 1994.

Tedlock, B. (ed.). *Dreaming: Anthropological and Psychological Interpretations*. Cambridge: Cambridge University Press, 1987.

Thompson, L. *A History of South Africa*. New Haven: Yale University Press, 1990.

Thompson, P. *The Voices of the Past: Oral History*. Third edition. New York: Oxford University Press, 2000.

Thompson, P.S. *Bambatha at Mpanza: The Making of a Rebel*. Pietermaritzburg: P.S. Thompson, 2004.

Thomson, A. 'The Anzac Legend: Exploring National Myth and Memory in Australia'. In *The Myths We Live By*, edited by R. Samuel and P. Thompson. London: Routledge, 1990.

Tick, E. 'Heal the Warrior, Heal the Country'. *Yes! Magazine*, 20 May 2008. http://www.yesmagazine.org/issues/a-just-foreign-policy/heal-the-warrior-heal-the-country.

Truluck, A. *No Blood on Our Hands: Political Violence in the Natal Midlands 1987 – Mid-1992, and the Role of the State, 'White' Political Parties, and Business*. Pietermaritzburg: Natal Midlands Region of the Black Sash, 1992.

Tutu, D. *No Future without Forgiveness*. New York: Doubleday, 2000.

UNICEF. *The State of the World's Children 1996*. Oxford: Oxford University Press, 1996.

Vail, L. (ed.). *The Creation of Tribalism in Southern Africa*. Oxford: James Currey, 1989.

Van Niekerk, J. 'Failing or Future: Responding to the Sexual Abuse of Children'. *SA Crime Quarterly* 3, 2003: 11–16.

Van Warmelo, N.J. *A Preliminary Survey of the Bantu Tribes of South Africa*. Pretoria: Government Printer, 1935.

Vetlesen, A.J. *Evil and Human Agency: Understanding Collective Avoiding*. Cambridge: Cambridge University Press, 2005.

Vincent, L. 'New Magic for New Times: Muthi Murder in Democratic South Africa'. *Tribes and Tribals* 2, 2008: 43–53.

Vines, A. *Renamo: Terrorism in Mozambique*. York: Centre for Southern African Studies, University of York, 1991.

Von Holdt, K. 'Vigilantes versus Defence Committees: The Maritzburg War; A Turning Point for Inkatha?' *South African Labour Bulletin* 13(2), 1988: 16–27.

Wa Afrika, M. 'Patient's Penis Skinned in *Muthi* Murder'. *Mail & Guardian*, 29 May 1998.

Waetjen, T. and G. Maré. '"Men amongst Men": Masculinity and Zulu Nationalism in the 1980s'. In *Changing Men in Southern Africa*, edited by R. Morrell. Pietermaritzburg: University of Natal Press, 2001.

Webb, C. De B. and J.B. Wright (eds). *The James Stuart Archive of Recorded Oral Evidence Relating to the History of the Zulu and Neighbouring Peoples*. Volumes 1–5. Durban: Killie Campbell Africana Library and Pietermaritzburg: University of Natal Press, 1975–2001.

White, K. 'Maintaining Meaning in Life: The Central Challenge for Palliative Care Practice'. PhD thesis, University of Sydney, 2000.

White, L. 'Telling More: Lies, Secrets, and History'. *History and Theory* 39(4), 2000: 11–22.

Williams, L.M. 'Adult Memories of Childhood Abuse: Preliminary Findings from a Longitudinal Study'. *APSAC Advisor* 5(3), 1992: 19–22.

Wills, T., D.H. Davis and R.H. Haswell. 'Maritzburg after the Group Areas Act'. Unpublished paper, University of Natal, Pietermaritzburg, 1987.

Winter, J. *Remembering War: The Great War between Memory and History in the Twentieth Century*. New Haven: Yale University Press, 2006.

Wright, J. 'Before Mgungundlovu'. In *Pietermaritzburg, 1838–1988: A New Portrait of an African City*, edited by J. Laband and R. Haswell. Pietermaritzburg: University of Natal Press, 1988.

Wright, J. and A. Manson. *The Hlubi Chiefdom in Zululand-Natal: A History*. Ladysmith: Ladysmith Historical Society, 1983.

Xaba, T. 'Masculinity and Its Malcontents: The Confrontation between "Struggle Masculinity" and "Post-Struggle Masculinity" (1900–1997)'. In *Changing Men in Southern Africa*, edited by R. Morrell. Pietermaritzburg: University of Natal Press, 2001.

Zulu, P. 'Durban Hostels and Political Violence: Case Studies in KwaMashu and Umlazi'. *Transformation* 21, 1993: 1–23.

Index

Reconsiderations in Southern African History

Masked Raiders: Irish Banditry in Southern Africa, 1880–1889
Charles van Onselen

Sol Plaatje: A Life of Solomon Tshekisho Plaatje, 1876–1932
Brian Willan

Bound for Work: Labor, Mobility, and Colonial Rule in Central Mozambique, 1940–1965
Zachary Kagan Guthrie

The Finger of God: Enoch Mgijima, the Israelites, and the Bulhoek Massacre in South Africa
Robert R. Edgar

The Cowboy Capitalist: John Hays Hammond, the American West, and the Jameson Raid in South Africa
Charles van Onselen

Historian: An Autobiography
Hermann Giliomee

Cradock: How Segregation and Apartheid Came to a South African Town
Jeffrey Butler, edited by Richard Elphick and Jeannette Hopkins

Imagining a Nation: History and Memory in Making Zimbabwe
Ruramisai Charumbira

A World of Their Own: A History of South African Women's Education
Meghan Healy-Clancy

The Last Afrikaner Leaders: A Supreme Test of Power
Hermann Giliomee

The Equality of Believers: Protestant Missionaries and the Racial Politics of South Africa
Richard Elphick

Slavery by Any Other Name: African Life under Company Rule in Colonial Mozambique
Eric Allina

One Love, Ghoema Beat: Inside the Cape Town Carnival
John Edwin Mason

The Rise and Fall of Apartheid
David Welsh

Art and Revolution: The Life and Death of Thami Mnyele, South African Artist
Diana Wylie

Murder at Morija: Faith, Mystery, and Tragedy on an African Mission
Tim Couzens

The Afrikaners: Biography of a People
Hermann Giliomee